JIM SHOOTER: CONVERSATIONS

Conversations with Comic Artists M. Thomas Inge, General Editor

Jim Shooter: Conversations

Edited by Jason Sacks, Eric Hoffman, and Dominick Grace

University Press of Mississippi / Jackson

www.upress.state.ms.us

The University Press of Mississippi is a member of the Association of
    American University Presses.

Copyright © 2017 by University Press of Mississippi
All rights reserved
Manufactured in the United States of America

First printing 2017
∞

Library of Congress Cataloging-in-Publication Data available

Cloth	978-1-4968-1179-0
Epub Single	978-1-4968-1180-6
Epub Institutional	978-1-4968-1181-3
Pdf Single	978-1-4968-1182-0
Pdf Institutional	978-1-4968-1183-7

British Library Cataloging-in-Publication Data available

Select Bibliography

DC Comics

Action Comics (1966–1970, 1975) · Adventure Comics (1966–1969) · Superboy (1967, 1975–1977) · Superman (1966–1969, 1975) · Superman's Pal Jimmy Olsen (1966–1969) · World's Finest Comics (1966–1968) · Legion of Super-Heroes (2008–2009)

Marvel Comics

The Avengers (1976–1982, 1986) · Ghost Rider (1976, 1977, 1981) · Daredevil (1977–1978, 1985) · The Spectacular Spider-Man (1977–1981) · Team America (1982–1983) · Dazzler (1983–1985) · Marvel Graphic Novel #12: Dazzler: The Movie (1984) · Secret Wars (1984–1985) · Secret Wars II (1985–1986) · Marvel Graphic Novel #16: The Aladdin Effect (1985) · Star Brand (1986–1987) · Marvel Graphic Novel #33: The Mighty Thor: I, Whom The Gods Would Destroy (1987)

VALIANT

Magnus Robot Fighter (1991–1993) · Solar, Man of the Atom (1991–1992) · Archer & Armstrong (1992) · Eternal Warrior (1992) · Harbinger (1992) · Rai (1991–1992) · Shadowman (1992) · Unity (1992) · X-O Manowar (1992) · Unity 2000 (1999–2000)

DEFIANT

Dark Dominion (1993–1994) · The Good Guys (1993–1994) · Warriors of Plasm (1993–1994) · War Dancer (1994) · Charlemagne (1994) · Dogs of War (1994)

Broadway Comics

Powers That Be (1995–1996) · Shadow State (1995–1996) · Fatale (1996) · Star Seed (1996)

Dark Horse Comics

Doctor Solar, Man of the Atom (2010–2011) · Magnus Robot Fighter (2010–2011) · Mighty Samson (2010–2011) · Turok, Son of Stone (2010–2011)

CONTENTS

INTRODUCTION

James C. Shooter, born September 27, 1951, in Pittsburgh, Pennsylvania, is among the most controversial and important comics writers, editors, and publishers of the twentieth century. A key figure in comics' transition from niche industry to vital pop culture force, Shooter reflects the changing times of the United States comic book industry during the latter half of the twentieth century and the first two decades of the twenty-first.

When Jim Shooter entered the comics field in the mid-1960s, he found an industry in flux. The conservative DC Comics had a reputation as a company in which editors kept tight control over their writers and artists, managing their fiefdoms with discipline and a focus on professionalism. These territories formed in the 1950s, when DC, following the creation of the Comics Code and with the closing down of competitors like Fawcett Comics, came to dominate a larger share of the market than it had before the Code's introduction. Though DC's 1950s business-like ethos continued well into subsequent decades, the surprising success of upstart Marvel Comics in the early 1960s confused and irritated them. Where DC's editors favored "puzzle stories" in which heroes with interchangeable personalities solved science fiction-themed mysteries, Marvel's editors—mainly the mercurial Stan Lee, who also wrote most of their stories—preferred narratives whose crises were inwardly existential as opposed to outwardly scientific. This humanity appealed to a certain sensibility in comics audiences. Jim Shooter was among those readers.

Shooter was primarily a fan of DC in his early childhood. However, he soon grew tired of DC's formulaic superhero stories and gave up reading comics when he was eight years old. Four years later, in 1963, Shooter rediscovered the medium while hospitalized in a Pittsburgh ward for minor surgery. There, he found comics from all companies, including Marvel, which by 1963 was delivering comics that emphasized character over plot. For many fans, that transition was a revelation. Shooter found that to be true: the DC comics were seemingly untouched, whereas the Marvel comics were clearly well-read. While reading a "Legion of Super-Heroes" story in an issue of DC's *Adventure Comics*,

Shooter decided to undertake a comprehensive study of the medium with the intention of learning how to write comics. He produced a full script and sent it to DC. That story prompted *Adventure* editor Mort Weisinger to request additional stories from Shooter. In response, Shooter submitted a two-parter that introduced new Legionnaires Karate Kid, Princess Projectra, Ferro Lad, and the Nemesis Kid.

On February 10, 1966, the fourteen year old Shooter received a call from Weisinger to inform Shooter of his intention to purchase all three stories and to request that Shooter write a twelve-page "Supergirl" story—his first formal assignment. Shooter's "Legion" stories, "One of Us Is a Traitor" and "The Traitor's Triumph," subsequently ran in *Adventure Comics* #346 and #347, with July and August 1966 cover dates. His first story, "Target—21 Legionnaires," appeared the following month in *Adventure Comics* #348 with a September 1966 cover date, while the "Supergirl" story appeared in *Action Comics* #344 (cover date December 1966). "One of Us Is a Traitor," a two-part story—rare in DC titles of the era—declared Shooter's concern for characterization, a concern which would be a key attribute of his writing for the duration of his writing career. Shooter focused on enhancing characters' emotional involvement in their relationships, adding a touch of characterization that was especially appropriate when depicting adolescents and teens like the Legion and Supergirl. In subsequent issues, Shooter ratcheted up the stakes of the series by killing Ferro Lad only six months after the character's initial appearance. Shooter's "Legion" stories arguably inaugurated the Marvelization of DC by emphasizing relatable, human problems and emotions for the characters he wrote; Shooter was, after all, a teenager writing about teenagers.[1]

Shooter's comics sold well—through the end of his run, *Adventure Comics* sold over 500,000 copies per issue at a time when DC sales were on the decline—yet the editors at DC believed Shooter was capitalizing on a fad that wouldn't last. For instance, stalwart editor Bob Haney referred to Shooter as their "Marvel writer" in a derogatory manner. Weisinger attempted to forbid Shooter from reading any Marvel books, but Shooter continued to do so anyway.

Nevertheless, Weisinger knew he had a talented writer on his hands. He commissioned several more stories from Shooter by the spring of 1966. "All were acceptable, all were purchased," Shooter notes; "Mort told me at that point he considered me one of his regular writers."[2] However, Weisinger did not offer praise to his protégé;[3] he was instead extremely abusive towards Shooter, heaping what seemed like endless criticism on the teenager. Shooter accepted the abuse, largely because he was bringing in much-needed income for his family. His father, a veteran of the Second World War, was a steel-worker who sometimes found himself without work through circumstances he could not control. "There were occasional steel industry layoffs and strikes," Shooter explains. "When those things happened he did anything and everything he could. He was never idle. He mowed lawns, did handyman work, and took odd jobs, anything. Sometimes it just wasn't enough." Shooter had to contribute. Writing for comics seemed like the best alternative.[4]

During his tenure at DC, Shooter contributed to nearly every Superman-related series other than *Lois Lane*, as well as to the Weisinger-edited *Captain Action*. He also proved himself to be something of a perfectionist; artists Gil Kane and Wally Wood were impressed by the young author's comprehensively researched scripts, which included complete rough layouts indicating how he envisioned the "action in the panels to be depicted." Shooter also provided suggestions for cover designs, an indication of his singular creative vision.

Shooter's tutelage under Mort Weisinger concluded in the fall following the young writer's graduation from high school. After over four-and-a-half years of writing for the domineering Weisinger, Jim Shooter had grown weary of the grind at DC. He never seemed to be able to earn enough money to really help his family, and professional recognition was scant.

In 1968 Shooter took and aced the National Merit Scholarship Qualifying Test. He received many offers from colleges and chose to attend NYU as a University Scholar in fall 1969, also hoping he could continue to work at DC Comics while in college. The award covered full tuition as well as room and board and provided a cultural stipend that could be used to attend Broadway shows or other cultural events in cosmopolitan New York. He also would have been able to design his own curriculum. (Shooter was one of only two University Scholars admitted that year.) As Shooter considered his enrollment at NYU, he hoped to move away from writing. He approached Weisinger about the possibility of transitioning to either freelance editorial work or part-time office work doing coloring or inking. Weisinger declined that request, so Shooter approached Marvel for work. To his amazement, he met with Stan Lee, who informed him that they needed someone to work there full-time. Shooter chose Marvel over NYU, giving up his scholarship for a life in comics. "On my first day at Marvel," Shooter recalls, Weisinger "called me there to scream at me about what an ingrate I was, after all he'd done for me [. . .] I hung up on him."

While at Marvel, Shooter took part in plotting sessions with Lee and others.[5] From a creative standpoint, the position was quite satisfying. Unfortunately, the pay was low; he was unable to afford New York rents on his modest income. Unable to work through the mail at Marvel and with no opportunities available to him at DC, the eighteen-year-old Shooter seemed finished with both the comics industry and New York City. Instead, Shooter embarked on a career in advertising in Pittsburgh, doing comics-format ads thanks in part to the exposure he received in the local press. He also worked some odd jobs in his home town, including managing a Kentucky Fried Chicken. Despite this early withdrawal from the comics industry, Shooter would soon stage an altogether auspicious and unexpected comeback.

In 1973, Harry Broertjes, one of the editors of the popular Legion of Super-Heroes fanzine the *Legion Outpost*, managed to locate and interview Shooter, who was flattered that anyone remembered his work. From the end of 1969 to 1973, Shooter had not so much as read a comic book, including any of his own, because he found the experience too depressing and frustrating.[6] During the interview—one of his earliest and included in this volume—Broertjes mentioned to Shooter that Weisinger had retired from comics. Murray Boltinoff now managed some of Weisinger's former editorial responsibilities, including the Legion, and Julius Schwartz managed other Superman-related series. Broertjes also contacted Duffy Vohland, an assistant at Marvel, who put him in touch with Shooter. Vohland invited Shooter to come to New York from Pittsburgh for an interview. There, Shooter met Roy Thomas, who offered him work on the Marvel title *Creatures on the Loose*, which then featured second-string Marvel monster Man-Wolf. Shooter considered the offer but wasn't excited about writing a character about whom he had no previous knowledge. During his New York visit, some Marvel staffers and freelancers recommended to Shooter that he visit DC's offices and attempt to find additional work there. "That would have been unthinkable in the sixties," Shooter remarks, "'working both sides of the street.' Few creators did so, and almost all used pseudonyms at the 'other' company." Yet the Marvel staffers insisted that this was now an acceptable practice and, as a result, Shooter visited the DC offices. He was introduced to Schwartz and Boltinoff, and the latter offered Shooter work on *Superboy* starring the Legion of Super-Heroes. Unlike Man-Wolf, these were characters he knew: "Superboy and the Legion of Super-Heroes hadn't changed that much. I could sit down and write stories for them that day." Shooter joined writer Cary Bates for a short run that began with *Superboy* #209 (cover dated May 1975). Unfortunately, Shooter's second tenure at DC was cut short due to personal conflicts with Schwartz.

This time, though, Shooter landed on his feet at Marvel. While Shooter was still working for DC, Marv Wolfman offered Shooter a staff position at Marvel, which desperately needed people skilled in comics production to help manage their massively expanded line. Marvel had doubled the number of books it published per month between 1970 and 1975—from twenty titles a month to nearly forty—and this volume of product proved to be unsustainable with Marvel's existing editorial structure.

The editorial staff consisted of an editor-in-chief and an associate editor, together with a handful of editorial assistants, like Shooter, who dealt with proofreading and other administrative duties. This structure created considerable pressure on the editor-in-chief and his assistant, which, when coupled with the amount of product being published by Marvel, led to rapid turnover of staff. Marvel attempted to reduce this workload in 1974 by establishing a separate editor for their black-and-white magazine line and a new writer-editor position through which certain writers edited their own material—though due to the massive workload, many Marvel books essentially never received editorial guidance.[7]

Shooter was hired under Wolfman's editorship as associate editor. He was responsible for catching problems early in the production process, before books were completed and errors were not easily corrected. Shooter's work ethic and careful eye were instrumental in making the production of books more efficient because he could prevent problems before they happened. The appropriately-named new hire was now Wolfman's "trouble shooter." Shooter was the de facto second-in-command to Wolfman, and to his successor, Archie Goodwin.

Goodwin assumed editor-in chief responsibilities in 1976. It was hoped that he would handle the job on a temporary basis only. Instead, Goodwin stayed on the job for over a year. Many systemic problems grew worse during Goodwin's tenure. Art and stories were delivered late, which drove up production costs. Adding to that, writers had nearly unfettered freedom to produce their stories without interference from the harried editorial stuff, with the result that, in Shooter's view, many creators (most of them working on a freelance basis) were delivering subpar work. This low quality in turn translated into a further decline in revenue. Furthermore, sales across all comics companies were down dramatically by the middle 1970s. Cover prices increased while paper quality reduced; moreover, the nation was undergoing a significant economic recession, coupled with an energy crisis. There was a pervasive sense among industry professionals that both Marvel and DC could be shuttered at any time by their parent companies. In fact, only the runaway success of Marvel's *Star Wars* adaptation[8] and the premiere of the commercially successful *Superman: The Movie* (1978)[9] kept Marvel and DC from going out of business.

By late 1977, though, Goodwin was exhausted and ready to leave the editor-in-chief position. Of the possible successors, Shooter seemed the only member

Jim Shooter in 1980.
Photo by Jackie Estrada.
© Jackie Estrada.

of Marvel's staff ready to assume this crucial, if challenging, role. At Marvel's informal 1977 Christmas party, Stan Lee and his wife arrived at the party unexpectedly. Lee used the opportunity to announce Shooter as Goodwin's replacement as editor-in-chief. "The announcement was greeted with silence," Shooter recalls. "The old guys, like [editor] Danny Crespi and [artist] John Tartaglione, congratulated me. The ones who feared having a new sheriff in town were freaked." Shooter began work as editor-in-chief on the first business day of 1978.

Shooter was keen to take on the job, having developed and expressed his own ideas about how Marvel's problems could be solved. He planned a thorough restructuring to create a system akin to the one he had seen work so effectively at DC, where editors who were each responsible for a group of titles reported to an editor-in-chief. Shooter envisioned a top-down system. Unlike his predecessors, Shooter took on each of Marvel's problems aggressively and decisively; in fact, he approached his job in a manner some observers found reminiscent of Mort Weisinger.[10] Shooter appointed line editors to manage titles, instituted a process of fill-in issues for comics that were behind schedule, and banned the practice of prepaying, where creators were paid in advance of delivering their manuscript or artwork. Shooter had no patience for creators who missed deadlines or demanded autonomy without responsibility.

In addition to the many internal issues Shooter faced, there were considerable challenges outside the company that affected the comics industry at the time of Shooter's promotion. One key issue was how to work with the growing direct-sales market. In 1972, Marvel's executives made an agreement with distributor and conventioneer Phil Seuling that allowed him exclusive discounts to sell Marvel Comics on a nonreturnable basis to the small but growing specialty comics shop market. Eventually, Shooter was approached by Denver, Colorado–based retailer Chuck Rozanski, who complained to Shooter about Seuling's practices, presenting to Shooter a plan for a mutually beneficial business arrangement that would not present antitrust concerns to the company. In meetings that included Shooter, Rozanski, Marvel Circulation Director Ed Shukin, and Marvel President Jim Galton, a new direct-sales marketplace was created that benefitted all publishers and led to the birth of independent comics publishers such as Eclipse, Pacific, and First Comics. The new arrangement allowed different distributors to exist with the same trade terms as each other. The direct market became a creatively and financially advantageous market for much of Shooter's tenure at Marvel and, eventually, the default method for distributing comic books in North America.

Under Shooter and Direct Sales Manager Mike Friedrich, as well as Friedrich's successor Carol Kalish, Marvel determinedly pursued the creation of comics sold exclusively through the direct-sales marketplace to comic shops. The first such book, *Dazzler* #1 (cover dated March 1981), sold a remarkable 428,000 copies, helping to prove the viability of the direct market as sales outlet. By 1982, Marvel transitioned fan-favorite series *Ka-Zar the Savage*, the successful toy-license tie-in *Micronauts*, and *Moon Knight* exclusively to the direct-only market while also launching new series targeted solely for that market, including *Marvel Fanfare*—printing both new and inventory stories on deluxe paper at a deluxe price—and Marvel's ongoing *Marvel Graphic Novel* series, which released original comics stories in a format reminiscent of European graphic albums. Though other publishers, notably independent publishers Eclipse and NBM, published works in graphic novel format prior to Marvel, the influence of America's largest publisher gave those formats considerable attention.

Moreover, in 1978, changes to copyright law allowed publishers to obtain licensing rights from authors—so that an intellectual property could be marketed for film or toy adaptation or for foreign publication—while also allowing the author to retain ownership. Previously, intellectual properties were indivisible and could not be licensed without retaining a copyright, requiring the publisher to assume ownership. In light of this new law, in 1980 Shooter and Archie Goodwin, under direction of Marvel President Jim Galton, who wanted to expand Marvel into new markets, and taking inspiration from National Lampoon's fantasy magazine *Heavy Metal*, created a new slick paper anthology magazine consisting entirely of creator-owned content, entitled *Epic Illustrated*, followed in 1982 by the Epic Comics line.[11]

Impressively, Marvel's share of the direct market approached 70 percent in some months. In 1982, in recognition of his efforts, Shooter was named vice president, by which time he was overseeing fourteen editors, over three hundred creative personnel, and some fifty to sixty titles. Much of Shooter's—and therefore Marvel's—success during the 1980s was due to Shooter's promotion of major creative talents and his commitment to producing quality material. He fostered creativity among many of his most popular creators, installing Frank Miller on the low-selling *Daredevil*, Walter Simonson on *Thor*, and John Byrne on *Fantastic Four* as solo writer-artists whose work on those titles resulted in considerable critical acclaim and substantial sales. Shooter lobbied for a sales incentives program in order to retain talent that might otherwise be drawn away to other, potentially more profitable employment in animation, or producing content for DC or upstart direct market companies such as Pacific, First, Comico, and Eclipse, who attracted talent by offering their creators intellectual property rights.

Having worked freelance for many years, Shooter understood that an incentives program might prove financially lucrative for creators whose comics sold over a certain determined level. Creators would also receive bonuses for remaining on a comic, resulting in writers and artists becoming more fully invested in their comics, thereby improving the comics' quality and thus salability. In addition to these programs, page rates tripled, and, according to Shooter, "every creator's income rose dramatically, some spectacularly."[12] Star creative talent such as Chris Claremont (writer of *Uncanny X-Men* and *New Mutants*, among other series), Byrne, and Miller enjoyed considerable personal financial gain. This incentives plan in turn had an impact on the quality of material that Marvel published. Thus, Marvel expanded their lead in sales both through newsstands and the emerging direct market as a result of Shooter's advocacy of creative talent, his willingness to experiment, and his efforts to build and, more importantly, retain a staff of the best writers and artists in the business.

Shooter's greatest financial triumph at Marvel was *Marvel Super Heroes Secret Wars* (1984–85). This twelve-part "event" miniseries was not the first of Shooter's career; he also wrote the well-received "Korvac Saga," which appeared during his run on *The Avengers* (1977–78). The "Korvac Saga" introduced a number of themes—expanding on those first introduced a decade earlier by Jack Kirby and Lee—that Shooter would repeat for the remainder of his career: the reluctant superhero or a god embodied in human form, their relationships with humanity, and the associated ethical considerations this often confusing and troublesome relationship demands, namely morality, duty, and responsibility. In *Secret Wars* that god-like being is the Beyonder, who kidnaps all of Marvel's major superheroes and supervillains, bringing them to the alien planet Battleworld, where they are forced into combat against one another.

Secret Wars was published as a stand-alone twelve issue miniseries, with a handful of storylines spinning out from the main series.[13] In keeping with Marvel's lucrative toy licensing from this period, it appeared in conjunction with a toy line produced by Mattel.[14] The series, while immensely profitable, was critically reviled, primarily because the comic acted in many ways as an advertisement for the toys. Nevertheless, *Secret Wars* represents a watershed moment in the comics industry, in that it is the first of the epic crossover comics, with events from its storyline intruding into and informing the narratives of a number of Marvel titles.

An inevitable sequel, the nine-part *Secret Wars II* (1985–86), followed only three months after the completion of the original series. Also written by Shooter, this decidedly philosophical, wickedly satirical series, which included, among other things, prostitution, drug use, and infanticide, brought the Beyonder to Earth to learn more about humanity. *Secret Wars II* was, notably, the first comic from any company to cross over directly to other titles, presenting a precursor to comics throughout the following decades, including the Shooter-written *Unity* in the early 1990s. Though *Secret Wars II* was another financial success, anticipating other similar crossovers, the series wasn't quite the sales success of its predecessor. Shooter delivered a story that was relatively short on action, the opposite of the first series. Furthermore, some readers and critics were annoyed by what seemed to be a cynical marketing ploy intended to coerce readers into buying multiple titles they did not normally read, in order to get the "whole story," only to find that in many instances the crossover components were trivial.

One constant element in the two *Secret Wars* miniseries was Shooter's insistence on clear storytelling techniques. Though he allowed exceptions for creators like Walter Simonson, Bill Sienkiewicz, and Frank Miller, who earned their creative autonomy, Shooter pushed his artists and writers to deliver work in which the stories could be easily understood, bereft of many of the storytelling techniques that he viewed as distractingly ostentatious. Shooter wanted to ensure that readership could grow, which meant that comics had to be easily accessible to new readers. He held internal classes on storytelling techniques that reminded writers always to identify their characters and to give readers an anchor to help them understand those actions.[15] A number of creators credit Shooter's lectures for their understanding of comics storytelling fundamentals. Yet some creators found Shooter's editing style heavy-handed and perhaps reminiscent of the work of his mentor Mort Weisinger. In fact, accusations abounded, especially in *Comics Journal* interviews with disgruntled and highly experienced former Marvel creators, of a lack of flexibility from Shooter. He gave a free hand to a handful of favored creators, "big guns you can't aim," as he calls them in our interview below, meaning creators talented enough for Shooter to allow them considerable creative autonomy. For less capable creators, Shooter's insistence on producing what he saw as storytelling essentials could be infuriating. He reportedly required establishing shots, characters clearly identifying each other, and panel arrangements that did not distract the reader.

Despite the frustration many creators felt, Shooter's approach paid off in sales, with Marvel comics dominating the market. This might explain the apparently paradoxical impression one may be left with when one considers the conflicting accounts of Shooter's tenure at Marvel: he is alternately described as a merciless dictator producing indistinguishable product, and a cultivator of talents undertaking decidedly unique, original, and envelope-pushing material. In fact, the former may in some cases be the result of the latter, which is to say, in his cultivation of accessible, professional comics, Shooter was often required to make considerable editorial inputs, which some creators saw as unwelcome interference as opposed to justifiable or necessary improvements. Shooter, however, maintains that his editorial decisions were the result of his core storytelling aesthetic and his professional obligation to act as "ultimate arbiter of the characters" and that he was "hired to protect [Marvel's] franchises."[16] Thus, Shooter maintains, his only true editorial infringement was his demand for an accessible, coherent, and technically proficient unit of entertainment.

The reality is that Shooter's editorial suggestions often improved stories; he encouraged what were at the time radical plot developments, such as the death of perennial *X-Men* character Jean Grey, then known as Phoenix. The original climax of the Phoenix story involved Grey being spared; Shooter, however, insisted that the ending to the story as drafted seemed anticlimactic. He explains, "with Jean Grey being 'cured' and everything going back to the way it was, I asked for a better ending; for instance, Jean going to prison for her crimes." In response, Claremont proposed killing her off, and Shooter agreed. At the time, the death of a major character was a novelty, and fans were outraged—yet the story was arguably improved by her death and, from a practical perspective, so were sales: *The X-Men* #137 (September 1980), the issue in which Jean Grey dies, sold twice as many copies as any other comic on the stands that month. Arguably, the trend of killing off a character to generate sales begins here; for example, Shooter followed this up with Jim Starlin's equally successful *The Death of Captain Marvel* (1982), the inaugural volume of Marvel's prestige Graphic Novel series.

At around this time, rumors began circulating in the fan community that Shooter was planning radical changes to the Marvel Universe: new costumes, new characters assuming iconic identities, even the deaths of characters (see, for instance, the 1982 interview with Chris Barkley, reprinted here, in which Shooter addresses these rumors). In fact, Shooter asserts that his motivation was simply to encourage creators to try different ideas. As he stated at the time, "I told [the writers] if they come up with some kind of wild, new idea or exciting new concept and it involves a change in character or a major change in a title, that they should not be afraid to propose it, that there is no rule or force that will prevent it. . . . We encourage people to go for it and do exciting things"[17]

Shooter, when asked if he had any ideas to help celebrate Marvel's twenty-fifth anniversary in 1986, recommended "Big Bang," a version of a line-wide reboot of the Marvel Universe. Sales executives, however, did not think such a radical change was worth the risk, so Shooter instead proposed his idea for a New Universe.[18] Though many of his business decisions were successful, sales on the New Universe represented the nadir of Shooter's tenure at Marvel.

Ostensibly telling the story of the "world outside your window," presenting ordinary people who unexpectedly gain superpowers as the result of a mysterious White Event, Shooter was initially given a generous budget of $120,000 to develop the new line. That amount was significantly reduced once Cadence placed itself for sale and had suitors such as New World Pictures and Western Publishing considering purchase. This process led to considerable tensions between Shooter and Cadence. "Because the company was on the block and the owners had no stake in the company's future and because making any investment in a project like the New Universe would take dollars off the bottom line, which would reduce their multiple," Shooter laments, "funding for the New Universe was, for all intents and purposes, eliminated soon after the project started." Yet Shooter remained obligated to go forward with the project and was instructed to "do it on staff," meaning that the work was performed "by staff people, mostly assistant editors, for free, after hours." When the line of comics, eight titles in all—Shooter wrote the flagship title, *Star Brand*—finally reached the stands, following considerable promotion and publicity and after many false starts and delays, sales results were disappointing, and the New Universe line was met with critical scorn. Resultant lackluster sales resulted in the cancellation, after one year, of four of the titles, half of the New Universe line.

One of the great paradoxes of Shooter's career at Marvel was that while he drove tremendous achievements in sales and creators' rights, he was often rendered a pariah in the fan press. He became the symbol for many for Jack Kirby's struggle with Marvel to recover thousands of pages of his original artwork, though Shooter maintains he "fought for Kirby from the inside." Moreover, because many of the creative talent believed Shooter too heavy-handed in his control of the stories and art, he also faced dissension among his own freelancers and staffers. A one-shot called *The Pitt* (1987), produced following Shooter's tenure at Marvel, depicts Star Brand carelessly destroying the entire city of Pittsburgh (in the "Black Event," contrasting with the "White Event"), pointedly Shooter's hometown. John Byrne, who co-wrote *The Pitt*, disliked Shooter, despite Shooter's having been instrumental in his financial successes. In fact, at a party at Byrne's home on April 4, 1987, creators burned a crude effigy of Shooter; a suit was stuffed with unsold issues of New Universe titles and a picture of Shooter was used for the head. When a videotape of the party at Byrne's home found its way to the corporate offices at New World, executives looking to eject Shooter found their justification.[19] Less than two weeks after the party, on April 15, 1987, Jim Shooter was fired from his position as editor-in-chief at Marvel.[20]

Yet Shooter was not without a plan. Entertainment lawyer Steve Massarsky had come to Marvel following Shooter's tenure as editor-in-chief in the hopes of obtaining rights to certain Marvel properties to produce a traveling arena show for children. Active in the entertainment industry in which he represented popular clients such as Cyndi Lauper and the Allman Brothers, Massarsky had an idea for applying his music industry success to the world of licensed characters. While arranging for the licensing, Massarsky inquired about obtaining creative talent to help write a story to accompany the show. They recommended Shooter, whom Massarsky hired, but when Massarsky submitted Shooter's book, *Spider-Man and the Night of Doom*, to Marvel for their approval it was rejected, according to Shooter, "on grounds that it misrepresented the characters." Shooter discusses this situation and other elements of his relationship with Massarsky at length in our interview below.

Shooter meanwhile followed the progress of New World Entertainment's finances in trade magazines and in the *Wall Street Journal* and deduced that the company was losing money. He rightly anticipated that New World would eventually have to sell its subsidiaries, including Marvel. Meeting with Chase Bank executives and, together with Massarsky and entrepreneur and former Time Inc. executive Winston Fowlkes, Shooter formed Marvel Acquisition Partners. The team assembled an $81 million offer, with a reserve to bargain with. However, that bid fell short of Wall Street investor, and New World insider, Ronald O. Perelman's offer. This setback did not stop Shooter, however. Since he knew comics publishing and Massarsky knew entertainment, they decided to combine their respective expertise on a venture that could provide a new home for intellectual properties. With the backing of the former investors from Marvel Acquisition Partners, Shooter and his partner Winston Fowlkes started a new company: Voyager Entertainment. That funding was complete in November 1989, and Shooter began redeveloping former Western Publishing properties Magnus and Solar for a new line of comics to be named VALIANT (Shooter insisted the name be presented in capital letters).

Barely a month after getting funding, though, things started to turn sour. Massarsky informed Shooter of his relationship with Melanie Okun, one of the principals at Triumph. That romance presented a clear conflict of interest, and Shooter at first considered walking away from the new company. Instead, he opted to remain at VALIANT, he claims, out of loyalty to his staffers and in the hopes of making the company profitable enough for him to buy out the financiers. Together, Shooter and Massarsky launched a new line of comics that featured work by industry stalwarts such as Steve Ditko and Bob Layton. Initial books were based on Nintendo games and the World Wrestling Federation, rather than on the tried-and-true stalwarts of Shooter's earlier successes, superheroes, and sales were poor. By 1991, Voyager was losing large amounts of money, at the very moment when the comics market was experiencing unprecedented growth.

Eventually, Shooter began publishing the Western Comics characters for which he had hoped to start the new line. In May 1991, VALIANT released the first chapter of "Steel Nation" in *Magnus Robot Fighter*, followed in September 1991 with *Solar, Man of the Atom*. Though fans were slow to recognize these revivals, Shooter was once again able to write comics that appealed to his sensibilities. If his new company was going to fail, Shooter figured he might as well fail while doing work that he cared about. For several months, sales were moderate, with the first issue of *Magnus* selling roughly 80,000 copies and *Solar* around 60,000, with subsequent issues selling in the 50–60,000 range. However, a prominent mention in the fifth issue of the new industry magazine *Wizard* noted, "Has anyone noticed that all of Valiant's (sic) titles are slowly climbing up the sales charts?"[21] Moreover, *Wizard* #7 included several VALIANT-focused features,[22] helping spur dramatic increases in growth. The titles were catching on as fans were embracing new comic universes. The line expanded to encompass additional titles, including *Rai, Shadowman, Harbinger*, and *X-O Manowar*. VALIANT's comics borrowed from Shooter's ideas for the New Universe, presenting ordinary men and women in the "world outside your window," with realistic adventures told in real time.

These were fulfilling but extremely trying times for Shooter. As the line grew, Shooter and the production and editorial team worked long hours producing the comics; Shooter reportedly worked over five hundred days straight, including holidays.

VALIANT's adventure titles' gradual increase in popularity culminated with the epic crossover series *Unity*. For two months, all of VALIANT's titles crossed over with each other in the type of extended storyline that Shooter pursued in *Secret Wars II*. The first issue of *Unity* was given away free in the summer of 1992—at approximately the same time that Image Comics launched their first titles—receiving considerable media attention and accompanying massive sales. Together, Image and VALIANT grew to represent novel comics universes for a new generation of readers, though early Image Comics emphasized flashy, exaggerated art, while early VALIANT comics opted for a subtler, more realistic style. As a result, these comics captured reader attention and delivered unprecedented sales, often surpassing even *Secret Wars* in the number of copies sold. Unfortunately for Shooter, just as the line took off, he was unceremoniously fired from VALIANT. The reasons given for his firing are many: Shooter alleges that Massarsky and his girlfriend-turned-fiancée pushed Shooter out in order to make more money for themselves[23] and that VALIANT's lawyers offered him an onerous employment contract.[24]

Shooter's feelings of defiance toward the industry that had treated him so callously and unceremoniously helped suggest the name for his next project. The appropriately-named DEFIANT (its name also always all in capitals) solicited its first title in August 1993. Again taking a cue from the New Universe, DEFIANT's titles would be oriented around a central plotline concerning a living planet called the Org, and five genetically modified humans who must work together to stop an impending alien invasion. Together with the comics, a massive merchandising effort was planned, including action figures, lunch

Jim Shooter with Debbie Fix, circa 1992. Photo by Jackie Estrada. © Jackie Estrada.

boxes, and trading cards. The River Group, which owned DEFIANT as well as a trading card company, licensed the properties as a card set and album. As a result, the first issue of their flagship title *Plasm* was released as a set of trading cards in a custom binder. The River Group made a large profit from the set while Shooter and his team received only a small royalty.

Facing a dramatically declining comic book marketplace in late 1993, the company started off somewhat unceremoniously, when Marvel UK decided to sue DEFIANT over the use of the name *Plasm*. They absurdly claimed it would be confused with the Marvel UK comic *Plasmer*, which at that point had only been registered "with intent to use" in the United Kingdom. Most observers, including Shooter, saw the suit as a transparent attempt to put DEFIANT out of business, preventing Shooter's new venture from being as successful as his previous one. (See Shooter's account of this case in our interview below, pp. 196–97). Though the case was ultimately decided in DEFIANT's favor in Federal Court, the financial damages from the massive court costs, which amounted to over $300,000, coupled with the loss of various merchandising deals and the bad comics market, put them into bankruptcy. Though representatives from other publishers and media outlets considered buying DEFIANT, the company went out of business on September 1, 1994, just a year after its first solicitation. Altogether the company released barely three dozen comics during the year, and nearly all the comics met with retailer and consumer indifference.

Several suitors considered purchasing DEFIANT, and some came close to consummating their purchase. New Line Entertainment sought a deal, and Shooter actually accepted a deal from Savoy Pictures before that deal was scrapped. Another potential investor was Broadway Video Entertainment, a video production company that delivered such popular TV series as *Saturday Night Live* and *Late Night with Conan O'Brien*. When DEFIANT folded, Winston Fowlkes made an arrangement with the president of Broadway, Eric Ellenbogen, to hire members of DEFIANT's creative staff to develop a property based on Harley-Davidson motorcycles. Following the expiration of his contract with DEFIANT, Shooter received a call from Ellenbogen telling him that the development team "needs a leader." Eventually, Shooter explains, Ellenbogen "offered to start a comics division, owned 50/50 by Broadway Video Entertainment and me, but with BVE/Lorne Michaels as the general partner." Though comics industry sales continued to slump badly as 1995 dawned, there were hopes that Broadway's wealthy investors would help the company to survive and thrive. Sales, however, were anemic, with series like *The Powers that Be* selling close to a mere 5,000 copies per issue. Eventually, Broadway Entertainment was sold to Golden Books, who had no interest in managing a line of comic books. They pulled the plug on the ailing company, and Jim Shooter once again was out of an editorial job.

Following this latest in a series of defeats, it appeared Jim Shooter, after working steadily in the comic book industry for over two decades as writer, editor, and entrepreneur, had reached a dead end. However, he has since attempted a handful of comebacks. In 1998, long-time friend Chuck Rozanski approached Shooter with the idea of launching yet another company, to be called DARING, again always capitalized. Rozanski and Shooter would cofinance the project, which would premiere with two limited edition titles. Though Shooter did some press for the comics, work on them never got beyond the talking stage. The following year, Shooter returned to the latest incarnation of VALIANT for a six-issue series entitled *Unity 2000*. That series aimed to unite Shooter's original vision for the VALIANT characters with a failed 1998 reboot of the line and would have led to revivals of Shooter-era characters such as X-O Manowar and Shadowman. Shooter completed work on all six issues of the series, but only three saw print before the latest version of the VALIANT line went bankrupt. A revival of *Unity* would have been an ironic and appropriate return to comics for Shooter, yet few readers felt the need to read a new *Unity*.

In 2008, Shooter also returned to writing the Legion of Super-Heroes with a twelve-issue run of DC's latest incarnation of the team, an effort that was met with mediocre sales and professional frustration. In 2010, at Dark Horse

Comics, he revived licensed versions of his *Doctor Solar, Magnus Robot Fighter, Mighty Samson*, and *Turok Son of Stone*. *Solar* lasted eight issues while the others only completed their initial four-issue arcs.

Though his latest efforts in the comics industry occur largely behind the scenes—currently, together with investment banker and attorney Joseph C. Lauria, Shooter runs Illustrated Media Group, a custom publishing group—and in a mostly noncreative capacity, Jim Shooter remains a key figure in the field as well as a true original. No other writer entered the industry at such a young age (though several artists did, including his frequent collaborator John Romita Jr.) or enjoyed such success and rancor—often simultaneously—as head of one of the major comics companies. His actions and editorial decisions during his tenure at Marvel Comics, while they do have their critics and detractors, contributed to a widespread revival of interest in comic books and helped revolutionize key aspects of the comics industry, such as creators' rights, compensation, and negotiation, or direct market distribution.

Moreover, Shooter's career has significantly impacted popular culture, the ramifications of which are still apparent today. From the structure of the direct market, to creator-friendly policies of the major comics publishers, to the concern with realism in comics, to the now perennial "event" comics with multi-title tie-ins—see Marvel's recent *Civil War* and *Secret Wars* revival (the latter including its own action figure tie-in) and DC's *Rebirth*—which now also inform the crossover nature of Marvel's on-screen adaptations with its big-screen version of the event storyline the Infinity Gauntlet, Shooter's imprint is everywhere in mainstream comics. His bible for the Hasbro toy line Transformers laid the foundation for the hugely popular, financially lucrative multimedia and multigenerational franchise. And he may not be done yet; in conversation, Shooter intimated that exciting new projects may be on the horizon.

Shooter's unique contributions to the medium as theorist, writer, and editor deserve further acknowledgment and critical assessment. We hope this collection of interviews will inspire such a reassessment.

The interviews included here cover a nearly thirty-year period, spanning from 1969 to a 2016 interview, conducted by this volume's editors, evidencing a Shooter confident in his stature and influence. Douglas Fratz's brief interview from 1969, a hard-to-find early conversation, provides fascinating insight into Shooter's thoughts about comics while he was still an adolescent. The interview also includes interesting information about the mechanics and economics of DC in the late 1960s.

The key 1974 interview with a post-DC, pre-Marvel Jim Shooter, conducted by Harry Broertjes, features a candid discussion about Shooter's early years within the comics industry. Shooter discusses the impetus for his submission of scripts to DC editor Mort Weisinger, his years as a freelancer struggling to make an income to support his family, with a focus on his Superman family and Legion of Super-Heroes scripts and characters. This interview also provides a window into Shooter's creative process, as well as his interactions with the various artists with whom he collaborated and his impressions concerning their contributions to his work.

Broertjes's discussion with Shooter is followed by four interviews covering Shooter's period at Marvel Comics. First, David M. Singer provides an in-depth, career-spanning (as of 1980) conversation, offering Shooter's reminiscences and thoughts about his days at DC as a writer and his then-current position as editor-in-chief, providing detailed and illuminating insights into his views on the art and craft of comics production. He also briefly addresses the character assassination engaged in by the *Comics Journal*. In Chris Barkley's radio interview from 1982, Shooter confronts the emerging controversies about his working methods, commenting on his relationship with many artists, and in Maggie Thompson and Hal Schuster's 1983 interview Shooter shares some of the struggles and triumphs of working at Marvel, discussing the freedoms and restrictions that come from working on a small budget. He also examines the lack of politics he feels between himself and the management team at Marvel, delivering comments that feel straightforward yet which are especially intriguing in light of some of the stories that he has subsequently shared. Finally, ten years into his tenure at Marvel, Shooter, in an interview published in the British fanzine *Speakeasy* in 1986, discusses his working methods and his publishing philosophies, explaining how his changes have led to Marvel's market dominance.

Joe Martin's interview from 1992 finds a post-VALIANT, pre-DEFIANT-era Shooter during a transitional moment in his career, and at a transformative moment in the comics industry. Shooter reflects on the state of the industry when he first entered it in the 1960s, as well as his role in establishing additional creator rights and royalties and the advent of the direct market and new, non-mainstream publishers. Shooter also discusses how he brought this creator-friendly environment into VALIANT. He then comments on the existing comics market, in particular the then-current prevalence of various marketing gimmicks, its accompanying market speculation, its detrimental effect on the medium, and his disappointment that VALIANT has contributed to these factors. Marty Grosser's 1993 interview gives us a Shooter reflecting back on the controversies involving Marvel and VALIANT, offering his frank opinion of the then-current comics landscape, and speaking in some detail, and with clear optimism, about his hopes and plans for DEFIANT.

This volume concludes with two interviews from the current decade, beginning with Richard Arndt's career-spanning recent (2015) interview, and concludes with an all-new interview conducted by the editors of this volume in the spring of 2016. Taken together, these interviews provide a multifaceted portrait of a sometimes divisive and controversial, yet always intriguing figure.

ACKNOWLEDGMENTS

There are two excellent interviews that, due to length restrictions, we were unable to include: Darren Dean's "Dissertations, Disclaimers, Defiance: An Interview with Jim Shooter," published in *Amazing Heroes Interviews* in 1993, and Bryan Stroud's "Jim Shooter Goes Back to the Beginning," first published on his *Silver Lantern Blog* in 2008. Both provide invaluable background and insight and are highly recommended.

We would like to thank all the interviewers for their work and for permission to reprint, in particular Steven Shamus for allowing us to reprint the Jim Shooter radio interview from Mr. Shamus's website and Richard Arndt and Roy Thomas for granting permission to reprint the recent discussion published in *Alter Ego*. We wish as well to thank Pam Singer, for kindly allowing the republication of her late husband's conversation with Jim Shooter and for sharing wonderful memories of David Singer. We are grateful to Terra Kushner for her permission to use her late husband Seth's photograph of Shooter as our cover image. We also thank Lisa Macklem for her assistance with permissions. Finally, we would like to thank Harry Broertjes for facilitating our contact with Jim Shooter, and to extend our deep gratitude to Mr. Shooter for his generosity in assisting us with his project, and for agreeing to sit down for an extensive interview specifically for this volume as well as his thoughtful and detailed notes on his career.

JS
EH
DG

Notes

1. See Jeff Barbanell, "Shooter's Marvelesque," in Timothy Callahan, ed. *Teenagers from the Future: Essays on the Legion of Super-Heroes*, Edwardsville, IL: Sequart Research and Literary Organization, 2008, rev. ed. 2011, 63–84.

2. Unless otherwise noted, all Shooter quotations are derived from comments Shooter made to the editors in July 2016.

3. There are many anecdotes to this effect, including Roy Thomas, "Two Weeks with Mort Weisinger; Or, Four Years with an Angry Mob (Take Your Pick)," *The Krypton Companion*. Raleigh, NC: TwoMorrows Press: 2006.

4. "Jim Shooter on the X-Men," https://www.youtube.com/watch?v=BxJSL6uqiCM&list=PLIq gi6UcSQ9YB_VrsjgD17fG6jVd-oV9D, accessed March 11, 2016.

5. Remarks Shooter: "Regarding plots, when I left Marvel that time, I asked Stan, who still did most of the writing, if I could work through the mail as I did with DC. There were no writing assignments available, so I suggested that I could be paid for writing plots since Stan seemed to like my plotting. But, Marvel had never paid separately for plots. It was just part of the writer's job. Payments for plots would have to come out of the writer's compensation. No writer, including him, would be willing to give up a substantial part of their money to someone for "only" doing the plot. Stan said he might be able to pay me five dollars a plot. That was a nonstarter."

6. Peter David, "*Marvel Age* Interview with Stan Lee and Jim Shooter," *Marvel Age* 8 (November 1983): 16.

7. See R. S. Martin, "Jim Shooter: A Second Opinion," http://rsmwriter.blogspot.ca/2016/06/jim-shooter-second-opinion.html.

8. The six-part adaptation of George Lucas's *Star Wars* (1977) by Roy Thomas and Howard Chaykin sold over a million copies in all editions in 1977 and 1978. Making the project even more lucrative for Marvel, the rights to adapt the film were given to Marvel free of charge to help promote the film. Director George Lucas had been a co-owner of the Supersnipe Comic Book Euphorium in New York during the early 1970s and was friends with Thomas.

9. *Superman the Movie* was the second highest–grossing film of 1978 in the United States.

10. See, for example, Christopher Priest, "Oswald: Why I Never Discuss Spider-Man." http://lamerciepark.com/legacy/comics/spidey.html, accessed March 20, 2016.

11. R. S. Martin, "Jim Shooter: A Second Opinion," http://rsmwriter.blogspot.ca/2016/06/jim-shooter-second-opinion.html.

12. Indeed, many creators were able to purchase houses on the royalties they made from some of Marvel's bestselling titles.

13. For instance, Spider-Man first wore his black costume in the pages of *Secret Wars*, and She-Hulk joined the Fantastic Four in that miniseries as well.

14. Mattel made a deal with Marvel because they feared that Kenner, who had recently acquired rights to DC characters, would otherwise obtain a monopoly in the superhero action figure market. Mattel required a comic book tie-in to help promote the toy line. Shooter had already planned a series entitled *Cosmic Champions* that would involve a number of superheroes and supervillains. Shooter's series, coupled with the success of the direct market, came about at exactly the right time.

15. Shooter had what he called the "Fifty-cent Storytelling Lecture." Using an issue of *Strange Tales*, illustrated by Jack Kirby (issue 114, November 1963), Shooter described the basics of graphic storytelling, a valuable demonstration that many comics artists still point to as one of the most straightforward and useful lessons they received. The basics included: "The characters must be introduced. Their situation must be established. The conflict must be introduced. Suspense must be built. A climax must be reached. A resolution must be achieved." Jim Shooter, "Bullpen Bulletin Special," all Marvel Comics titles, August 1982. See also Jim Shooter's blog, http://jimshooter.com/2011/05/storytelling-lecture-strange-tales-par.html.

16. "Jim Shooter on the X-Men," https://www.youtube.com/watch?v=BxJSL6uqiCM&list=PLIqgi6UcSQ9YB_VrsjgD17fG6jVd-oV9D, accessed March 11, 2016.

17. Schuster, Hal. "Doug Moench, Jim Shooter, and Death in the Marvel Universe." *Comics Feature* (No. 21): Nov. 1982: 5–7.

18. He used "Big Bang" as the chapter title for *Secret Wars* #12 "because it was appropriate and it was a good title."

19. "A Look Back with Jim Shooter," https://www.youtube.com/watch?v=boMX4q5mUoo, accessed March 10, 2016.

20. The complexities of Jim Shooter's sudden departure from Marvel in 1987 are addressed at length by Shooter in a 2016 note appended to the editors' interview, conducted specifically for this volume; see note on pages 205–7 below.

21. "Wizard Market Watch." *Wizard: The Guide to Comics* #5 (January. 1992): 80.

22. "Among Them Is the Notable 'Straight Shooter,'" an interview with Jim Shooter conducted by Patrick Daniel O'Neill, which provides an interesting early history of VALIANT.

23. Bryan Stroud also discusses this topic with Shooter; see Stroud, "Jim Shooter Goes Back to the Beginning," http://comicsbulletin.com/interview-jim-shooter-goes-back-beginning-0/, accessed March 10, 2016.

24. Michael David Thomas, "Jim Shooter Interview: Part 2," http://www.comicbookresources.com/?page=article&id=146, accessed March 20, 2016.

CHRONOLOGY

1951   James Shooter born 27 September 1951, in Pittsburgh, Pennsylvania, to Ken and Ellie Shooter.

1963   While hospitalized for minor surgery, Shooter discovers Marvel Comics.

1965   Shooter writes and lays out a story for DC Comics featuring the Legion of Super-Heroes.

1966   First professional sale, "Brainiac's Blitz," is published in *Action Comics* #339, cover dated July 1966. First "Legion" story follows shortly thereafter in *Adventure Comics* #346–47 (July and August 1966). Contributes to numerous other titles.

1967   Story published in fanzine *Sense of Wonder* #4. Shooter contributes script and some art.

1967–69   Continues writing numerous titles for DC.

1969   Graduates high school. Ceases writing for Weisinger. Briefly works at Marvel Comics. Retires from the comics industry at age eighteen.

1969–73   Works in advertising for the Pittsburgh office Lando-Bishopric Advertising, at the Joseph Horn Company, a Pittsburgh department store and as a manager at a Kentucky Fried Chicken.

1973   Fan Harry Broertjes contacts Shooter, resulting in an interview for fanzine the *Legion Outpost*. Subsequent to that fanzine appearance (1974), Shooter begins writing "Legion of Super-Heroes" stories again.

1975   Leaves DC Comics. First Marvel script published, *Super-Villain Team-Up* #3.

1976   Joins Marvel's staff as an associate editor. Writes for several Marvel titles.

1977   Writes "Korvac Saga" for Marvel, among many other stories. Final DC story published (*Superboy* #224).

1978   Begins work as editor-in-chief at Marvel. Helps establish a new distribution system that allows for multiple distributors to sell Marvel Comics directly to comic shops. Continues to write, primarily *The Avengers*.

1979–1984 Contributes scripts to a number of Marvel titles.

1981   Marvel Comics embraces the direct market. *Dazzler* #1 released exclusively to the direct market.

1982   Begins the Epic Comics line, overseen by Archie Goodwin.

1984   Kirby artwork return controversy begins.

1984–85   *Marvel Super Heroes Secret Wars*.

1985–86   *Secret Wars II* published. New World Pictures purchases Marvel Comics from Cadence Industries.

1986   Marvel's New Universe unveiled. Writes the first four issues of the flagship New Universe title, *Star Brand*.

1987   Fired by Marvel's new owners on April 15. Shortly before he leaves the company, meets Steve Massarsky, an entertainment industry lawyer. Final work for Marvel published.

1989   Along with Massarsky, unsuccessfully attempts to purchase Marvel. Shooter and Massarsky turn to creation of a new comics company called VALIANT.

1990   VALIANT line launches with comics featuring Nintendo and World Wrestling characters.

1991   VALIANT launches line of superhero and science fiction–based comics, including *Magnus Robot Fighter* and *Solar, Man of the Atom*. Shooter contributes scripts for *Magnus Robot Fighter* #0–8, along with art for several issues under the pseudonym Paul Creddick.

1992   VALIANT line expands with launch of *Harbinger*, *X-O Manowar*, *Rai*, *Shadowman*, and other titles. *Unity* storyline crosses over between all VALIANT titles. Writes nearly fifty VALIANT comics, across several titles. Fired from VALIANT.

1993   Launches the comics company DEFIANT, beginning with *Plasm* #0. Marvel objects to the name *Plasm*, which results in a court case. DEFIANT releases approximately sixty comics.

1994   DEFIANT closes.

1995   Broadway Comics founded.

1996   Golden Books purchases Broadway Entertainment, including Broadway Comics. All comics cancelled. Broadway releases thirty-three comics.

1997   Attempts to purchase Marvel Comics.

1998   DARING line, to be copublished with retailer Chuck Rozanski, is announced but does not see print.

1999   Writes *Unity 2000* for Valiant/Acclaim Comics. Only three of a scheduled six issues see print before Valiant/Acclaim ceases publication.

2008–9   Returns to write *Legion of Super-Heroes* at DC Comics with artist Francis Manapul. Run lasts thirteen issues (#37–49).

2010–11   Launches a revival of former Gold Key characters *Mighty Samson*; *Doctor Solar, Man of the Atom*; *Turok, Son of Stone*; and *Magus, Robot Fighter* at Dark Horse Comics. Writes *Doctor Solar, Man of the Atom* #1–8; *Mighty Samson* #1–4; *Turok, Son of Stone* #1–4; and *Magnus, Robot Fighter* #1–4.

2012   *The Omega Point: A Science Fiction Screenplay* published.

JIM SHOOTER: CONVERSATIONS

Jim Shooter Interview

DOUGLAS FRATZ / 1968

Originally published in *Comicology* #3 (1969). Reprinted by permission.

Doug: Well, to start off, can you tell us when, how, at what age, and what you sent in to get you the job at DC, and all other whos, whats, whens, hows, and whys that you are probably so tired of telling everyone?

Jim: When I was fourteen and still occasionally reading comics, it dawned on me that people actually got paid for creating such junk. Immediately, I set out to get in on a good thing and wrote (and illustrated) a script for "Legion of Super-Heroes." I had written other such scripts before (usually Spider-Man) but for once I did it in real earnest. I was so pleased I sent it to "Editor" DC Comics. It took quite a while, but I finally got a reply—a nice letter from Mort Weisinger asking me about my career plans, telling me about opportunities in comic books, inviting me to New York for a visit, and best—asking for another script. That was enough for me—I wrote a giant two-book Legion plot and poured my heart into the story and art. I mailed it and waited. It clicked. On February 10, 1966, a Mr. Weisinger called me from New York to offer me $200 for my story and assigned me a "Supergirl" script. I've been receiving assignments ever since. Later, my first story was also bought and used.

Doug: What work have you done since and under what editors and what artists? Had any artwork used?

Jim: I've had all of my work under Mort Weisinger. Usually Curt Swan interprets my layouts, but I've also worked with other DC artists like Carmine Infantino and Wally Wood. Living in Pennsylvania, I can't work as an artist, but my layouts are used.

Doug: Exactly how does the editor/writer/artist set-up at DC work?

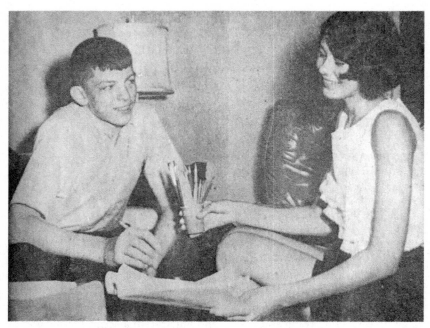

Fourteen-year-old Jim Shooter with his sister.

Jim: The DC machine works a little different for me than for normal writers, but . . . Mr. Weisinger will call me and either give me an idea or ask me for one. Either way, I will end up sending him a synopsis, usually with a cover sketch. He will call again and approve or reject it. With an approval comes suggestions, comments, and helpful information. Then I write the story and draw the panels. Usually I send two pages or so a day, so Mr. Weisinger can edit it as I go along and keep the artist supplied with material. From the artist, of course, it goes to be lettered, inked, and colored.

Doug: Whose gem was "Sharp" Shooter, by the way?
Jim: Mr. Weisinger, I think. Possibly his assistant, Nelson Bridwell.

Doug: Who are your favorite comic book writers and artists?
Jim: [Joe] Kubert, Wood, Infantino, Swan, and many others whose names escape me. I can't narrow the list to one or two. Of the few writers I know, I'd say that Edmond Hamilton had a way with plot that few could equal.

Doug: Oh yes, the old "Legion" writer. He's a prominent science fiction writer too. Any other DC comics you'd like to try to write?

Jim: Maybe *Doom Patrol* and *Metal Men* and several others of our lesser-known efforts.

Doug: How long do you plan to stay at DC, and what do you plan to get into after that?
Jim: I plan to stay at DC at least through college. I'd like to get into science fiction writing or maybe commercial art on a higher plane. I'm also interested in science.[1]

Doug: What is your favorite DC comic?
Jim: "Legion of Super-Heroes"–it has unlimited potential. It is not bogged down by time or by place criteria. My imagination can run wild—all in all, a writer's dream.

Doug: Do you wish credits would be given in the "Legion"?
Jim: I understand they soon will be.

Doug: Do you think the comic TV shows (Marvel and DC) will help or hurt the comics?
Jim: I think the worst the TV shows can do is spark interest in comics. I've only seen a couple, and they look like harmless TV distortions of what we write—a little simplified, maybe.

Doug: Do you read other comics?
Jim: Not really—I wouldn't say never and make it a law, but I can't remember the last time I read a competitor's magazine. I read what comes my way, which is what Infantino sends me. (He's the one in charge of keeping everyone posted.)

Doug: Do you plan to go to New York?
Jim: While in college (NYU) hopefully. That's next year.

Doug: What's your advice to the potential comics pro?
Jim: It's a good profession, but I wouldn't want to spend my whole life there. I consider it a springboard from which you can go almost anywhere—serious writing, TV, advertising, et cetera. Don't get bogged down.

Doug: Here's the question we've all been waiting to hear. What's your pay?
Jim: Per page: $14. Per story: $322. Per year: Well, shall we say upwards of $5,000, depending on how much I want to work.

Doug: How did you happen to get in on *Captain Action* with Wally Wood?
Jim: Luckily, I had just finished a particularly good "Legion" story and he picked me.

Doug: With all the changes at DC and so many titles being dropped, is DC in financial trouble?
Jim: No problems that I know of, but the way I understand it, comics are only barely profitable. The big money is in gimmicks like Superman t-shirts, et cetera. All that garbage you get royalties for.

Note

1. Shooter's interest in science, in particular quantum physics, remains a lifelong passion, and a repeated source of story ideas throughout his career. —*Comicology* eds.

Page of a non-existent story, drawn by Jim

Bill Schelly, "Profile No. 1," from *Capa-alpha* zine *Ivory* #2 (1969). © Bill Schelly.

IVORY #2   Bill Schelly   Page 4

Jim knows almost exactly what Mort
wants. Then, the pages are turned
over to Curt Swan, Ross Andru, Al
Plastino, Wayne Boring, or the other artists, who do the finished
artwork. (Boring varies the most
from Shooter's originals, while
George Papp sticks very close to
them.) (Often, they add or sub-
tract panels to get the correct
page count, because Jim is always
told the lengths in even numbers.)
And that's how it's done!

To encourage this young pro, Mort
Weisinger paid for Jim and his mother to visit DC headquarters in
New York. While there, Jim met
Murphy Anderson, and commented that
Anderson's pencils are just a mass
of indistinguishable squiggles.
Then Murphy inks them and somehow
knows just which lines to use and
which not to. Unlike some artists,
Murphy does not do the panels in
order. Then, Mr. Weisinger took
them to his huge home and to the
Superman broadway play which
greatly impressed Jim. (Shooter
says that Mort had to approve the
script before they could put the
play on; all those Superman-ori-
ented things are passed through
this comic-veterin's experienced
hands. Shooter had only the highest
regard for Weisinger, and considered him a genius at coming up with
plots and new angles. He said that
while other writers may be able to think up a plot, it is Mort that
'puts the meat on the bones'.)

Some of you may recollect the Fatal Five battling the Legion of Super
Heroes. Jim created this group of villains, and his explanation is
interesting. He classifies all villains in six categories: robots,
evil scientists, special-power villains, magicians, gimmick villains,
and strength villains. Then, with the help of Roget's Thesaris, he
chose a villain for each category, combining the robot and evil scientist into one. This group is a favorite of his which he tries to
have reappear often. Another villain was the Parasite, which came a-
bout when he was musing over names while in Biology class. While
daydreaming of this, the teacher was going around the room asking for
definitions of biological terms. When she named parasite as his term,
he thought: "That's it! I'll call him the Parasite!" He was so jubi-

lent he forgot the teacher until she'd repeated the term several times.
Dr. Mantis Morlo, another opponent of the Legion, received his name
from a 'Formula 44' cough syrup bottle. The list goes on and on.

I was amazed at Jim's ingenuity and talent. On the spur of the moment,
he could build up a plot with so many original details that it's as-
tounding. Sometimes, though, he is irked when some Superman-family
concepts are scientifically wrong. He claims that a Kryptonite <u>ray</u>
could not exist according to the laws of physics and chemistry.

When I suggested that we publish a fanzine one-shot as a team, he was
enthused, but insisted he be allowed to pay for an all-offset, four
color edition by doing an extra story for DC in his SPARE spare time.
It was to be for WORLD'S FINEST, and did appear in #172. We planned
to call the magazine <u>Shades Below</u> (a synonym for Hades) and introduce
as the main character, Brimstone. Sadly, Jim discovered he could not
donate the money to our cause after all, and the fanzine was scrapped.
(Brimstone later appeared in <u>Sense of Wonder</u> #4 to meet unanimous approval.)

However, Shooter cannot understand why anyone but children or pros
would be interested in comics, and to the extend that Fandom is. He
says that they are strictly for kids and he is only in it for the
cash benefits (although he enjoyed his work); for some reason, he
thinks Fandom must be a little crazy to be so enthused over them. Of
course, Jim couldn't explain why <u>he</u> has such a huge comic collection!
He claimed 'professional interest', but <u>we</u> know better ..!

          0   *0*   *0*

Ivory

IVORY #2, intended for the 53rd mailing of Capa-Alpha.
Pubbed by: Bill Schelly, 2211 Carol Drive, Lewiston, Idaho, 83501.
Phone: 208 - 743 - 5464.
Superman c 1969 by National Periodical Publications.

Welcome, all and sundry, to a second excursion into IVORY! (Okay, so it's _not_ an original opening ... but how _else_ do you start off an editorial?)

Yes, inconsistency again rears its ugly head; a few of you have possibly noticed that thish is printed mimeo and ditto. Now, if you'll all turn back to IVORY #1, you'll read that I prefer _ditto_ as a printing process. Then why the mimeo? In this case, I just want to see how it will work out. I hope the insides of the O's don't all fall out as they're apt to do. This is my first experience with mimeo, so please be kind.

<u>Mailing Comments:</u> Since this is being written far in advance, I have yet to receive K-a 52 which contains my first K-a contrib. However, I did receive the C.M. COMMENTS section in #51, so here are some thoughts on that: I didn't think Maggie's comment: "'You can quote us on any of this, if it pleasures you.'" was necessary, at least not the sarcastic last part. It seemed rather childish to me. :: While I have been stapling IVORY separately, largely to save Fred the work, I'd prefer to have K-a stapled together into one (or two, if one would be too large) big zine(s). For one thing, K-a is turning into a bunch of little entities, too easily mixed up, lost, or spoiled. I guess I oughtn't complain since that is probably the main reason I'm a member now (it cut down on C.M.'s chores). :: The Style Sheet was helpful to me in a number of ways, as I'm sure it was to most of the new initiates. For one thing, it cleared up my confusion on the subject matter we can use. I'll see if I can't stick more to comics stuff. But, if movie or miscellaney sneaks in occasionally, well -- it must be remembered that we comics fans have _other_ interests too! :: Interesting point about THE #3. I didn't make the rules, but I have no objections about the 5½ ppg. of advertizing in a genzine, as long as Harold Smith obtained no bonus points for them. (I assume he didn't.) However, I must side with Maggie on the subject of dated material. No one wants to read it, it clutters up the zine, and

Legion Outpost Interview

HARRY BROERTJES / 1974

From the *Legion Outpost* #8 (1974). Reprinted by permission.

Five years have passed since Jim Shooter ended his phenomenal career as a comic book writer. He was eighteen then.

Today he still lives in the suburban Pittsburgh home where he wrote dozens of Superman-family stories including, from 1966 to 1970, most of the "Tales of the Legion of Super-Heroes."

In a phone conversation this May with *Outpost* editor Harry Broertjes, Jim discussed his years as a DC writer and what he's been doing since leaving comics.

OUTPOST: You quit writing comics when you were eighteen, I believe, which is younger than most of today's writers were when they started in the business. Why did you get out so soon?

SHOOTER: It's a long story. You have to remember that I was thirteen when I started writing. For me it wasn't a whim or a juvenile fantasy that prompted my stab at authorship. It was the need for money, in a big way. What else can a thirteen-year-old do? Sell papers? I did that, too, by the way.

For four years while I was in high school I earned very good money writing for National.[2] The money went for necessities. There I was, an otherwise normal school kid, engaged in a very serious business with adults who were very serious about earning their livings. It's difficult to be fifteen and be very serious about anything. It leads to neurosis. You see, adults justify their existence by earning a living. In their peer group, jobs and earning a living take on much status significance. In a high school peer group, however, things are different. Writing comic books can have peer significance, in the same way that doing macramé or climbing the flagpole does. Making money can have significance

11

but only to save for college or buy a car or waste. Earning a living is adult—it has no high school peer group significance!

So, as a typical high school kid turned writer, the money—or more precisely, earning a living—quickly lost its charm. It ceased to be an incentive. It paid bills, but it had no personal meaning. What all this adds up to is that my former neurotic, teenybopper self lived and worked for praise. Pats on the back. Recognition. The local papers ran a couple stories on the "boy cartoonist." *This Week* magazine and *American Youth* published my picture. I loved it. This was my pay.

But [Weisinger] didn't have a hint about that. He was a hard-nosed businessman; he paid for my work and thought that was enough. He caused a kind of pathological fear of telephones in me. Every call from New York included liberal griping from Mort—too many words per panel . . . over the page limit . . . not on time . . . why can't you write like you used to . . . how the hell can we get a cover out of this—typical editor stuff. I knew the complaining was natural, and I knew Mort just wasn't the type to hand out praise. But this didn't help; it got so I was afraid to pick up the phone.

Mort was always right—businesswise, anyway. I was invariably naive, uninformed, and often downright stupid. I'm sure that in many ways I caused him more problems than I was worth . . . He made it clear that he expected the same from me as he would from any writer on his staff. On the other hand, it was very hard to deal with him, the situation being what it was. As it progressed, our relationship became more and more strained. I felt more and more inadequate. I can't say it was Mort's fault. Let's call it extenuating circumstances.

At any rate, it reached its worst when I became a senior in high school. I was tired of trying; the money never seemed to be enough for my mother; the stories never seemed to be enough for Mort—and my last chance to be a kid was slipping by! I tried to do it all—write for Mort, go to school and get good grades so I could nail down a scholarship, and have a little fun, like football games, dances, parties, and stuff. But it was too much, and it all suffered. I missed sixty days of school that year, my grades fell, my work output dropped, and I still missed a lot of high school life. The bright side was that I did get the scholarship, thanks to the fact that I clobbered the NMSQT [National Merit Scholarship Qualifying Test]. And I think I did some of my best work that year, though not nearly enough to please Mort.

The scholarship was a University Scholar's appointment at NYU—$17,000 plus an overlapping National Merit $6,000 maximum, so I was all set to go to New York. But by this time my difficulties with Mort had reached a head. We had a telephone argument about what my working arrangements would be

Jim Shooter, 1967.

when I came to New York. He really wasn't prepared for that, and although the lecture I got was probably justified, I had just about had it with him. On top of the financial disaster and personal chaos of my life, I just couldn't take the harassment.

So I decided to try Marvel. I flew to New York and got Stan Lee on the phone—and that, by the way, was amazing. He had never heard of me, but he agreed to give me fifteen minutes to talk to him—and getting to see him, I found out later, was an incredible feat. Anyway, talk I did, for almost two hours, and in the end he hired me. Though I couldn't swing the kind of deal I wanted—so that I could work and go to school at the same time—at least I had a job. Actually, scholarship or not, I wasn't really sure I could stand four more years of working and going to school. I gave up the scholarship to give Marvel a try. The deal was that I got a regular salary for a forty-hour week at the office and freelance for anything extra.

OUTPOST: Freelance for the writing . . .
SHOOTER: Yeah, and I was going to try some inking, coloring, and what have you. I did some editing—art corrections, little story corrections, and stuff like that. They showed me how to color, and I hassled Sol Brodsky until he let me do some inking samples for him. And boy, he was a slick one; he gave me these two splash pages, one by Jack Kirby and the other by the guy who did *Daredevil*.

OUTPOST: Gene Colan.

SHOOTER: Yeah, Gene Colan. [Sol] said, "Here, see what you can do with these." And I was impressed, inking Jack Kirby . . . I thought that was cool. Anyway, I did it and I tried to be as faithful to his style as I could—and that was my big mistake. I inked it like I thought he wanted it, the way the pencils suggested, because Kirby does a real thick job on machines and everything else. I took it in and then Mr. Brodsky told me that this drawing had been rejected originally, and it had been rejected because it was too cluttered and had no depth. And I had so accurately interpreted Mr. Kirby that it was still too cluttered. Brodsky then told me what I should have done; he's a good art critic. By the way, everyone else in the office loved it. And let me tell you, Marie Severin at Marvel is one of the gentlest, kindest, nicest people on Earth.

OUTPOST: The same thing happened to the Gene Colan sample?

SHOOTER: It came out all right, but it wasn't anything special. Anyway, Brodsky really showed me how an illustration should be done, and then he started showing me all the art that people from all over were sending him. Some of it was fantastic, but I thought mine was pretty good, too. At least some people— like Gil Kane—thought so.

OUTPOST: When did you do anything that Gil Kane drew?

SHOOTER: All I remember is that he did something I wrote, and he wrote me a little letter saying it was nice.

OUTPOST: *Captain Action* #2, maybe?

SHOOTER: Right, that was it. Anyway, I only worked at Marvel for about two weeks, wading through a mountain of books. They had collections of their own books, but they weren't complete. I'd read a series with a few issues missing, and I couldn't keep up with the continuity. Then one day Stan told me, "Okay, write something." Well, I was involved in all kinds of story conferences and stuff, contributing ideas on a bunch of books, but he wanted to see something of my own. I wrote him a whole bunch of story synopses. At the same time I was trying to find a place to live, at least temporarily. I was staying with one of the guys from Marvel then, and I was broke. . . . it's expensive to live in New York City.

OUTPOST: Yeah, I've heard.

SHOOTER: Things just weren't working out. I tried to see Stan, but he wasn't there half the time since he only came in on certain days; the other half of the time he had something else to do. I gave up and came back to Pittsburgh to see what kind of trouble I could get in here.

OUTPOST: What happened when you got back?
SHOOTER: The job market in Pittsburgh for eighteen-year-old comic book writers is pretty sad. First I wanted to try to get into some advertising, and that's pretty difficult.

OUTPOST: Was this writing ad copy or doing art?
SHOOTER: Anything involved with it; I wasn't too particular. I got good interviews but nobody wanted to risk hiring me, a kid just out of high school. My background wasn't exactly something I could sell. Some places gave me some freelance assignments. I did a billboard for Pittsburgh Outdoor Advertising; I did various little jobs, signs and whatever, but I eventually had to get a normal job. I figured, okay, what I'll do is just earn a living until I decide whether I want to go to school. I did that for a couple of years, working freelance on the side when I could. The latest thing I got to do . . . one of the advertising agencies I was interested in called me up; they wanted me to do a cartoon series for U.S. Steel, which I did. It was very successful. I've done several other things for them, too. I'm working fairly steadily now as a freelance writer-designer, brain-for-hire for an ad agency here. My name is coming up in advertising circles in Pittsburgh and possibly I'll get a job in that direction, which beats managing a chicken store.

OUTPOST: Which beats what?
SHOOTER: I managed a Kentucky Fried Chicken store for about a year. I quit when I decided to go back to school. I don't think I'm really sure what I want to do.

OUTPOST: Have you ever considered going back into comics again? Especially since Mort has left DC?
SHOOTER: Yeah, sometimes. I mean I really feel like I'd like to go out and just see Mort, now that I'm not working for him anymore. There'd be no hassle. I really like him, and I'd like to straighten things out. Actually, he was very generous in a lot of ways. For instance, after I was writing for him for a couple of months, he called me up and he said, "I want you to come to New York." He said he'd pay my plane fare, my hotel, the whole thing. That was a thrill. I was only fourteen then. My mother and I went. We visited his house and he took us to see Superman [the musical *It's a Bird . . . It's a Plane . . . It's Superman!* played in

the Alvin Theater from March 29, 1966 to July 17, 1966] on Broadway. I mean, it was fantastic. A fourteen-year-old's dream come true. I don't feel bad about everything. I've been in New York City several times since, and every time I've been there I've thought I should go up to Third Avenue and drop in on people.

OUTPOST: They aren't even there anymore; they're at Rockefeller Plaza now.
SHOOTER: Oh, are they? They'd just moved to Third Avenue . . .

OUTPOST: Yeah, they keep switching around pretty quick; they made the move last summer.
SHOOTER: I kept thinking I ought to go see Nelson Bridwell, but I don't really know if I'd identify with any of the people there anymore.

OUTPOST: Did you ever do any work with Nelson while you were writing at DC?
SHOOTER: Only when Mort for some reason wasn't there. Nelson would occasionally send me a letter and tell me to do something and I'd do it. Working with Nelson was pretty good. He was so tactful. Like, when he'd talk to you about something, he made you feel like you were right all along even though you were doing it his way. Then when I'd do a story and he'd send me a letter with the check, he'd have a nice little paragraph or two telling me how well I handled it. I was impressed. I could work for Nelson again. I mean, I guess we had a lot of other differences, but he was so easy to talk to and work with. Same with Carmine Infantino. It was a good deal.
    Say, is Cary Bates working there full-time?

OUTPOST: He's more or less working full-time, although it's on a freelance basis. He's been trying to get into film writing, I understand. But right now he's writing the Legion, the Flash, and about half of the Superman stories.
SHOOTER: The thing Mort always used to tell me about Cary Bates was he always had a good cover to go with a story. That was my problem; I was a good verbal thinker sometimes, but I couldn't get a cover. Cary would always come up with a cover first. I understand he had some rejections, but Mort told me when he had a cover it was a good one and he had a story to go with it. I always used to hear about Cary Bates and how he did it. I guess Cary heard about me, too.

OUTPOST: Did you ever try to do any art for DC or sound them out about the possibility?

SHOOTER: Not really. It was too hard to do *Superman*. I talked about it a couple of times with Mort, and he said if I were out there in New York it would be different since he could have somebody help me out. But all he ever wanted from me was scripts and layouts. At one time I wanted to just write scripts, without layouts, but he said no. The artists liked my layouts, so I always did them.

OUTPOST: You mean actual layouts of the pages?
SHOOTER: Oh yeah, a comic book page with simple sketches, a little more complicated than that.

OUTPOST: That's not the policy at DC, though; it's more or less just a plain script.
SHOOTER: Right. I think I was the only person who ever did that. I mean, in the summer when I was thirteen, I was reading *Adventure Comics*, and it occurred to me that somebody got paid for writing this. I remember I was reading a particularly bad story, and I thought, "I can write better than this." So I did. I wrote a story and sent it in. It was like a comic book; I had a cover on it and all the pages drawn, like a kid would do. But this story was reasonably coherent. Mort sent me a letter which didn't really say much except, "You're a nice kid. Send me another book." I did. I did the same thing again, the same way, written and drawn together like a comic book. The drawings were kind of amateurish, but anyway, the second time he called me up and said, "Look, I'll pay you for these, and let's do some more." And he bought them both—including the first one.

OUTPOST: Was that the story that introduced Ferro Lad and the others [*Adventure* #346–47]?
SHOOTER: Yeah, that was the one. Actually, the first one I wrote was the Doctor Regulus story, with the big golden spaceship [*Adventure* #348]. Looking back, it was kind of corny, but anyway, Mort liked it.

OUTPOST: That was the one George Papp drew later on.
SHOOTER: Right. And the second one I wrote was the two-parter with Ferro Lad. Then after that, for a while I did "Supergirl" and some other little things. I did a whole bunch of different books. I guess Mort wanted to try me out. Later I settled on the Legion.

But like I said, I've often been in New York, and I've thought about writing again. But I don't know how I could go about it. I don't think I would want to

Sample of Jim Shooter guide art.

work through the mail again; I know I don't like the work well enough to do that, but I do have a sister in Ithaca which is quite a way upstate but still in New York. It would be a bit closer than I am now. There are people who commute on a weekly basis. Of course, I don't know what kind of reception I'd get back there. I've got a feeling they'd say, "Jim who?"

OUTPOST: I doubt that, but I can see how working by mail could be rough. How did you and Mort work out the arrangements? I mean, plotting and all.
SHOOTER: Sometimes I simply submitted a story synopsis or a cover idea. Mort called me regularly to discuss my ideas and his. Often he'd suggest an idea and ask me to develop it into a synopsis. Mort got his ideas from readers' letters, TV, movies. Often he'd tell me to see a particular movie or TV show to pirate an idea. Sometimes Mort would veto an idea of mine and then, weeks later, suggest the same thing to me. Or sometimes he'd detail a plot to me. But more often he'd add things to one of my plots. Lots of times he'd select a subject, like "Send me a plot for a Super-Pets story, twelve pages."

Once we had hashed out a good synopsis, I'd take a big sheet of paper and do a storyboard, page by page—sort of a super-rough outline to get the length right. Then I'd plan what the villains would look 1ike and do some of the settings on scratch paper. After I had a reasonable idea in my mind of how I was going to do everything, I laid it all out on facsimile comic pages, complete with word balloons and dialogue, and mailed the results off to Mort, generally two to four pages at a time.

All the editing was done in New York, and only on one occasion did I have to do a rewrite—four pages of the Mantis Morlo story [*Adventure* #362–63].

OUTPOST: You always managed to keep a good sense of continuity in the "Legion" strip, even though DC never was big on that type of thing . . .

SHOOTER: That's what I wanted to do. Marvel comics did that for quite a while. Each story was complete in itself, yet there was a continuing thread. With the Legion I wanted to get into people's backgrounds and stuff. They all seemed so much the same to me. You could switch characters in the middle of a book and unless somebody knows the costumes they'd never even notice.

OUTPOST: Yeah, it's like somebody said in a letter column once, "You can't tell the Legionnaires without a score card."

SHOOTER: Right. I wanted to muddle around in their past lives and stuff like that. I hate to use the word again, but like Marvel did. Everybody had a past. It was kind of cool; I liked that. I didn't necessarily want to get sordid about it, but I wanted to make it interesting. Whenever I tried to do something like that, though, it was toned down.

OUTPOST: What kind of ideas did you come up with that didn't make it?

SHOOTER: I wanted to . . . well, in some of the stories I did I'd take a Legionnaire and I'd go through his past. I can't remember a lot of the specifics offhand, but for different ones . . . oh, like with Princess Projectra, I thought it would be cool if she were a real princess. And since she and Karate Kid got it on, I wanted to bring in all the royalty shtick, where she wasn't allowed to fool around with these commoners, and have hostility there, a degree of subterfuge—investigators checking up on her to make sure she wasn't running around with a commoner. But Mort vetoed that; "No way," he said. It was this kind of thing that he didn't like in the Morlo story. He sent back the four pages and said, "This is just rejected; write me four more pages." He said, "I don't want this shit; get this outta my book." So, okay, I had to rewrite part of it to suit him because in the synopsis I hadn't come on as strong as I did on the pages. He OK'd the synopsis, but he didn't like what it came out to be. That was the closest I ever came to getting a rejection. But I was sowing seeds there for future things between the princess and Karate Kid, getting her parents and everybody interested in what was going on. Anyway, that didn't work out too well. I didn't particularly like that story—it got too chopped up.

OUTPOST: That was the story that everybody appeared in too, I think.

SHOOTER: That's how Mort wanted it. I liked to get just three or four or five of them, but he wanted great hordes of Legionnaires in each one—thousands of bodies. And he wanted things like . . . well, for instance, he wanted me to write Super-Pets stories, which was all right, I guess, but really, my heart wasn't in it. Then, there were some good story ideas which I thought were terrific, but he didn't want them because they weren't in the Superman tradition.

OUTPOST: What kinds of stories were those?
SHOOTER: I had one that I sent in that he said got dangerously close to alcoholism, and he didn't like that. It involved one of the characters in the Legion, and Mort wouldn't have anything to do with it. His idea of human interest was the secret identity–type story.

OUTPOST: There was "The Forbidden Fruit," a Legion story that ran in the back of *Action* [#378].
SHOOTER: The drug addiction story?

OUTPOST: Right.
SHOOTER: When I suggested that he fought me for a while and we argued about it, the Comics Code and everything. Mort finally told me to write it. I wrote it, and he bought it; then they rejected it, and he wouldn't print it. I was mad about it for a while, but later on it was printed.

OUTPOST: That was kind of a forerunner story in that it came out before the famous Spider-Man story that involved drugs and didn't pass the Code [*Amazing Spider-Man* #96–98, published May–July 1971].
SHOOTER: In my case it wasn't only the Comics Code. It was the way in which I wanted to write—a little more serious. Like, somehow or another I got hold of a Batman comic around the holidays, I think, and it was a Batman Christmas story [*Batman* #247]. I just thought this was good. I picked this up and I was all excited—I was all ready to write comic books again. It was a terrific story; the whole thing tied together—several stories but all involving the same criminal. Batman was the kind of Batman that I'd always pictured, the figure lurking in the shadows. The lines he used! The gunman had Batman and a family held at gunpoint, and he's going to kill them. Batman says, "You'd better kill me first because if you fire that gun and it isn't at me, I'll be on you before you fire a second shot." That stirred my blood! This was cool; this is the Batman I want to write about. This is just the way. Oh God, this is what I wanted to do with Superman, Superboy, and the Legion of Super . . . y'know . . . idiots. I wanted to do this stuff, and Mort said this isn't our tradition. He said when you write that way, three college kids like it and two thousand little kiddies who buy

the books could not care less. He'd rather sell it to the two thousand kiddies. I suppose he had a point, but it stifled my creativeness or something.

But I had fun with a couple of the stories right at the end there. I had one with Duo Damsel in the back of an *Action* book [*Action* #380] where her two personalities had a little fight with each other. I enjoyed that. I didn't have a lot of room to work with, but it came out pretty much like I wanted it to.

OUTPOST: The artistic style of the strip has changed quite a bit, too, since you left. What did you think of the artists who drew your stories?

SHOOTER: When I'd have a story and an artist that I didn't particularly like would draw it, it really seemed to affect the story. Curt Swan was pretty good. He used to take my layouts and either, A) use them or B) improve on them. Some of the other guys really did a poor job as far as I was concerned. I like Curt Swan; the only thing I didn't like about Curt was that whenever somebody was hitting something or picking something up or doing anything, his figures didn't look like they were really trying, didn't look like they were under any strain or particular effort. But it was always so interpretive, very good. But the action scenes lost something.

For instance, I'd have Karate Kid smashing a tank or something like that. It just didn't have any impact. I'd give it four panels—I'd want this scene to really sing. I'd play it up big, but it wouldn't have any real zip to it. Curt always seemed to prefer to draw Lois Lane or something. He preferred to do a single character, like Superman, instead of an army like the Legion. He wrote me a couple of letters, gave me some interesting hints about how to do things.

OUTPOST: I remember that in your origin story for *Captain Action* [#1] and a few of your other stories—I'm thinking especially of the Legion story in which you introduce Universo [*Adventure* #349]—ancient history was the backdrop for the story's plot. Are you an ancient history buff?

SHOOTER: Sure. You don't have to dig very deep into history books to get into some fantastic heroics—Thermopylae, for instance, or Sergeant York or Gordon at Khartoum in the Sudan. Great stuff and fuel for any writer's imagination. I read history and comics in about equal amounts while growing up. They're often much alike—the best of both show the dark sides of their heroes as well as the bright.

OUTPOST: I don't know if I'd make such a sweeping comparison, but I see your point. What about the Fatal Five? I've been told that when you created them, you included five different concepts of super-beings: the robot; the powerful, mindless monster; the man with the gadget; the female; and the young kid. Is that the way you actually approached the FF?

SHOOTER: I didn't know there were five concepts for super-beings. In any event, I didn't follow an alleged formula that closely; as far as I'm concerned, I invented the half-man, half-robot in Tharok. The way I saw it, the biggest problem with the group was that it needed an opponent for Superboy. I solved that with Validus, the big monster, so naturally the others had to be different. Of course, the group needed brains and a woman-who I tried to make as seamy as possible. Mano and the Persuader just evolved into opponents for the princess and Karate Kid. In fact, most of my villains were created as opponents made to suit a particular hero, rather than just to rob banks. With the Five, the thing I wanted to stress was their professionalism. They weren't meant to be patsies. One of the things I hated about Thor comics was that he was so damn superior I found myself rooting for the villains. On the other hand, in the Iron Man stories, the hero was having so much trouble just staying alive; he lost credibility as a fighter. I aimed for the happy medium–powerful heroes struggling against high odds, heroic if you will. That was my concept. The Fatal Five were tailored to suit that idea.

At one time I wouldn't have given a nut for DC's being able to compete in what I created for the college market. But contrary to public perception, the people who appear in DC's comics do want to show human characteristics—and are consistent. The heroes in Marvel comics are always coming up with convenient super-human efforts to overcome anything, no matter what precedents have been established. But you can always count on Superman to be overcome by kryptonite . . .

OUTPOST: Cary has brought back the Fatal Five a couple of times in the last year or so. Did you ever meet him?

SHOOTER: No, and I'd really like to. I have a mental picture of him, and I'd like to see how accurate it is.

OUTPOST: If you can find the latest issue of *The Flash* [#228], it features Cary Bates in just about the starring role.

SHOOTER: Really?

OUTPOST: It was kind of like a couple of earlier Schwartz stories in which the Flash would go to a parallel dimension and discover how different things were there from Earth-1.

SHOOTER: Julie Schwartz always came up with stories like that. He asked me to send him an idea once—I guess Mort made a deal with him.

OUTPOST: An idea for what?
SHOOTER: For a story. Just to see if I could write for him. I wrote him a story which was very acceptable, I suppose, by Mort's standards anyway. But Julie wants you to think in terms of Earth-1, Earth-2, and tricks with the mind, things like that, and he didn't like my plot. Another thing I did—I . . . oh well, I'd better not say that.

Do you remember a Julie Schwartz story where Superman fought against the rest of the Justice League? The cover was terrific—all the Justice Leaguers lying around and Superman standing there, saying, "I told you who was going to win!" [*JLA* #63]. I suggested something exactly like that, the same thing to Mort, and then Julie turned up with that story. I thought that was kind of cute. But anyway, he and I never got anything together at all; I just sort of . . . when I was in New York I'd see him. I was introduced to him every time I was there. I guess neither of us remembered each other.

OUTPOST: Did you ever meet Murray Boltinoff? He's editing the Legion now.
SHOOTER: Again, I think so. I think I met just about everybody there. What usually would happen was that I'd miss my deadline—my mailing deadline—so I'd get on a plane and I'd fly it to New York personally. They had to have the story or else it would cost them air freight to ship the plates to Sparta. Then I'd go in the office in the morning, and I'd hand Mort the stuff. But it was awfully hard to hang around until he looked at it. During that period of time I'd just sort of wander around and bump into people. Carmine was great at those times because he'd always take me and introduce me and show me around. "This is what we do here, and this is what we do here."

OUTPOST: That's interesting. But you've never really seriously considered getting back into comics?
SHOOTER: Oh, I don't know. I've come within a hair of writing a couple of scripts. I'll tell you what I'm doing right now—I'm writing a book. I don't know what kind of a book writer I am.

OUTPOST: A novel?
SHOOTER: Yeah. I also wrote a couple of short stories, but I never did anything with them. They're just lying around somewhere because I never felt

they were good enough to pursue. When I was still working for DC, I wrote a story about a spy in the future, a James Bond–type, but instead of carrying an attaché case with trick weapons, I had them built into his body, like a Six Million Dollar Man. This was in '67. But now they have the Six Million Dollar Man, and if I were to submit my idea to somebody now, they'd say I copied it.

But the novel itself is about a fictional young lad who amazingly enough has many of the same things happen to him as happened to me in my foolish youth. Move over Peter De Vries![3]

OUTPOST: Speaking of things happening to you, after you quit comics I heard all sorts of weird stories about you. Like once you'd supposedly gotten into the cycle scene and had gone out west to California, and you were living out there writing underground comics under a pseudonym.
SHOOTER: I have a bike and I'm thinking of riding to California, but I haven't yet.

OUTPOST: And you haven't written any undergrounds.
SHOOTER: No, definitely not.

OUTPOST: Another thing that I'd heard was that you'd just kind of dropped out and you were in the Village in New York by now.
SHOOTER: Lies! I'm here in Pittsburgh where I've always been.

OUTPOST: Yeah, and my phone bill will show it, too. Thanks, Jim, and good luck to you.
SHOOTER: You too, Harry.

Notes

1. In 1976, National Periodical Productions was renamed DC Comics, Inc.
2. American editor and novelist known for his satiric wit.

Chatting with Jim Shooter

DAVID M. SINGER / 1981

Portions of this interview were conducted at a later date with Mr. Shooter by Mark Gasper. Reprinted by permission.

David M. Singer (1957–2013) indulged in creative endeavors that ran the gamut: he wrote poetry/essays, created board games, and brainstormed new inventions. In addition to being a lawyer and public relations consultant, Singer was also the founder/owner of Singer Publishing, Deluxe Comics, and Lodestone Publishing. Among Singer's cherished mementos sits a letter signed by Jim Shooter, dated November 27, 1984, in which Mr. Shooter congratulated him on the debut of Deluxe Comics, calling it "a fine beginning."

"MY PLAN IS TO MAKE THIS PLACE BIGGER THAN DISNEY"

DAVE: At the ripe old age of twenty-eight, you have been writing comics now for most of the past fifteen years. What prompted you, at the age of thirteen, to decide to write a comic book?

JIM: A desperate need for money. I mean, when you're a kid and you're thirteen years old and your family needs money, selling papers, delivering newspapers doesn't bring enough money in, what choices do you have? You can't get a job. I had this crazy notion that somebody got paid for writing and drawing these comic books. It looked easy enough. I wrote a script, and I sent it in. I got a nice letter telling me to send in another script. So I sent in two more, and I got paid for all three of those. I got regular assignments from that point on. I was too dumb to know better, that it just couldn't be done, so I did it.

DAVE: When you say that you needed money, are you talking in the sense that every kid wants to buy baseball cards, or did you mean your family needed . . . ?

JIM: I'm talking about paying the rent and eating regular meals.

DAVE: Hard times.

JIM: Yeah, stuff like that.

DAVE: Were they paying you like they'd pay any writer, or were they treating you like a kid?

JIM: That's hard to say. The only source of information I had was Mort, obviously . . . I've never really done a great deal of research to see whether or not I was screwed. All I know is that when I sold my first story it ended up being for a little over $4 a page. Shortly thereafter, Mort doubled my rate with no explanation to me or anything like that.

I heard years later, and I have no way of knowing if it's true or anything like that, that one of the writers who I was competing with found out that I was not being paid well enough. Here I am, this guy's competition, and he went into Mort's office and raised Cain. They ended up paying me a more reasonable rate. I got several more raises, and by the time I got out of the business, I was making $14 a page. This was not great, but it was respectable in those days. Now, the trick is this: That's not a bad rate for script, but I was not only providing script, I was also providing script and complete pencil breakdowns.

DAVE: You did the breakdowns?

JIM: Oh, yeah. You bet. I drew every single little picture. See, when I sent that very first script in, I had no idea what a script looked like. I drew all the pictures, all the characters, wrote all the little balloons, the little captions in . . .

DAVE: When you say "draw," do you mean stick breakdowns or fully fleshed-out panels?

JIM: No, I draw pretty well. I'm not a professional, but I draw pretty well. I drew as complete as I could draw. I mean they were finished drawings. I put every brick in the wall and the whole thing. Now, Mort told me a couple of times that I really didn't have to get that complete. As a matter of fact, I got some letters from Curt Swan that he told me I could be a little simpler with the stuff. I didn't have to noodle it quite as much.

DAVE: He didn't feel you were impinging in his area?

JIM: Oh, no! As a matter of fact, they were delighted. That was one of the things that Mort said was one of my selling points. That since I gave them pictures, they had visuals. I mean, let's face it, at the ripe age of thirteen, I didn't have the command of the language. I didn't have as strong a technical background as most of the people I was competing with. What I really gave them was pictures. That was, I gave them more visual stories, I think, than most of what they got. It was also much better to get a story—even if it's crudely illustrated—that's illustrated because then you can say, "Okay, this picture's wrong," and tell the artist to make a different one. You don't have to visualize, so it's much easier to edit.

But for the most part they used everything I did. I have a splash page that Curt Swan was nice enough to give me, and it turned up in our warehouse. I don't know how it turned up in the Marvel warehouse but it did.

DAVE: When you were writing comics at fourteen, did you feel closer to the readers by virtue of being the same age as your audience?

JIM: Recently, I wrote a piece for Jack Harris at DC that hasn't seen print which talks about exactly that. I'm disappointed it's not in print because I'm real proud of that piece. I think that I had a unique situation. I was the same age as my audience and also very close to the age of the characters that I was writing: the Legion of Super-Heroes. The audience that I was writing for were my friends. It was an incredible synchronization because my friends became my characters; my characters became my friends; I was my characters; my characters were my audience. Everything was just all together; it was weird. I think as a result of that, some good things occurred in the stuff that I wrote and that I was very fortunate.

DAVE: Could you write as fast as a teenager as you do now, or have done before you assumed this position?

JIM: I'm actually a very fast writer. When I was a teenager, don't forget, I was going to high school. Every day I'd come home from school, and I'd have to sit there and do pages because as soon as I finished one job I'd start on the next. Mort always wanted more from me than I could give him. First of all you have to understand that I already sort of worked an eight hour day, and I had homework and things like that—

DAVE: Chores, I guess, as well.

JIM: Oh, yes, sure, and I didn't have a whole heck of a lot of time to devote to it. The second thing was that the pictures took a lot of writing time. I did more work than some of the writers in the industry today who write as a full-time job.

DAVE: Were you that good, or was DC that weak, that they had to take a thirteen-year-old kid?

JIM: I just happened along at the right time in the right place. Mort had mostly older writers working for him, like Edmond Hamilton and Leo Dorfman, and I think he needed another writer. He just happened to be [in] the market for another writer. Basically there had been no new faces in comics for years and years and years when I came in. I was part of the first wave of new faces in comics. There was a ten-year gulf, and then three people came into the industry: E. Nelson Bridwell, Roy Thomas, and Jim Shooter. All of those people came into the industry through Mort Weisinger. Roy only lasted two weeks with Mort, but nonetheless, we all came in through Mort Weisinger. We were the first of the new wave. Shortly thereafter, Cary Bates showed up. Somewhere in there, Archie Goodwin did his first stuff.

We were the first new people in a long time. They couldn't get by with just the old people anymore and they needed new people, so I just happened to be there at the right time. It wasn't that they were booting people out to make room for me. It was that the guys were getting old, and there weren't very many of them.

DAVE: One of the big differences, right away, when you started the "Legion" series, was that you started emphasizing characterizations . . .
JIM: Yeah.

DAVE: . . . whereas, prior to that, the first two pages would be almost the same every issue. "We're a club. These are our members. These are our powers." It was as though they were meeting each other for the first time each issue. It always seemed as though the dialogue was interchangeable among the characters.
JIM: I agree. That's how I thought about it.

DAVE: Did DC like this change, or was it that your stories overall were so good that they were stuck with your change?
JIM: No, they liked it. See, a lot of people think that there was this huge difference between Mort Weisinger's approach and Stan Lee's approach to comics. You know, that Mort liked bad comics or something. Now I want to tell you something: I worked for Mort for five years, and I got endless lectures from him. I've worked for Stan for almost five years now, and I've gotten endless lectures from him. It's like déjà vu because sometimes in the very same words Stan will tell me the same things that Mort told me. Mort knew technically how to put a comic book together. So does Stan. Mort knew characterization

and plot and action and the whole thing. From a technical standpoint, they are virtually interchangeable.

The difference between Mort Weisinger and Stan Lee was that Stan Lee had the best comics writer in the world writing for him, namely himself. And Mort had a bunch of kids and old guys who were really science fiction writers.

Mort just didn't have the fire power that Stan had on the front lines there, so when I was providing some Stan Lee–inspired characterization and stuff like that, it wasn't against Mort's wishes for sure. I mean, that's what he had wanted all along. As a matter of fact, he wanted a lot more of it and a lot better than I could do, but I did the best I could. Their approaches were really not all that different.

Basically they both observed the fundamentals of good writing and the fundamentals of good storytelling. They both approach comics cinematically. The other difference is that Mort aimed a little lower. He'd do a Super-Pets story and stories where the heroes would all turn into super-babies and stuff like that because he was shooting just a little bit younger.

DAVE: What do you feel is the basis of the appeal of the Legion of Super-Heroes?

JIM: I think that is a book that succeeded on concept: It's got a bunch of young heroes (which is an appealing concept) in the far future with science fiction connotations, and it has characters who were easy to understand; the youngest kid could figure them out. Yet there were enough things that you could do with those characters that it would keep some of the older readers interested. Maybe not as many as the X-Men, but a substantial number. I think that the fact that it was concept-strong enabled it to survive some bad writing and pretty average art.

DAVE: Once you began writing the Legion, I noticed a greater experimentation with panel layout while you were breaking down the book. Was this a conscious effort on your part, or was this influenced by the editors?

JIM: Frankly, it wasn't my fault at all. The panels that I laid out were always nice, square, regular panels. In those days it's no secret that the people at DC were just desperately trying to figure out why Stan Lee's comics were selling better than theirs, or were creeping up on them, actually. They tried everything.

If you look through my run of "Legion" comics, you can almost see the gears turning in Mort's mind. One time he tried strange panel arrangements because he saw that some Marvel books had strange panel arrangements. Another time they tried coloring in the gutters, because they thought it would look more colorful and brighter (it looked terrible). They were just desperately fishing around, trying to find some magic ingredient that would make it as popular as the Marvel books.

I think that's one of the reasons that Mort appreciated me because I was obviously very influenced by the Marvel stuff. Not to denigrate his other writers, but being younger, I was a little more hip to the kind of things that appealed to people my age. Some of these guys were superior writers, but I might have been a little more aware.

DAVE: Were you able to adapt your stories to Bridwell's and Weisinger's plotting of the future history of the Legion? For instance they had decided who was going to die and who was going to marry . . .

JIM: Actually when I started writing the Legion, it was unique. It was sort of a miniature Marvel Universe. Basically I was the only writer, there were only four stories done by other people, in my four or five years of work there. They didn't affect what I had done. In that little corner of the DC universe where I could govern everything and I could keep everything consistent, I was a miniature Stan Lee guiding things along. All by myself I had all of these plans about the futures of these characters, right from the beginning. I would be setting things up which Mort or the casual reader wouldn't realize, but that six issues down the road they would say, "Oh yeah, he said something about that in issue . . . whatever it was."

For instance in the story that I introduced Ferro Lad, I knew that the guy was going to die. I didn't know exactly how, but I created him to die. "Oh, I know, I'll create a character who'll be a martyr." I put him in there. His future was sealed on the day he was created.

I had been writing the Legion for six or eight issues, and Mort said, "OK, write a story where the Legionnaires are all grownups, a future Legion story, the adult Legion." I thought about it, and I said, "Gee, well then I've gotta know what's going to happen to all those guys." And he said, "Nelson will help you." I don't know whether he and Nelson got together, or it was just Nelson or what (Nelson would be a good guy to interview on that), but he laid it out to me: "OK, these two will get married. . . . they'll get married . . ." They pretty much gave me those kinds of things. They didn't so much pick who would die as they decided who would get married. I think they told me some other things. I'm not sure now. At any rate they locked me into some stuff.

The only objection I had to it was that it was sort of the most obvious choices. They had all of the couples who were going together then, getting married later. No one had any girlfriend troubles, everything just came out like you figured. As a writer that bothered me somewhat. I said, "Let me see what I can do with this." I muddled with that story for a long time. I did some stuff in that story which wasn't obvious at that time, but I set some stuff up that I thought was pretty good. For instance, I had a statue of a dead character that wasn't even in the regular Legion yet. Night Woman . . . Shadow Woman, I don't know . . .

Whatever . . . A couple of issues later when I had a story where I could introduce a new character, I introduced Shadow Lass. After she became a member, I had her interested in one of the guys. She was interested in one guy for a while, then I had her going through two boyfriends before she ended up with the guy she was really going to go with, which I think was Mon-El. That also related to something back in the adult Legion story because Mon-El had gone out into space because his wife had died or something like that . . . Aha! Shadow Lass, who had died. Okay, well, why'd he go into space? That doesn't make any sense; it sounds corny. The reason is that here's this guy who'd spent a thousand years in this shadowy, nebulous place where you are just sort of floating, conscious the whole time.

A lot of people would say, "The Phantom Zone would be great; you could watch the world going on." But imagine, it's not like having a panoramic movie view of the world. Watching history unfolding minute by minute, hour by hour for a thousand years of a constant, sleepless myopic view of the world must be really dull. I mean, this guy has to be on the verge.

What does he do when he tentatively comes out into the world? I picture him as having a lot of trouble getting adjusted to life. "Oh, yeah, I can touch things, oh really. Wow!" Finally, he gets very tentatively adjusted to the world, falls in love with a woman, they get close, and she gets killed. Pffft. Back to the womb. Space, man, it's just like the Phantom Zone out here. It's dull. Of course, he would have to be alone; he would go back to the womb. The Phantom Zone experience would set him up for that beautifully. I had all that in mind and I got to carry some of it out, but I didn't get to carry most of it out. But. . . . I was slowly unfolding these things and trying to make them more interesting than what I was stuck with. For instance, I had Colossal Boy being a bachelor, and I had Shrinking Violet marry whoever the hell her obvious boyfriend was. My plan was that she would fall in love with this other guy, and, because of this unrequited love, he would go off alone and remain a bachelor. My intention was to slowly build a romance between Colossal Boy and Shrinking Violet over the years, and then when she would finally marry this other guy, Colossal Boy would be heartbroken and remain a bachelor. I did have all this planned.

When I came back to the Legion, I tried to carry off some of this stuff. The problem was that I no longer had my own corner of the universe because I was sharing it with Cary [Bates]. Murray [Boltinoff] always liked to have more than one writer on the strip. I would be trying to slowly build things, bring things along and establish characterizations, and Cary was doing things that broke up my continuity and characterization that disagreed with mine. I'm not blaming him. I never had any control.

DAVE: Was there any communication between the two of you?
JIM: Oh, no. I mean, I suppose I could have, but in a way I felt kind of strange about walking in and getting half of Cary's book. Cary kept insisting that it was okay, but I was real worried about that. Anyway I didn't have the control that I once had.

DAVE: Why was the Legion moved from *Adventure* towards the end of your tenure?
JIM: It didn't have anything to do with the Legion's sales. It had more to do with *Superboy*'s sales. The *Superboy* book was failing, and I think they felt they were diluting the impact of Superboy by having him under two titles at once. The Legion was doing just fine at the time; but Superboy's own magazine was failing, so they tested having a couple of issues of the Legion without Superboy and it didn't do well. They decided, "We'll put Superboy in his own book and put Supergirl in *Adventure* and boot the Legion out," figuring that Supergirl could carry the title. That worked out terribly. It didn't work out at all. They should have left it the way it was. It wasn't my fault. We were doing okay. It was that stupid *Superboy* book that screwed it all up.

DAVE: Were there political factions between the DC editors at that time over the use of talent?
JIM: I only had contact with Mort. Once in a while I'd go up to the DC offices and shake everyone's hand and say, "Yes, nice to meet you," but that was the only contact I ever had with them. Since I wasn't slated for other people, it was easy to believe what I'd heard, which was that each editor lorded over his own little company, kept his own little stable of people and guarded them jealously.

Once Mort asked me if I would like to try a story for Julie [Schwartz]. I said fine, so he told me to come up with a plot and a cover for the *Justice League*. I did and I sent it to Mort. I didn't even send it to Julie. I wouldn't presume to send it to him because I had always dealt with Mort. Mort told me that it was no good, and I accepted that and forgot about it. Sometime later there was a Justice League cover which looked a helluva lot like the one I submitted to Mort along with the story. It could have been a coincidence, but when I saw that cover I said, (postured indignation) "Wait a minute, that's my cover." It's the one where Superman is standing over a bunch of fallen Justice Leaguers saying something like, "I'm the toughest one." [*Justice League of America* #63, June 1968, cover art by Mike Sekowsky, story by Gardner Fox].

Another example of that is Captain Action. Mort called me up and said, "Would you like to create a new hero, in his own comic book?" I said, "Great." Then he started telling me what had to be in it: the name has to be Captain Action; a drawing of his uniform would be sent to me; he has to have a pet panther, a kid sidekick; he gets his powers from mythological coins . . . By the time he read me this list of stuff that had to be in it, it was like a travelogue.

I was just trying to find a way to fit it all into seventeen pages, or whatever it was. Anyway, I only wrote two of them, whereupon the book was turned over to Julie. I couldn't go with it because I was one of Mort's writers. It went to someone else, even though I was the guy who had started the series. It wasn't even brought up whether or not I'd continue to do it.

When it was time for the third issue, I said to Mort, "Do you need another Captain Action plot?" and he said, "Oh no, Julie's working on that now." The subject wasn't even broached. It went to another editor and being one of Mort's writers, I couldn't touch it.

DAVE: Why did you leave DC?

JIM: Because Mort Weisinger, who was a great help to me and a fine editor—who gave me my start, and who I owe a lot, and on and on and on—was a tough guy to work for. He told me up front when he said, "Look, you're going to be a writer. I'm going to treat you exactly the same as I treat any of my writers. No quarter given because you're a kid." And he meant it. He was very rough on me.

DAVE: I understand you had almost a psychological fear of the telephone.

JIM: Oh, yeah. When Mort had complaints, he delivered them in no uncertain terms. He was capable of being harsh.

He'd call me once a week for sure, and then he'd call me any time he had anything to say. Very often it was more than once a week. I got this weekly telephone call from this big important man from New York who would tear me to ribbons, talk about everything I'd done and point out its flaws. He was tough when he did this, he didn't mince words.

He sort of had a way about him; he'd put you down. That was the way you did it back then. I've heard a lot of similar horror stories about other editors. It wasn't horrible from their point of view; it was just how you do it. I guess they pictured themselves as gruff foremen.

That's fine now. I can understand that intellectually. But when you're fifteen years old and the executive vice president and head editor at DC comics—a big, important guy who could show you his name in *Who's Who*, when he calls you up to tell you, "You've done it all wrong again" and that you're "his charity case" and that "you can't write like you used to" and on and on . . . I mean, you believe it.

I used to be in fear of answering the phone. It got to the point where I'd hear a telephone anywhere . . . in school . . . in a phone booth, and I'd jump three feet in the air and my knuckles would get white. It took years, years for me to realize that I had some sort of telephobia and could stop jumping at the phone. "No, it's not Mort. Even if it is . . . (Bronx cheer)." It took me a long time to be able to deal with it because he was right when he told me how tough he'd be.

Later I found out that he considered me one of his better writers, that I was the guy that he could depend on. He felt that he could throw me any title, and he knew I'd give him a good product. But that was just how you handled people in those days. If you talked nice to them, they'd want a raise.

I think that if I was older I could have dealt with it. I would have been able to fire back. Actually that's what happened because when I turned eighteen I just started telling Mort, "No."

What happened was that when I was coming to the end of my high school career, I decided I wanted to go to college. I had a scholarship to NYU, an academic scholarship. I wanted to come up to New York and go to school here. I was in horrible debt, so I had to keep working. I had gone to school and written comics at the same time for over four years. I didn't think I could come home from school every night and sit there at the drawing board.

I asked Mort if I could have some kind of office job that I could do part-time to earn the money that I would need while I was going through school. He said, "No," but he wanted me to keep writing. I thought about that, and I just couldn't take it. I called up Stan Lee, who had never heard of me, and I told him who I was and that I needed a job. It was amazing just to get him on the phone, and then he said, "Okay, I'll give you ten minutes, and I'll look at your stuff."

I came up to his office, which was at 625 Madison Avenue at the time, and I spent two-and-a-half hours with him. He hired me and gave me a staff job and everything. But, there was a catch. It was a full-time job, so I couldn't go to school. That was all right because I really didn't know what I wanted to do. The only thing I knew was comics at that point, and I guess I just wanted to settle [down] for a while and figure out what I wanted to do.

Anyway, I started working for Stan Lee at Marvel Comics. My official title was staff writer, but I did everything. I did editing, art corrections, stats, paste-ups, mechanicals, everything. You name it. But it only lasted for about three weeks. It was too tough. I was eighteen years old, all alone in the big city, fresh out of Pittsburgh and having trouble finding a place to live. Everything is expensive here. I just said, "What am I doing here?" I owed the whole world money. Life was too tough. I went back to Pittsburgh.

DAVE: Coming from Pittsburgh, the son of a steel worker, did you feel intimidated by your better educated and more cosmopolitan co-workers once you came to New York?

JIM: No, because Pittsburgh is a pretty cosmopolitan place. Except for New York and Chicago, it has the most corporate headquarters and major universities of any city in the country. It's actually a metropolitan area of three million people, so it's not a small town. I dealt with a lot of very creative and intellectual people in Pittsburgh, particularly in the advertising agency. The difference was more in the city itself. New York is an oppressive place. Kamikaze cab drivers . . . a lot of people who don't speak English.

When I was eighteen and didn't have a lot of money and didn't have a place to stay, it was a big hassle. The people didn't overwhelm me. I was actually more comfortable at work than I was walking around on the street.

DAVE: What kind of work did you do in advertising?

JIM: I was a freelance art director. I wrote copy; I did design work; I wrote a billboard. I did studio work, consulting, paste-ups, and mechanicals, and I even did finished illustrations. I just did anything that needed to be done.

Towards the end of my tenure, I evolved a nice little situation with this one agency that had a very strange political situation. They would keep getting these jobs that were political hot potatoes, and the regular art directors would be afraid to touch them. What they did was get someone from the outside, so they would throw those to me. Being freelance, they couldn't fire me. I would do them, and none of them would have to face the danger of being on the wrong side of the political problem and getting fired.

That was good while it lasted, but I got real tired of taking my work into this agency and sitting there with one of the art directors and having to figure out in which order we should show it to this string of people in charge. If you went in the wrong order, you could get really mixed up. If this guy signs it, then maybe that guy will sign it. If we've got two signatures on it, then maybe the third guy will sign it. If we've got three signatures on it then maybe we can take it to the creative director. If the creative director OK's it, we'll go to the copy chief. If the copy chief OK's it and there are five signatures on it, then we can take it to the vice president. God, I couldn't believe it. People worry about comic books being overedited . . . they're crazy! You have almost total autonomy if you work in comics, compared to "the world." The real world sucks. This is one of the last places you can do anything, any kind of commercial enterprise, and have any kind of reasonable control over the product that is produced. Certainly more than films or television unless you're Alfred Hitchcock or somebody like that.

DAVE: Did you miss not going to college?
JIM: Yes. I sort of feel I missed both of the experiences which are the experiences for most people: being in the service and going to college. You talk to someone and most of their anecdotes about themselves are based on those experiences. I missed out on both. That's okay, I kept busy. I wanted to go to college, but the circumstances weren't right. Basically, I needed to earn a living. I didn't have any choice. That's okay.

Actually, I would have gone to college if my parents were wealthy and I could have just gone to college. If I only had to study and have fun, that sounds fine. That sounds like a ball, so I'm sorry I missed that.

But as far as it affecting me in my work, it hasn't at all. That's the nice thing about being in a creative business. No one ever asks to see your degree, they just want to see your samples.

DAVE: How did you get back into comics?
JIM: When I left DC in late 1969, I did not exactly part on good terms with Mort Weisinger. He felt that I'd stabbed him in the back. I worked for Marvel for three weeks before I went back to Pittsburgh. I didn't really leave Marvel in the lurch but working in a place for three weeks and then leaving is not exactly a great way to endear yourself. So I figured that I had burned my bridges behind me, and I never picked up another comic book. I didn't even

pick up my own, which were still coming out on the stands. It was goodbye to comics.

I was mostly doing advertising work when I got a call from Harry Broertjes who had apparently been trying to track me down for a long time to interview me for this *Legion Outpost* magazine. I couldn't believe it. I didn't know anyone was interested in this stuff. In the process of the interview, Harry wanted to know why I didn't get back into comics. I said, "I don't think I could work for Mort anymore." Harry told me that Mort had left shortly after I did, of which I wasn't aware. I said, "If DC really wanted me, they would have called me." But he insisted that nobody at DC knew where I was. I couldn't believe it because I could still be reached at my mother's address, which was the address they always had. But I also knew that Mort was the kind of guy who was very protective and might not tell anyone that address.

Harry called some friends of his in New York who worked at Marvel and DC. One of them was Duffy Vohland. Of course, I had no idea who or what a Duffy Vohland was, but when this person named Duffy Vohland called me and said he worked at Marvel, I presumed that he was some sort of editorial executive. He told me, "We'd love to have you working here. Why don't you come up and see us?"

I thought about it overnight and then I flew up here and pretty much just showed up on their doorstep.

I got an enthusiastic reception at both companies, and they both offered me work. I was amazed. Marvel offered me things that I'd never heard of like Man-Wolf. DC offered me Superman and Legion of Super-Heroes again which was exactly the way I'd left them. I could just step right in and write them. The stuff that Marvel offered was a lot different than anything I'd ever done. It was very complex, and it looked as though I'd have to read six years' worth of comics before I could even begin. It seemed very complicated and very hard to understand, which is not my style. I had enough reservations about Marvel, though I frankly would have preferred to work at Marvel. But the fact that I could just step in and begin writing at DC is what made up my mind. That's how I got my job through Harry Broertjes.

DAVE: When you were working on Superboy and Superman, did you handle Superman as a separate character, or as the adult extension of Superboy?
JIM: I don't know that I ever really thought about it. I wrote Superboy as Superman's younger self. I guess I really figured it that way. I always figured Superboy as being a lot better character than the other people did. I felt trapped a little bit with some of the Superman stuff. But I always figured that Superboy

would have to be a really terrific guy to be that powerful and still be that nice. He must be an incredible guy.

DAVE: You came back to the Legion after being away from comics for three or four years. During that time you must have grown considerably as a person. Had your approach to the series changed at all?

JIM: To tell you the truth, I really wasn't sure I could still do this. I just buckled down and tried it. I didn't have any sweeping plans for changing directions, I wasn't striving for a difference. The fact that I was more mature surely must have had some effect on the stuff, but I certainly wasn't conscious of it. I wasn't sure I could do it. It was scary, walking into an entirely new situation.

I was hailed when I walked into the office: "Oh, Jim Shooter's back. Oh my God!" Carmine Infantino walked up to me and said, "Oh, you're the guy who created the Legion." I said, "Well, no, but . . ." They were just thrilled to see me, but I just kept thinking, "What if I can't do it? What if I'm not that good?" Because you gotta understand, when I was working for Mort, he never gave me the impression that I was good.

DAVE: Besides *Captain Action*, which I guess was the first toy merchandising comic book, did you create your own series?

JIM: I created Karate Kid, and they later gave him his own series. I wasn't real thrilled at that. The thing was that I happened to be working at DC at the time, and I found out third hand that they were giving one of my characters a series. They didn't feel any obligation to ask me to write it or anything. But I never created another series. I never really had the opportunity to do it, and now that I have the opportunity, I don't have the time.

DAVE: Why did you leave DC and go over to Marvel?

JIM: I was working for Murray Boltinoff and Julie Schwartz, and they were very difficult people to work for—Julie especially. Our personalities didn't fit well together.

I really feel that the editor is responsible for the books, and it's his right to be in charge of them so I defend to the death their right to conduct business any way they want. But they were not conducting it in a way that I was all that enthusiastic about. They didn't seem to be getting into the stuff I was doing, although I really tried to give them what they wanted. That's why people have told me that my work for Murray doesn't sound like me. Well, no, it sounds like what Murray wanted. I was trying to be a professional writer and give him what he asked me for.

As a matter of fact, Murray sent me an old Edmond Hamilton comic book because he just couldn't communicate to me what he wanted. I think that it was the origin of Element Lad. He said, "This is the ideal comic book, the best comic book ever done. Read it and write like this." It was an old 1950s style comic book, where every panel is a new scene. If a scene lasted two panels, it was remarkable. Every panel would start with a caption like, "Soon, a fateful meeting on the Planet Zoon," and then you'd have a bunch of Legionnaires around a table and one of them is saying, (in an affected Saturday morning cartoon baritone) "We must find Timber Wolf!" Then the next panel would say, "Meanwhile on Earth, a dreadful accident occurs!"

If that's what he wants, fine, it's his job, and he's supposed to make that judgment. But I had trouble doing that; it's just not my style. But you can't really knock it because Murray was selling books. Apparently, there are a lot of people out there who want that, and Murray was giving them what they wanted. I'm not making fun of that stuff because a lot of it was good stuff, especially for the time that it was done. It might have been one of the most exciting comics of its time. I had trouble relating to it. It was inevitable that I would try to find something else that I could do better and feel better about.

Also, he kept rewriting things, and I wasn't happy with what came out. Eventually what happened was Marvel made me an offer, and I came over and started working for Marvel. Or, I tried to come over and start working for Marvel. They gave me Man-Wolf, and before I wrote my first issue, it was cancelled. Then they gave me *Super-Villain Team-Up*, and I wrote one issue. Then they took that away from me, and I was just about to give up on the whole thing again, when they called me up again and offered me a staff job: associate editor, second in command. And I thought, "That's interesting. I'll try that." I always thought I had an enormous amount of background in editing, that it might be fun to edit. You know, to use all that stuff that Mort had taught me.

DAVE: In your *Daredevil* stories, particularly in the issues that Gil Kane did, I notice a very relentless, vicious quality in the fight scenes. Was this a conscious effort on your part, was this Gil's addition, or was it simply what the stories dictated?

JIM: When I took it over *Daredevil* was very convoluted. Marv [Wolfman] had basically been expecting to get off the book for quite a while, so there were all these dangling plot lines. A character had been kidnapped six or eight issues ago and forgotten. So, I was just trying to tie it all up.

And I was working with Gil. Gil is really concerned with graphics, and he'd give me very intense faces, very powerful graphics, very dramatic scenes, and very intense fights, which is good but he's not the sort of person who pays a whole lot of concern to the plot. I would plot something which I had all figured out as being dramatic, a good story and very clear. Then I would get back pictures which didn't have a whole lot to do with what I wanted. But they were great pictures. I tried to make do with what I got. Some stuff was brilliant because Gil's graphics were just brilliant. Some stuff just fell flat because we were not telling the same story. I felt that some of it failed. Since I'm the writer and my input came after Gil's, then it's my fault. If it wasn't right, I should have fixed it, or I should have changed the story to make sense. Like I said, we all make mistakes. But we did some good stuff.

The issues that I think are the most comprehensible are the ones that Carmine [Infantino] did because I virtually did a full script for Carmine. He doesn't like working from plots. With Carmine I got more or less what I wanted. I think the series gets better, and I wish I could do it again because they were good stories. If they were well told I think that they might have been memorable.

DAVE: How did you approach Matt Murdock's blindness as a writer? For instance, did you find it necessary to find an incident in virtually every issue that would indicate that it was a "day in the life of a blind man"?

JIM: Oh, yeah, I think that was the key thing to the character. I read the previous issues, and Marv apparently didn't think that that was important. You could read lots and lots of those issues and not realize that he was blind. He was wisecracking and swinging around on this cable that sort of goes off panel and must be attached to something, and it came off as second-rate Spider-Man. Of course that may not be too bad.

But I wanted to focus on what makes this character unique, while they'd been focusing on what makes him the same. I focused on his blindness and his super senses and the advantage that gives him. I really tried to make it apparent that this guy is blind. I did a bit where he gets hit on the back of the head with a golf ball and temporarily loses his radar sense. Matt tries to get around his office, and he starts tripping over chairs and things because he's never bothered to count the steps. Everybody's surprised at him because they thought that he had the place memorized. I always tried to do something like that.

In that same story, I had him walk into a gun shop, and the guy behind the counter said, "Pardon me fella, you sure you know where you are? This is a gun shop." He has to explain why a blind man is in a gun shop. "I'm here for a gift." That kind of thing. Yes, I thought that was very important.

DAVE: Do you feel that Daredevil is similar to Batman?

JIM: I was accused of making him like Batman. I made him grimmer and less wisecracking. But, one of the first things I set out to do in that first story that I did, "In Search of the Purple Man," [Shooter's first issue (144, April 1977) features Man-Bull and the Owl; his Purple Man story appears in issue 147, July 1977] was to emphasize his difference to change his motivation. From reading Marv's stories, it seemed to me that the only motivation this guy had was that it was fun catching crooks. There was one scene where a sniper's shooting people at an ice skating rink. There are people dying all over the ice; Daredevil swings in, making wisecracks, gets the sniper, knocks him out, and swings away—leaving all these people bleeding on the ice. He caught the bad guy, and he's a happy guy.

I tried to think: "What can I do that's different? We've got lots of guys that catch bad guys. How about if we have a hero that's concerned for the victims?" Great. This guy's a lawyer so it fits! This guy's a crusading lawyer, concerned for the victims. Aha! I couldn't just change his character with no explanation; I had to have an event. I set up this thing where he's so busy searching for the Purple Man that he forgets about everything else. Foggy is drinking himself to death. His girlfriend, Heather, is suffering because her father is in jail. The father thinks he's really guilty. Only Daredevil can solve all their problems. But what's Daredevil doing? Chasing the bad guy. I build to the point where her father is so upset, so sure he's guilty, that he commits suicide. This is the event that brings it home to Daredevil that he's been doing this wrong. You screwed up and you've been doing it wrong, and it's cost this guy his life. Now don't you feel like a schmuck? That was the event I created to make exactly that change in character.

My intention was that Daredevil would be the hero who would be concerned with the victims. Gil and I plotted the redemption story. First we had the story where the father was dead, and Daredevil felt terrible [issues 150–51, January–February 1978]. Then came the redemption story, where he would be just lost in this fog, and this little kid would get hit by a bus or something like that. The kid's scream, of course, is a lot louder to him than it is to anyone else. He can't get away from being Daredevil. By saving the kid, and getting the bad guy, in that order, he redeems himself. He decides, "I blew it once but now I understand, and I'll never do it again. I'm going to be concerned for the victims." And that was going to be the new Daredevil. I felt I was stuck with a creature of the night, a guy who's blind and has super senses is either a creature of the night, or he's crazy. I figured that anybody who runs around in this red suit with horns on it in the middle of the night, sneaking up on people, has got to be a scary figure—and that smacks of Batman. What I was doing different than Batman was to give him a characterization as Daredevil which fit with his characterization as Matt Murdock.

A crusading lawyer is a person who's concerned for victims, and so is Daredevil. Daredevil would have his outrage based on the victim's suffering. His primary goal would be to take care of the victims, not to just happily chase after the bad guys while the victims are bleeding to death. That was what I intended.

Unfortunately, at that point, I was forced to get off. I didn't have time to write it anymore. Roger McKenzie took it over. He and Frank Miller got really heavily into a Batman riff. They just lost what I had set up. They went a different direction, which is their right.

I think that Frank, who's now writing and drawing the strip, realized the error of their ways and is coming around to what I was saying. My feeling is that Daredevil really is a guy who's different from Batman. He's not a psychotic and he's not hung up on avenging his parents. He's a creature of the night, but he's a whole different kind of creature. I think there's room for several different creatures of the night.

DAVE: How did you approach the Avengers? Did you find it difficult to handle so many diverse characters?

JIM: One of the letters I got that I was proudest of was a letter from a fan that picked out something I was deliberately trying to do. In one *Avengers* story, every character under the sun appeared even though there were a couple of characters who only had a couple of lines. He said that even from those couple of lines, you could tell what kind of people these were, their character was conveyed, even though they only had a couple of key lines. I spent more time on that than anything else. Not only what they would say but just how Captain America would say this, or just how the Beast would handle it. Things like that.

There was an issue of the *Avengers*, it may have been the last one I wrote, where Iron Man gives the order for the Wasp and someone else to start trying to get in touch with the Avengers who aren't present. They're coming in to give their report, and he asks, "Who'd you get in touch with?" The Wasp says, "We got in touch with Black Panther, somebody else, and oh, yeah, Captain Marvel called us, he said something about being aware of our need." That wasn't in the plot, and it wasn't in the pencils, but when I'm writing this, and I came to the part where they were supposed to have gotten in touch with Captain Marvel, I felt, "No! He would get in touch with them because he would know;

he's cosmically aware." It leaped up and screamed at me, and I put it there. I'm so proud of little things like that because anybody could write, "Yeah, we got in touch with Captain Marvel," but it's the essence of the character, that Captain Marvel knew. In every place where a person talked or did something, I tried to find something unique about them to emphasize. I got that letter, and it was a real thrill.

DAVE: Did you ever consider writing outside of comics: a novel or a screenplay?
JIM: Oh, I don't know. Let me tell you this. I think that as far as stories go, I can write stories with anybody. I think that I know how a story is put together, and I can put together a story as well as anybody anywhere. I could do stories for TV or novels or anything. What I'd have to do, if I went outside of comics, is I'd have to learn the form. Just like I learned the form and researched it when I was thirteen years old. Just like I figured out how to do it so they'd like it. And it's a lot of hassle to learn the form.

Comics is really a good place to be. It pays well; it's something which is easy for me. It is virtually untapped as far as its potential goes. It's an incredible medium. I'm not under any pressure or in a terrific hurry to leave it. It might be interesting to try something else someday. I tried writing one of those novellas [*Stan Lee Presents: The Marvel Superheroes* (1979) was the ninth volume in the Marvel Novel Series and included Shooter's prose story about the Avengers, "This Evil Undying"] for the Simon & Shuster Marvel series, and it was my first effort ever in prose. My peers told me I did okay for the first time out. I felt a little awkward about it because I kept feeling that if I really studied this and had a command of what I was doing, then I wouldn't be feeling my way along so much. But I don't feel too incompetent to do other things. I just feel that I'm okay where I am.

DAVE: Do you foresee yourself going back to writing in the future?
JIM: Oh, gee, I don't know. Sometimes I wake up in the morning and I just can't face another day as editor, and I think, "Nope, today I'll tell them I quit and be a writer." But I really don't think I'll do that. I'm a pretty stable, secure person, and I like this job. It has its rough moments, like when your character is assassinated in the *Comics Journal*, but that's part of the territory.

DAVE: Do you want to discuss whatever you just alluded to?
JIM: The trouble with this job is that I don't think anyone really understands what it is. It's the ultimate flak-catching job. To the people—the publisher and the president and all the financial people and everyone who is one of the

upstairs executives here—I am responsible for everything that goes wrong at Marvel Comics. To the fans and the pros and everyone else I am responsible for everything that goes wrong in Marvel Comics and with their lives. It's part of the package deal. Archie really sympathizes with me.

DAVE: Archie Goodwin?

JIM: Yeah. Because having been here one-and-a-half years, he is one who knows you're just constantly getting blamed for stuff that you may or may not have had any control over. But what's the difference, as far as the *Comics Journal* is concerned? What I was alluding to is since I've been here, I've had to let Rick Marshall go, and he made a lot of comments about Marvel and me to anyone who'd listen. A lot of that stuff got printed in the *Comics Journal*. When Marv Wolfman and I couldn't reach a contract settlement and he went to DC, he had a lot of stuff to say that got printed. When Roy Thomas and I recently couldn't reach a contract, he had a lot to say. And it all gets printed in the *Comics Journal*. The fans really don't know what goes on; they only know that they read these vituperous letters, and I guess they think I'm this monster that lives in this cave here and slays anyone who comes in. It's kind of frustrating because you can't reply to anything like that. It'll just make it worse. You can't say anything. It's really unfortunate, but it's part of the deal.

DAVE: To address that for a minute, there are rumors circulating about George Pérez's departure. Anything you want to talk about?

JIM: There's not a lot to talk about. We parted on very friendly terms. Basically, what happened was that George used to do an incredible work load here—four books a month or something like that. I guess he started having personal problems, and he had to substantially cut back his workload. He cut down to only one book a month, and finally, his contract expired. We knew how much he had been doing.

He was still quite welcome to be here and draw for us and everything, but after his contract expired the people at DC went after him in a big way. I can't blame him for wanting to do some work for them. They paid him very well. I guess he got over his problems, and he started being able to do more work. So, he picked up, aside from the regular book that we had given him here, some regular work there. Now, the trouble was that he picked up too much, and he had to give up something. I guess, he ultimately decided he wanted to work for them since they had more for him than we did.

He wrote a nice letter saying that being under the deadline pressure for two companies was too much, and he wanted to simplify his life. He still intends to finish up the stuff he has been doing for us and to work for us in the future if he has the time. There is no hostility that I'm aware of.

DAVE: You mentioned earlier that when you first worked at DC, each editor jealously controlled and guarded his creative people from the other editors. As Marvel's editor-in-chief do you fear a similar sort of situation at Marvel, which is now divided into a similar system of editors controlling a stable of books?

JIM: I don't think that having several editors necessarily creates that situation. I think that it may create the danger of that situation. But if you'll notice, we don't have editors with their own stables of people. We have got the same writers working for three or four different editors. I encourage that. My whole job as far as I'm concerned is to make sure that these guys are not working at cross-purposes, to coordinate between them. And we're all very friendly; people get together all the time. I insist that everyone on my editorial staff either do artwork or writing or something like that. They all work for each other, not for themselves, and that helps cross-pollinate.

I think that way as long as we have one person in charge we preserve the best of the Marvel system which just had Stan in charge, guiding everything. But by having all those people who have a degree of power over their books, that gives us the best of the DC system, which is that it brings in many thoughts, much variety. I don't want all the books to be the same. I want to have a difference between Al Milgrom's books and Louise Jones's books. I don't want them to be contradictory. I do my best, we all do our best to keep in line with the Marvel Universe because I think that's great—it's great to have a consistent universe. I've learned a lot about what not to do, how not to handle people, and also positive things about how to work with people, from the string of editors I've worked for. I'm trying to avoid the pitfalls and accentuate the positive. The books will tell if we're working right. If they get better then we must be doing it right. If they fall apart, then I screwed up.

DAVE: Has not being familiar with most of Marvel's books, the continuity of the Marvel Universe, which you've referred to as being a very beautiful thing, hurt you, in this position?

JIM: I am very familiar with the early ones. The early Marvel stuff is what got me interested in comics in the first place. Those books got me to write my first story. Afterwards, I kept track of the Marvel stuff because I wanted to know what was going on. If nothing else, it was my finger on the pulse of comics. Towards the end of my first tenure at DC, I didn't follow it as much. Then when I got out of comics the first time, I didn't follow it for a period of years.

Since I've been working here, of course, I've been keeping on top of it. I read every single thing published. I do have a gap in my knowledge, but I've found that it really doesn't hurt me. If something comes up that I'm not familiar with, we've got the bound volumes so I can research it. In my five years here at Marvel, I have acquired a nodding familiarity with what went on. If someone mentions the Kree-Skrull war, I can say, "Oh yeah, that's in the *Avengers* that [Steve] Englehart did." I don't remember it as well as I remember . . .

DAVE: You mean [Roy] Thomas. Thomas did it.

JIM: Did he? Oops. Well, anyway, I know it's there. I can go look it up. I know what they're talking about. But if you ask me about the first Molecule Man story, I can give you that panel by panel. I can tell you what happened because I remember that; I remember it clearly. I read it when I was a kid. I liked it, and I probably reread it a couple dozen times. So, in the time that I've been here, I've probably at least paged through all that stuff, looking for things. If you know the fundamentals of writing and have a reasonable background in the Marvel Universe, between the droves of experts we have around here, your own general knowledge, and the bound volumes, you can get by. I got the writer wrong on the Kree-Skrull War but that is not really going to affect anything. If I would write something in a Bullpen Bulletin about that, I certainly would go look it up. I wouldn't trust my memory. That's never going to be a problem. Stan doesn't know it all either, and even when he was doing it, I don't think he knew it. He got along.

DAVE: What do you feel makes a good editor?

JIM: Back when I was working with Mort we'd do some talking about the plot and sometimes we'd hash it out. Once the plot was OK, he said, "Write the story." And when that plot was OK'd and the story was written, sometimes Mort would fix a few little mistakes. It was usually pretty much what I'd put down. Then he'd call me up and tear it apart panel by panel, telling me everything I did wrong. Hours and hours on the phone, telling me everything I did wrong. Now that sounds bad, but in a way it was good because I got to the point where I had the confidence that after I wrote it (unless I went crazy), that was the way it came out.

In the four or five years I worked with Mort I had a total of four pages rejected. They weren't rejected because of the writing. They were rejected because after approving the plot and after I wrote the pages, Mort had thought about something and decided, "I don't want to do this, so restructure it." I actually cut out panels from those pages to save the panels, so I didn't even have to rewrite the whole four pages. I just rewrote panels here and there.

I think that's good and that's how an editor should work. You should put your input in at the beginning, and after it's all over, you should sit down, go over it, and say, "Look, next time you come to this situation you can do something more exciting."

That's how I work it with my editors. They deal with the writers however they want to because that's their problem. The way I deal with the editors is I get the printer's proofs, the make-readies, and I go through them with a ballpoint pen and make my comments. After I'm done with that, I sit down with the editor, and I go over it. Now this is printed already so nothing can be changed. If I come to a lot of stuff that I don't like, then I know I have to have a lot of long talks with the editor. But generally, I'll have comments like, "This dialogue is too convoluted," or whatever, and I'll say, "When you come to this again I think you should do it differently."

Most of the time they'll say, "Oh, OK." A lot of the times, especially with Milgrom, they'll say, "No, I did this on purpose, it works because of this—." Sometimes he convinces me; sometimes he's right. Those guys shouldn't feel that someone's looking over their shoulder. They should have the confidence that once they finish it, the book will go out the way they want it. Then if we have a fundamental disagreement, we should work it out. I think that's real important, and that's the way we do it here.

Traditionally at Marvel, the writers have had more or less that kind of latitude. The writers have been given a lot of input into the books. That's the Marvel tradition. I think that's just great. Same with the artists. You criticize the efforts and try to make it better next time. You don't mess with it in progress.

DAVE: That's one of the things that Steve Englehart mentioned in his interview. You had your shot, and either you did it or you were out.

JIM: Yeah, I agree in principle with what Steve said, but with the qualification that that applies to people who are capable of being reasonably on the mark. Which Steve usually was, his stories were usually acceptable. The only thing is that even in the stories I did for Mort, I would do things wrong and Mort would fix them sometimes.

I can recall Steve Englehart stories, where for instance, Thor throws his hammer and it returns to the spot where it's thrown from, rather than to his hand. Now for the sake of the plot, it was convenient for Steve to have it return to the spot it was thrown from rather than to his hand. That's wrong! It's a mistake that should be fixed. And if that infringes on somebody's creativity I'm sorry, but that's too bad.

If he's defending that kind of stuff then he's wrong. If he's saying what I'm saying—which is you can't get into anything or do something wonderful unless you have some kind of reasonable understanding with your editor that you'll get your differences ironed out first and that what you finally write is basically going to be printed—I agree with him. I think that his implication that that used to be the way and isn't any more is wrong. The people that are capable of handling things that way, the Goodwins, the [Dennis] O'Neils, and even newer guys like Roger Stern, don't have people rehashing their stuff. Basically, it's the new guys, the younger guys, the guys who need more training who are the ones that are getting more stuff rearranged or whatever.

Ideally, I would like everyone to be in that situation. I'm sure the editors do too because they don't want to work. They want the stuff to come in, be ready, and go out. When Archie Goodwin turns in a script, you read it, it's nice, and you send it to the letterer. That's how they want to do it; they don't want to have to hassle with the stuff.

I sort of agree with the principle of what Steve said, but I disagree with his assessment that we want it otherwise. I also find it strange that he's condemning comic books that he admits he hasn't read in years. I think there's a lot of stuff that's being condemned because people aren't reading it. Walt Simonson's done some wonderful *Galactica*s; Frank Miller's *Daredevil*; Mary Jo Duffy's *Power Man*. It's good stuff! And it tends to be written off by people who haven't read comics in years. I don't understand that.

DAVE: Some people say that the four-color comics industry is slowly on its way out now and that it's just too big to fall overnight. Do you see that, or do you see a viable future?

JIM: I think they're crazy. I think that, especially here at Marvel, the regular comics are the backbone of the operation. They're doing fine; they're selling well. They're profitable, and we're very happy with them. I think there may come a day when you just can't get letterpress printing in that kind of volume. If the presses at Sparta ever break down, I sincerely doubt that they'll replace them, so we may have to change the package in that we may have to go to offset printing at a slightly higher cost.

But the point of the matter is this: I think that Marvel will always publish a package that is the least expensive package that we can put together. And if the least expensive package we can put together costs 75¢, that's what it will be. I think it will sell just like the regular comic books. I think there is a market out there for inexpensive entertainment. As long as we're producing whatever the most inexpensive package we can produce is, we'll sell those.

We'd like to open up other markets. We'd like to open up the trade paperback market. We'd like to open up the magazine market more than we have. We'd like to open up a lot of other markets that we haven't even explored, like videotapes and stuff like that. And we're doing all that. I think the fact that we're doing market research and testing and trying things out like the magazines, the trade paperbacks, stuff like that, people say, "Aha, see, that's because the comics aren't selling." No. That's because the comics are selling well enough that we can afford to expand.

It's good business to diversify. If I were in business and I had one product, I sure as hell would want to have more than one product, so that if disaster happened, I would have some kind of hedge. So, we're comfortable enough that we can afford to mess around and try different formats.

That (pointing at a rack of comics) is not comics. That's one way to package comics. Our product is graphic stories. We can package them any way you want. That's not an expensive package. Epic is a more expensive package. There is lots of stuff in between these two. There's lots of stuff that I don't have with me now that I can reach to show you. We can package graphic stories in many ways. Graphic stories is a medium which is just as viable, just as powerful as film or television or any medium.

DAVE: In years past, there were several Marvel-oriented shows on television, *The Merry Marvel Marching Society* had five different superheroes and *Spider-Man* cartoons and *Fantastic Four* cartoons. Basically, they represented quite accurately, the comics. Now, whenever you have something on TV, a cartoon or live action, it seems like it's been changed drastically for some type of audience that you think is out there. Why is that?
JIM: That's not us. Until recently when we acquired our animation studio, we had no facilities to do animated work, and all the animated work that's on television is controlled by the networks, really. Because you have to make presentations to the networks, and if they're interested, they put up the money. Since they're putting up the money, you better do it their way.

What happened was, we signed some deals with the TV people for some of the live action stuff and some of the animation stuff in which we really didn't have enough of a veto power. There was nothing we could do about it. They had an option to do twelve characters, or something like that, and until they ran out their contract they could continue murdering our characters on the tube. All that has done is to convince us how important it is not to let them let Spider-Man have a dog and stuff like that. We are older and wiser, and we have a large commitment now to making sure that we don't get our characters screwed up again.

In recent years, we've had a lot of interest in our characters and a lot of people want to use our characters on TV, but we haven't had any control over them. The networks use them the way they want to, and the studios that produced them were not capable of understanding the Marvel stuff and treating it the right way.

I don't think you'll ever have 100 percent control over it as long as the networks are involved. As soon as you do a movie, you're using a lot of other people's money, and when it's their money, they obviously have things to say about it. But we're working on it. That's why Stan's out there.

DAVE: Does the licensing restrict you? For instance, you can't turn Conan into a homosexual because it destroys his value to the other licensees?

JIM: Yeah, of course we have to respect the property. This is a great argument against people who say comics are losing money or comics are going bad. A lot of people will tell you, "Hey, comics just exist on the merchandising." We don't own the merchandising for any of those licensed books. Look how many licensed books we have here: *Rom, Conan, Tarzan, Micronauts, Shogun Warriors, Star Wars, Battlestar Galactica*. I can't think of them all. We don't own any of the licensing or any of the merchandising on any of that stuff. The only way we can make money is if the comics make money. We've got a lot of them.

They must be making money because the comics are our only source of revenue from those characters. We're very happy with licensing good properties as well as with licensing our characters to other people for their use.

DAVE: As editor-in-chief of Marvel comics, if a thirteen-year-old kid wrote in with a plot synopsis with breakdowns and a cover layout, probably in color, would you consider him in the same way that Mort considered you?

JIM: Yeah, I think that I'm a reasonably objective person, and I think that I could probably tell if the guy really had it. The thing is, though, that I don't have the time that Mort did to work with him. He'd have to be better than I was. He'd have to almost be a finished product when he came in. Whereas when I came in, I really needed a lot of work and was fortunate that Mort cared to take the time to work on it. But regardless of age, race, national origin, or what planet they're from or anything, if the stuff is good, we'll make them an offer.

Shooter and Stan Lee at the 1986 San Diego Comic Con. Photo by Jackie Estrada.
© Jackie Estrada.

As a matter of fact, when I started working here, they had this standard answer that they'd give everyone who'd send in, "never send samples; we don't need writers; you can't get work by sending in samples." That's what they were telling people at conventions and stuff. There was this little form letter they'd send out, saying, "Thank you very much but we don't need writers; we already have writers." And I said, "Wait a minute. Now I'm the editor. How am I going to tell people that you can't get a job by sending in samples? That's how I got my job. Furthermore, that's how everyone I know got their job. We're not going to lie."

It's a lot of work for me to go through all these samples and write all those letters, and I often spend my weekends doing it. Anybody who sends in reasonable samples gets a reply. If it's on the back of a paper bag, in crayon, probably Virginia [Romita] will just send them a postcard, but even those I see and go through before I tell her to send these people postcards. If it's a sincere submission, I'll read it, and if it's got any merit at all, I answer it.

I have a memo right here to call one of the people who sent in samples. They were good, we corresponded a couple of times, and she's going to come up. I'm going to spend a couple hours with her, give her the

$1.98-how-to-write-Marvel-Comics lecture, and let her try and apply. If it doesn't work, she loses. If it works out, it'll be yet another case of somebody who sent samples and got work.

DAVE: What is Stan Lee's present role? He's listed as publisher and he's general spokesman for Marvel, but does he have any direct input anymore?
JIM: Oh, sure, but not really in the day-to-day stuff. His title is executive vice president and publisher. What that means is that he is the second officer of the company. The president of the company, the president of Marvel Comics, is Jim Galton—oh, by the way, we just changed the name of the company. The president of Marvel Entertainment Group is Jim Galton.

Stan also has another title that has to do with our film projects, but I don't know what that is. Probably executive vice president and producer or something. At any rate, he's the creative director. He literally has the final say on everything that has to do with the business.

DAVE: It's more like a veto power than an input.
JIM: No, not true. He doesn't mess around with the day-to-day stuff. He mostly spends his time out at the coast overseeing movie projects, TV projects, and the animation studio we just acquired. And that's fine. As far as comic books go, what Stan does is, we send him a Xerox of every cover, and he makes his comments on the covers. When he's in town, we get together and talk about whatever the major issues are. Like, if we want to make a major change in a book, if we're going to kill Aunt May, I'd have to sit down and talk it all out with Stan and the editors, writers, and artists involved.

Quite often, we'l have general meetings where we'll go over a batch of books and sit down and really talk in general terms about how to make good comic books. Any time there's any major decision made regarding the books, cancelling or starting titles or anything like that, he's involved in the decision. Very often he goes along with what I suggest because he knows I'm on the firing line and I have the most information, and I think he trusts me.

When we start a book, a lot of times I'll go over the plot with Stan. He doesn't read every script. He doesn't read every finished book. He doesn't work with them constantly day to day, but he is still the ultimate creative authority on the stuff. And that suits me fine.

DAVE: You give the impression that you're going to be in comics for a long time to come. Are there any editorial levels left between you and Stan Lee, or is he now a man with his neck on the line?
JIM: That's a funny way to put it. Uh, no, I report to Stan Lee and Jim Galton.

DAVE: Until Stan leaves, you can't move any further up?

JIM: I don't want to move any further up.

DAVE: But if you wanted to?

JIM: I guess not. But Stan Lee has already left. He's already out on the West Coast, and he's functioning as creative director rather than, in a technical sense, the publisher. But that doesn't matter because if they said, "Look, you'll be a publisher now. You'll sit in Stan's office, and you'll talk on the phone all day," I don't want that. I am as high as I can go and still have any real contact with the creative process. And that's where I want to be.

Now, they can pay me lots more money. They can change my title. They can call me anything they want: head bottle washer, that's fine. But leave me here. Leave me alone. That's the nice thing about this job. I really feel that with my guys here I can make Marvel Comics wonderfully successful. There's really no limit on what we can get done and how wonderful we can become. My plan is to make this place bigger than Disney. It's not something I can do, of course, but I feel it's also Galton's plan. I'm not in a holding pattern here. We're going to charge ahead. And, yeah, I plan to be in comics for a while. I don't see why not. It pays well; it's pleasant. I got my own room. What more could you ask? I mean, look at this luxurious office, right?

Jim Shooter Radio Interview

CHRIS BARKLEY / 1982

CB: This is Chris Barkley with another edition of *Bad Moon Rising*. Tonight is probably going to be one of the toughest shows I've ever done. I have on the line here Jim Shooter, editor-in-chief of Marvel Comics, and over the past month or two, there have been allegations as to whether he's going to kill off certain characters, set up certain situations . . . and I felt it only fair to present this forum to all you listeners who like comics and to find out the truth of the situation. . . . Now, why don't I stop stalling and get on with the interview. Hello, Jim Shooter.
JS: Hello.

CB: Before I say anything else, I wanted to thank you for agreeing to tonight's call. I'm very nervous about this.
JS: Ha, ha! It's my pleasure.

CB: Now, over the past . . . maybe month, there have been allegations of you making certain changes in the Marvel line, mainly *Master of Kung Fu*, *Moon Knight*, *Thor*, and specific changes with *Captain America* and *Iron Man*. The talk is that you are going to kill off Tony Stark and Steve Rogers and have someone else replace those two.
JS: Yeah, well, uh . . . None of that's true.

CB: At no time did you ever say that in front of anyone or even muse it?
JS: No, no. What I said was, as a rhetorical example, I said that there are no sacred cows, meaning that if some writer came to me with a brilliant plan to revamp or make Captain America exciting—more exciting—that it would be considered. I chose Captain America particularly because I thought that

Undated photo of Jim Shooter,
Marvel offices. © JayJay Jackson.

was probably the most extreme, unlikely example I could think of—trying to demonstrate to one of our writers that he shouldn't be fettered, he shouldn't let his mind be shackled by imaginary constraints.

CB: Was the writer in question Doug Moench?
JS: Yeah. See, Doug was writing *Master of Kung Fu,* and *Master of Kung Fu,* like every other Marvel book, is doing pretty well. Sales are going up steadily and anyone else would be real happy to have it, but Marvel right now, everything is doing very well. *Master of Kung Fu* has been our third from the bottom book for years. I was approached by the editor of *Master of Kung Fu* [Ralph Macchio], a fella who works for me directly who was unhappy with the way the book was going and felt that they were sort of in a rut, so I talked to him about it, and I said, "By all means, if you can come up with some great new direction for it then go ahead. You shouldn't feel constrained that there's any particular rules that you have to be bound by." The editor approached Doug with what I thought was a great opportunity to create new things or make changes or do anything he wanted to try to make it catch fire. Apparently Doug wasn't thrilled with that concept, and I ended up talking with him. The editor gave up trying to convince him and asked me to talk to him, so I talked to him. Doug felt that it was, I guess, just fine the way it was. What I was offering him was

an opportunity to just sort of go wild and create something exciting. We'd done that recently with *Daredevil* and *Fantastic Four* where a writer . . . we just told him, "Look, don't be afraid to do things," and as a result we've seen dramatic new increases in the interest in those titles. That's basically what I was looking for.

I have no plans to kill off anybody. I have no plans to make any specific changes on any titles. However, in general, I'm willing to listen to anybody who does. Basically there is no plan afoot, and there never were to kill any . . . I have no plans or desire to make any changes with Captain America. *I did* use those as rhetorical examples for what I was looking for in one title, our third from the bottom title, and I'm still . . . If somebody comes to me and says, "Hey, I've got a terrific idea; you'll love it; it'll make Thor wonderful. We're gonna kill off the Asgardians." I'll say, "Well, let me hear it." If it's brilliant, who knows? But, uh . . . don't hold your breath.

CB: What do you see as the responsibility of the writer or an editor in this case?
JS: I think the editor's responsibility is to . . . he is the guy who's solely responsible for that book, whatever book that he's in charge of. He answers to me, and I basically edit the editors. I feel that I'm responsible for the general priorities and very, very fundamental directions of the line mostly and the characters on a very broad basis and responsible for the cohesion of the universe because Marvel books all form one universe. I have to make sure they all interrelate properly, so the editor is basically in charge of the book. He works with his creative people to bring each title along. Each creative person's input and effect on the book varies from individual to individual by how much they're willing to take, how much responsibility they're willing to take. I'll give you an example: John Byrne, on the *Fantastic Four*, he likes to be left alone. He likes to carry the ball, and essentially he's doing terrific. Basically we read his work and enjoy it. The same is true of Archie Goodwin when he wrote *Iron Man*. He really didn't need a lot of help, and his work was sufficiently good that it really didn't require a lot of correction. So we knew well enough to let him alone. There are other writers—some of them are very good—who like to evolve things slowly and like to talk to a lot of people in the course of developing their stories and so forth. Chris Claremont for one—Chris will start talking about ideas for issues he has months and months and months in advance and bounce them off of a lot of people and get their reactions and so forth. He has a very organic relationship with his editor creating things, and Chris is regarded by most people as kind of the number one guy in the business.

CB: A couple more questions I want to ask you. What about Bill Sienkiewicz and Gene Day? I'm wondering why they left.
JS: Gene never left. Gene, unfortunately, died last week.

CB: We're talking about Gene Day?
JS: Yes, of a heart attack, but . . . at the point when he died he was still doing a regular series for us, *The Further Adventures of Indiana Jones*, and quite a lot of other work besides. I know that Gene, like many other guys, was doing some work on the outside for independent, smaller publishers and like that.

CB: And Bill Sienkiewicz?
JS: Bill Sienkiewicz told me about three months ago that after doing twenty-eight or so issues of *Moon Knight*, he was looking for a change. He was specifically interested in doing a graphic novel with me as the writer, so I said, "Fine, we can't hold a gun to his head and make him stay on *Moon Knight*." He certainly gave us yeoman service in the meantime. He is staying on, I believe, through issue thirty, and we're still talking about what he wants to do after that. Bill is, of course, such a terrific artist that we'll work with him on whatever . . .

CB: Working at Marvel in the near future, though?
JS: Oh, absolutely.

CB: Why'd Frank Miller [leave] after such a successful run in *Daredevil*?
JS: Frank . . . He was interested in developing one of his own characters and right about the time when we were starting out our Epic line of comics in which we buy limited rights to the creators' own characters . . . we were in the process of talking with Frank on that and right about that time the publisher of DC Comics called him up and made him a firm offer on the spot. He thought it sounded pretty good, and he agreed to it. He told me that he was gonna do a twelve-issue series with them. There were no hard feelings or anything. It's just that they gave an offer, and he took it. As I understand it that was almost a year ago. I don't think he's signed a contract with them yet, so I don't know. In the meantime Frank has been coming around and talking with us and making plans to do things with us as well, so if he eventually does go with a series at DC, I'm sure he'll be back. If the negotiations fall through since they've been going on for a long time, then he'll probably come and do that series for us and . . . whatever. We can't own everybody. We want to have the best people we can. We try hard to get them, but there's gonna be some good people everywhere.

CB: There's also the question of George Pérez, Gene Colan, Roy Thomas, Steve Englehart, Craig Russell, Marshall Rogers, Gil Kane, and Ross Andru. Do you feel that all these artists and writers going over to DC or smaller independent publishers will hurt Marvel?

JS: First of all, approximately half of those people you named work for Marvel more or less exclusively, and if they left they didn't leave . . . for any period of time . . . they didn't leave while I was in charge. Craig Russell, for instance, has just done a graphic novel for us and has done a lot of jobs for *Marvel Fanfare*. I don't think Craig works exclusively for anyone. He sort of likes to shop around on a frequent basis. Steve Englehart, as far as I know, is working exclusively for us right now on one of our Epic comics. I can't remember who else you named.

CB: . . . Gene Colan, Roy Thomas . . .

JS: Gene Colan and Roy Thomas. When Roy Thomas's contract came up, he wanted things that . . . we didn't want to give him. Even though DC was not offering those things, he felt obliged to go over there because he couldn't get what he wanted . . . same sort of thing with Marv Wolfman. Those guys both are very talented, and they're both very good. I think stylistically they belong at DC.

They kind of come from a different school than Stan and I come from, so that doesn't bother me. I don't think we've been hurt at all by that. In the meantime, we've gotten from DC Al Milgrom, Larry Hama, Frank Miller for a good long time, Terry Austin, Dennis J. O'Neil, Denys Cowan, Dave Michelinie, and Bob Layton, and the list goes on and on and on. I can't think of it off the top of my head, but the flow of people has pretty much generally been the other direction. And the people who have left have more or less left with my blessing. George Pérez left because he wanted all his life to draw the Justice League from when he was a little kid. He wrote me a very nice three-page letter explaining that there was nothing against us and that he really felt we were fine, but that he was given the chance to really sort of fulfill a childhood dream. He said he wanted to do that for a while, and he'd probably be back. We'd be up against that sort of thing, and I don't know what I should have done. As far as I'm concerned, right now, creatively we're stronger than we've ever been before. We have a terrific editorial team. We've got the people I want to have , almost without exception, and the proof of it is we are in the midst right now of our best year ever in our history. We're up some phenomenal percentage in sales and the money we're making and so forth, and this is the best year in our history—better even than last which was the previous best year in our history, better than the year before that which was the previous best year in our history, so I gotta figure we're on a trend here?

CALLER: Are you planning to simplify the Marvel Universe, and if so are you afraid of losing some of your older readers?
JS: Well, no. No, I have no plans to simplify if he means by that to make it sort of childlike or something.

CB: I think he means eliminating some of the extraneous, sort of out-fringe stuff like Baron Strucker coming back every so often and Hydra and AIM . . . things like that.
JS: I've been plotting some stories with Tom DeFalco recently that use Hydra. I really think Hydra's kind of a great concept . . . No, I have no plans along those lines. You see, people run into a problem . . . If something is sophisticated, then it's generally pretty easy to grasp. If it's just complicated, then it's usually pretty boring. I'm not in favor of things being complex for the sake of complexity, but I'm also not out to take away the subtlety or the intricacy or the sophistication of anything we do. I think that's an essential part of making it a real place. I don't wanna simplify it if that's what it means. I'm not at all interested in that. I want the Marvel Universe to work. I think it's a valuable thing, and I think we should protect it.

CB: Why did you have to have Yellowjacket divorce the Wasp? [Janet Van Dyne decided to divorce Hank Pym in the Shooter-penned *Avengers* #214, December 1981].
JS: It was the other way around. The Wasp divorced Yellowjacket. I saw that as . . . My question is, how could it *not* happen? I read everything those two characters ever appeared in, and I went to the trouble of finding a psychiatrist and asking him about behavioral symptoms and so forth to check my storyline against practical experience. I felt that, considering the history of the Wasp and Yellowjacket, that it was kind of inevitable. Here we had a woman who was clearly a very intelligent, very strong, very smart woman who clearly had been sort of suppressing herself and sublimating herself to this man who has an awful lot of on-panel mental difficulties. I saw . . . it's a situation where . . . In the past she always flitted around his shoulder and flirted with him and teased him, and he always said, "Not now. Can't you be serious, Jan?" and . . . you know, she had everything. She was wealthy and smart and glamorous and heroic and so forth, and even though he started out being a renowned scientist, in the last however many stories he's appeared in, I think very, very

seldom was he the solution to any problem. I think the only thing he ever did of any note was to create the most horrendous villain the world had ever seen in the form of Ultron. This guy's gotta have some serious self-doubts, so I saw it as a volcano getting ready to explode. I started preparing for the story when I wrote my first *Avengers* story in 1976. I started laying groundwork for this to occur, and I saw it as a very natural development of the characters. I think that . . . maybe . . . I've gotten a lot of mail to protest it, but it's been the kind of mail that expressed concern about the characters. "How can you let Yellowjacket suffer like this?" mail rather than "You're a moron who can't write." From what Stan tells me, that's exactly the kind of mail that he used to get on *Spider-Man* back when he did the . . ."How come Peter Parker can't have a girlfriend?" rather than "You're a moron, and you can't write" which tells me that the people care about the character which is what it's all about. So that doesn't bother me at all. I think we did real good. Besides I think people are going to be very pleased by issue 227 of *The Avengers* where there's some real significant developments with Yellowjacket and the Wasp.

CB: Okay. Let's see. A couple of questions about Bob Layton. What happened to Bob Layton, and, if Steve Ditko's style is low quality, when will Bob Layton do *Iron Man*?

JS: Steve did one fill-in issue of *Iron Man*, and Steve's style is kind of a style that a lot of people aren't real interested in these days although he's really one of the all-time greats of comics. But styles go in and out of vogue, so I kind of understand if people aren't interested in the look that he has. Steve's not doing a whole lot of stuff for us although, as far as I'm concerned, since he's one of the guys that created Spider-Man, he can come work for us anytime.

CB: You wrote "Legion of Super-Heroes." Any idea to get Mike Grell, and why do some artists work exclusively?

JS: It comes down to personal taste. I mean, we'd like all of the best guys to be exclusive to us. Yes, we've talked to Mike Grell many times. Mike has got so many projects going. He's always said he'd love to work for us but he's gotta get this, this, this, this, and this done first. By that time something else comes up, so I expect sooner or later he'll get around to doing a job for us. There are just some guys who kind of like to play the field and can't get settled at one company or another. That's okay.

CB: When will Epic arrive?

JS: Okay, the first Epic Comic will be published in October. It's *Dreadstar* by Jim Starlin, all new, all original, featuring characters which he did in *Epic Illustrated*. It'll be bimonthly after that. The second series, the first issue goes on sale in January, and that's *Coyote* by Steve Englehart and Steve Leialoha. There'll be more, but that's all we have so far.

CB: When will Chris Claremont end the Brood story in *X-Men*?
JS: I believe in the next issue that'll be on the stands. The one that's on sale in November—a dramatic conclusion.

CB: The last question I want to ask you . . . the *Cincinnati Enquirer*, the paper here, has an editor who may have a specific gripe against you because they took a swipe at the Pope John Paul II comic that will hit the stands Monday . . . Tuesday. . . . They said it was atrocious, but as far as I know they don't have a copy. How do you respond to people like that who don't know anything about comics and take a swipe at things they don't understand?
JS: Well . . . what can you say?

CB: I mean, I'm no fan of Pope John Paul, but it seems to me to take a swipe at a comic book about him without ever seeing it . . .
JS: Ignorance has never stopped people from attacking things. All I can tell you is that we did the best we could with it, and the Pope saw the drawings and pronounced them good. That's good enough for me. I think the overwhelming response we've gotten has been positive. This is the first comic book that I ever remember certainly and, as far as I know in comic book history, that the wholesalers across the country have come to us and asked us for. Usually they just take the comics and really kinda don't care too much, but we have had them calling constantly asking us to make sure they get enough copies and so forth. This was done more or less at the request of the Pope and the Pope's people and working with his biographer, Father Malinski, who has been the Pope's friend since childhood, so let 'em take swipes at us. We did the best we could.

An Interview with Marvel's Head Honcho

MAGGIE THOMPSON AND HAL SCHUSTER / 1983

Reprinted by permission of Maggie Thompson.

COMICS FEATURE: What is your educational background?

SHOOTER: Just high school. I had scholarships, but I couldn't afford to take advantage of them. The only other training I had was seat-of-my-pants training at various other jobs. I wangled my way into some advertising work and managed to work with some good people there who helped me quite a bit. My justification for being where I am is that I worked very closely with Mort Weisinger for five years, and Mort, even though his approach was not something that most comics fans appreciate, really, on a technical basis, knew what he was doing. Then after I came to Marvel to work as an editor, I worked very closely with Stan for several years and discovered that Stan, on a fundamental level and on a technical level, agrees almost to the letter with everything Mort ever taught me. It's only the fact that Stan was a better writer and much more with it. That was really the difference. The difference wasn't any magic, wasn't any actual technical part of the writing that made Stan's books better. Marvel books were better than DC comics because Mort Weisinger had me and other writers, and Stan Lee had Stan. I found that working with Stan and Mort Weisinger was the kind of training you couldn't get anywhere else. You can't get that in college. It's pretty much unique. There are very few people in comics who can claim to have as many years of training as I had, working closely with two biggies like Stan and Mort Weisinger. Almost no one.

CF: Now that you're a biggie, do you offer that kind of training to other people?

SHOOTER: I certainly try to. I certainly try to pass along everything I picked up.

CF: What is your literary background? Do you have any input from movies, TV, or literature?

SHOOTER: I don't watch television at all. I watch a few football games. I don't go to movies too much. Not that I don't like movies, I just don't seem ever to have time. I end up reading a huge amount of screenplays, as part of the job. We're always getting screenplays sent to us to look at for possible adaptation. When I was a kid, I pretty much stopped reading comics when I was eight, but I was a voracious reader. I read everything that wasn't nailed down—you know, cereal boxes, newspapers, soup cans, classics, anything that had words in it. I read a lot of books. I read a huge number of books between first grade and high school.

CF: Do you have any favorite authors?
SHOOTER: No. I like a lot of them.

CF: What has kept you in it?
SHOOTER: I've sort of awakened to the fact that we have something unique here. We've got a creative field that, for whatever reason, is not burdened with all the many problems of the other creative fields. If someone walks into my office today and they say they've got a great idea, "We'll do a comic book about . . . ," I say, "Fine, okay good. Let's do it." You don't have to have committees and many layers of management approvals, and it isn't dissected. There aren't networks to screw it up . . . it's really a place where you can go and you can create something and have a reasonable expectation of it coming out like what you intended. There is such spontaneity. There's just an incredible electricity about this thing and the way it's set up. Maybe it's just because we're still small enough that we're not subject to the kind of pressures that the TV people are and the movie people are. One of the reasons television is all so homogenized is because everyone is afraid to become different 'cause they want to do something like something else that worked. We're not like that. We don't have to be like that, and that philosophy has paid off better for us. If you blow it on a comic book you may be out thousands of dollars, but that's thousands. If you blow it on a major motion picture you may be out millions. I'm sure the people who are investing millions, therefore, are more of a nuisance because they're worried about their millions. Look, I can relate to that, but I really like it here where I don't have to worry about someone looking over my shoulder. I've never had any executives from upstairs come down and say, "Hey, do this," or "Don't do this." The common belief is that merchandising people come down and make demands or give orders. No—that never happens. Sometimes they ask me something nicely, and I usually say no. I'm always amused when I get these letters with these kinds of paranoid fantasies of what goes on here or

why something was done. We're almost always doing the best we can. If it doesn't come out right it's because we don't have the time or the people or something else necessary to do it right. A lot of fans perceive all kinds of enemy actions that just aren't there.

Now, do you want a list of what's wrong? What's wrong is kind of a flip side of the same coin. Because it's a business which is still not a huge money business, we make money the old fashioned way—in relatively small amounts, a little at a time. We're enormously successful, but we're small. We're a small company. There's a difference between a small company succeeding and Warner Communications succeeding. I'm sure that movie companies count their profits in the millions and the hundreds of millions of dollars. We're on a very small level. For the amount of money that's invested in this, and it's very cash intensive, we don't make over much. An enormous amount of money has to be invested to make a comic book, so a comic book when it's sold has got to make that money back first before it's even profitable. We are profitable on everything we publish, but title by title we count our profits in thousands, not millions. What that means is that you have a very limited number of people you can have on staff and so forth. You might want to do something spectacular and the money isn't there. I'm sure if you go out to Lucas Films you can count hundreds and hundreds and hundreds of people. One guy's whole job is to turn the switch on, and another guy's whole job is to make sure no one comes through that door. There is no lack of personnel. The resources [are] there to fine tune everything. They can still screw it up, but it's not for lack of resources. Now with us, because this is such a small business—it's just like a small business man who owns a grocery store and finds himself doing his own little repairs, painting the place himself and doing all the maintenance jobs and everything himself. That comes with being a small business. It's not like the A & P where he can bring in a crew of painters. We have a situation here where each editor is in charge of six—eight books. Most magazines have a big staff of people for just one magazine. I don't think comic books are substantially easier to put together than other kinds of magazines. It isn't easy to get everything right no matter how hard you try. If we publish a clinker, some people say, "This book is terrible, and it's because you don't care." I hate it when they presume our motives. Okay, they're right, it's terrible, it's not good. The reason is Denny [O'Neil] took his first vacation in two years. He went away for a week and was as one with the Rocky Mountains, and the book didn't get the attention it deserved. You're right, this went wrong and that went wrong, and there was no one here to fix it. It's not because we don't care. It's because Denny would have died if he hadn't gone to the Rocky Mountains to be one with nature. This business has all kinds of little irritations like that, little problems. I think that since I've been here, thanks to me, thanks to a lot of cooperation I've gotten from people upstairs, we've largely overcome a lot of these problems, and we're making things better all the time. I'm trying to preserve the spontaneity and preserve the kind of seat-of-the-pants way we fly around here and get rid of the down side, get rid of the limitations that have been imposed by the fact that this is still a small business. I think a trap that you can fall into when things are running pretty well, things are selling and you're making money, the temptation is to get very conservative. Like, "Okay, now we've got to be real careful." That's what happened to DC years ago.

CF: So that we have Superman perpetually frozen in a cast of unchanging characters.
SHOOTER: Superdog and Supermonkey and Superhorse and this and that. That's a huge mistake. I don't want to have that. I want to avoid it.

CF: Peter Parker doesn't even own a pet spider yet, after all these years.
SHOOTER: If he does it will be a big joke. We'll do it in a way that will fit in character. It will be something he would do.

CF: What is your method of preserving spontaneity?
SHOOTER: My method of preserving spontaneity is to simply not make rules. I don't make rules. I analyzed everything Stan told me and everything Mort told me and everything I learned in years of looking into things myself and analyzing everything I saw and read. I've come up with priorities, which are not rules. Basically, my theory is to keep an open mind. When somebody has an idea, they need not just set it aside because they think, "Oh, I know they won't like that." Maybe we will like it. I want to keep everyone feeling they can walk in with anything and get it listened to and maybe it will be done. Here's a for instance: I personally think that if a character dies, to me, that's just pretty irrevocable. I think it's important that we have a credible universe, and I don't see a whole lot of people jumping up after they die. I mean dead. I'm not talking about a guy whose heart stops for a couple of minutes, and they bring him back. I'm talking about, you know, dead. So, I generally frown upon the concept of when the character has died that you should bring them back. Don't confuse this with the fact that when the villain falls into the volcano, he'll be back next issue for sure. That's different. Maybe the guy has a teleporter on his belt or I don't know what he had. If we don't see him die, who knows? But, I think if we establish that a character has died, that is a fact of enormous importance.

THE OFFICE HANDBOOK OF THE MARVEL UNIVERSE
VOLUME ONE

JIM SHOOTER

Real Name: James Charles Shooter
Occupation: Editor in Chief
Identity: Publicly known
Legal status: American citizen with no classical records
Other current aliases: Big Jim, The Big Guy, "Trouble" Shooter
Former aliases: Mister Warmth
Place of birth: Pittsburgh Pennsylvania
Marital status: Single
Known relatives: Ken, Ethie, Carol, Pete, Liz, Johnny, Chris, Jimmy, Margie, Toots and Grandma
Group affiliation: Marvel Comics Group
Base of operations: New York City area
First appearance: Noon, September 27 1951, in Saint Anne's Hospital
Origin: Young Jimmy Shooter, at the age of 13, was picking up a new supply of comics at his local candy store when suddenly a Marvel Comic, glowing strangely as if charged with some sort of radiation seemed to leap from the rack toward the startled boy. The comic's slick cover grazed Jimmy's hand inflicting it with a nasty paper cut. Later Jim found that he had been endowed with strange and wondrous skills. The next day, he sold his very first comic story. Jim then worked his way through school selling comic stories and by playing the shoe-horn down at a local Jazz club, *Le Club Foote*. About a week later Jim came to work for Marvel Comics and has since been a leading force in the battle for honesty, honor, fair play, and nifty-keen comics.
Height: 6' 7" and a smidge
Weight: 228 lbs
Eyes: Two
Hair: Yes
Unusual features: See above information.
Powers: Jim Shooter possesses the editorial ability to sniff out the plot holes of any story at 40 paces. This power itself is not so uncommon, however, Jim also possesses the power to plug up said plot holes. Jim Shooter can also hold his breath for 86 minutes — in his hands. He can lift (press) spirits and he reads the Long Island Press (Lift). Jim Shooter is able to cut a maximum of 450 miles of bureaucratic red tape in the interests of fair play and common decency. He can split an atomic infinitive. Possessing just *this much* above average strength he can support his end of a conversation. He knows the ancient mysteries of 'Why the Chicken Crossed the Road. and has a license to drive points home. He can recite several area codes without looking and has been known to lick his weight in ice cream.

From *The Office Handbook of the Marvel Universe*, a parody of *The Official Handbook of the Marvel Universe* (1982), one of the projects Shooter launched at Marvel. © Marvel Comics.

And it should be treated with respect. It should be treated as if it were real. I've conveyed that at various times to the editors here . . . so . . . when Frank Miller wanted to do the resurrection of Elektra, he and Denny felt obliged to ask me about it. They came in and said, "We want to know what you think of this before we do it." They told me all about the story they had planned. They said, "We want to bring back Elektra." I said, "How are you going to do that?" And he explained it to me and it made sense. It convinced me; I could get behind it. It worked. If it works, if it's good, then it should be done. It shouldn't be prevented from being done because of some stupid rule. The point of what I'm telling you here is that resurrecting dead characters is one thing I'm really disinclined to do—but when someone pitched a resurrection story that was good, and made sense, I said okay. There is no rule. It's just that I want it to be good. I want it to make sense. When anybody brings in anything I'm ready to hear it; I'm ready to listen to it. Some people have brought in some wild stuff, and those people tend to be everybody's favorite artists and writers. Usually when their wild ideas hit the book shelf, everybody likes it, and everybody goes crazy over it and everybody writes fan mail. Most people who are not free with ideas are the ones that are having the trouble.

CF: How much attention do you pay to fan mail?
SHOOTER: I read each and every letter. I read every piece of mail. Everyone here will open and read every single letter addressed to him or her. I swear up and down in the Bullpen page that I don't reply to any, but I do reply to some. There are some that I cannot let go. Somebody has a question, and I say, "Oh, okay, thirty seconds . . . ," and I write it on the back of a post card. I pay an awful lot of attention to fan mail. And submissions, submissions are always welcome here. They're not opened by and screened by somebody down the hall. I open them and I read them. Maybe not the whole thing every time—sometimes I don't even have to go all the way through a plot to know it's not professional quality. I don't necessarily read every word of every plot, but I certainly read a big chunk of it—enough to know. I think that's incredibly important. I think that the mail is our most direct communication with the readers. They're the guys who are buying these things; we ought to listen to what they say.

CF: How long a day do you work, and how on Earth do you fit everything in?
SHOOTER: I've had that problem lately. That's been a big problem lately. This job is enormous here. It's enormous for all of us, the editors and everybody. One of my big problems is that I don't have any time . . . I haven't had a

vacation, really, for a long time. I've stolen a couple of days here and there, but for maybe five . . . or seven years I haven't had a vacation. Last night at two a.m. I was still answering fan mail. It's going to be an all-work weekend because Denny went on vacation. I've got to take care of one of his books and that means working over the weekend. I've got to write a Bullpen Bulletin over the weekend, a Bullpen Bulletin Special and a plot for *Team America*. That's more work than you can fit in a weekend, but I'll do the best I can. A while back, I was away for a couple days; I went to Atlantic City. I went there because a) I needed a day off and b) I was meeting David Michelinie and Brett Breeding there to discuss business. They had a lot of stuff pending, they had ideas, they had questions about the Epic comics, and all kinds of things. So, I figured I'd combine the discussions with a day off. But when I come back I have a sixteen-inch high stack of art submissions. I have another stack of plots—a small hill, actually. They're hard to stack because they usually come in small envelopes. I've got a mountain of stuff here.

CF: What does go on there as far as the procedure? Say in producing a comic or, from your point of view of running a line, how does your day go?
SHOOTER: I really try to stay out of everyone's way and let them create. I really do confine my input to fundamentals and helpful advice and being available to help with problems, and give sort of broad general direction–type of stuff. In general, I figure that I hired eight of the best editors I know of, and if I stay out of their way and give them what they need to operate, then they'll do just fine. We have meetings, and I tell them what I think—I go over their stuff after it's in print. If I read every book before it went out, that's a real different psychology than if they know they're the last word. They're responsible. They're doing it; they're in charge of it, and they know it. It's going to be whatever they say, and if it's not right I'll tell them later. "Aw, gee, you really shouldn't have done that. That's not good because of this or that . . ." Okay, then they'll get it right next time. I think there's some stuff that gets into print that isn't perfect or that I could have made better if I could have picked up a mistake or a spelling error or something like that if I'd read it before it went out, but I really feel that I'd rather not inhibit anybody. I'd rather have them feel—I'm talking about writers, artists, and editors—that what they do is given that respect. Whatever they do is really good, and if there's something not exactly right about it, we'll get it on the next one. I think that's important. I'm in charge of all the comics and all the regular publications here. A lot of my days are all administrative kinds of stuff, unfortunately. I'd really rather just kind of bury my nose in comics, but it's important that I represent all the

artists, writers, editors, correction people, and creative people of all kinds to the company—and I represent the company to them. A lot of my days are involved with doing what I can to get anything they need for them. I deal with Jim Galton and Mike Hobson, who is the vice president in charge of publishing. Hopefully I come away from those guys with policies that I can represent to the creative people. If they say, "We're spending too much money, cut all the rates in half," they're going to have to get someone else to represent that point of view. But they've never yet put me in an untenable position. They've never asked me to represent anything bad or unfair. I've been very effective so far—I've been very good at getting what we need to operate and very good in terms of their point of view, in getting the best creative people, and keeping the best creative people and sustaining the creative effort and keeping it running and running well. In other words, I've served both the company and the creative people, I think, pretty well. That may sound surprising—because people have been conditioned to believe that management people are evil exploiters and that creative people are oppressed victims. That's not true—here at least. At Marvel, we're of the opinion that the company and the creators are in this together—and that it is possible, make that essential, that we work together for our mutual benefit. Nothing that hurts creators can, in the long run, help Marvel. Nothing that hurts Marvel, in the long run, is truly beneficial to creators. The last three years have—each year succeeding has been the best year we've ever had. What I do is I say, "Okay, this is what I need." And I've gotten it. These people are great people, Jim Galton and Mike Hobson, and the other people around here I deal with. They don't always understand everything that goes on in the Bullpen with the comics and everything like that, but they've been extremely cooperative. Years ago, if something went wrong, some people who occupied this chair found it easier to say, "It's Cadence's fault." They passed the buck—just blamed things on the parent corporation rather than trying to fix them. When I took this job, I expected there to be corporate ogres that I would go talk to who would say, "Captain Marvel has to be green this month." I never found any of those people; all I found were people who were absolutely eager for someone to tell them what should be done. "Tell us what to do: we'll do it!" I said, "We need this and that," and they said "Okay, here you go." Usually, what I asked for—raises for the talent, more editors, whatever—worked out. And every time I got good results the people upstairs were even more eager to try to cooperate with me and give me what I needed the next time I asked. I never ran into any ogres. I ran into some people who didn't understand what I was talking about sometimes and I had to explain it, and people who occasionally had a slightly different point of view on the subject. They'd say, "Hey wait a minute. That won't work. Will it?" But in general, I've never had the antagonism that I was told to expect. I now believe that all that stuff about upstairs being the enemy was just a cop out. That was a lie. That was what people said so they didn't have to work. It was easier to just pawn off the blame on some nonexistent people than it was to get stuff done. I don't understand the origin of that. All I know is that I've had nothing but cooperation, as much as you could possibly expect. We are dealing with people here—I mean they're not just going to automatically agree with everything I say. But they are reasonable. Dealing with them is a big part of my job. It's unfortunate that it's a big part of my job because I'd rather deal with the creative things. But, somebody has to do this, and I feel I'm qualified to do this sort of dual role thing.

CF: Do you want to make any comments on the shake-ups in staff recently?
SHOOTER: Are you talking about Doug Moench?

CF: Yeah, and someone else—an inker or a letterer?
SHOOTER: As far as I know Doug was the only one who left. The rumor was that Gene Day was quitting and Bill Sienkiewicz was quitting . . . none of that was true. Doug and I disagreed about *Master of Kung Fu* and in the end—he decided to go elsewhere. Everybody here has standing offers—I mean, if you work for Marvel it's like playing for the Yankees; you can always go to other teams. Virtually everyone who works here has a standing offer from DC, and they're always getting letters from Pacific Comics and letters from First Comics. We're number one, and everyone is always after us. If someone really feels that they're upset by something or they think we're wrong or something like that, they can go elsewhere. With Doug, I'd been talking to the editor of *Master of Kung Fu* for a long time; it's Ralph Macchio—and I felt that there were things in it that were—kind of the same every issue. It was not as good as it could be. I'm interested in things being exciting and moving. I'm not interested in getting into stagnation. I saw it on *Master of Kung Fu*. It seemed like—I pick up an issue from a year ago and I pick up an issue now, and it's pretty much the same. I said, "Look, why don't you get Doug to come up with some way to jazz it up: to come up with some way to do whatever it is he's always wanted to do and was afraid we'd say no, to go crazy and come up with some ideas. The sky is the limit. The title is *Master of Kung Fu*. It doesn't even have to be the same guy; you can do anything. Tell Doug, 'Look, why don't you come up with crazy and weird, and let's do it.'" If I was a writer, I think I would have been excited by the concept. I would have said, "Wow, what an

opportunity!" Of course if he created something we would have paid him for it, many thousands of dollars. Then he would get the creator's piece of the incentive payment. There would be a lot of benefit to it. I also said, "Look, if you don't want to create something for us, then, you know, maybe we can get someone else to do it, and you can still write it." The editors on the book agreed entirely with me. They said, "Yeah, you're right. We really feel the same way." They called Doug, and Doug didn't agree at all. Doug thought *MOKF* was just fine; he liked it just the way it was. He thought we were crazy. After they talked to him for a while, they said, "Jim, maybe you better talk to him." I talked to Doug, and I told him the same things. He didn't understand why I wanted to mess with it. I told him, "I'll mess with anything. I don't want there to be sacred cows that you can't mess with. I want brilliant ideas! I want things to move and develop. People like that." He interpreted what I said to mean that I was going to kill off all of our characters and told everyone so. That's not true. I don't have any particular plans for any characters. I'm here to listen. If anybody comes in with a great plan for *Spider-Woman* or *Master of Kung Fu* or *Thor* or anything, I'm here. That's what I feel the job is. Doug, after talking to me, said he'd think about it, and then the next day he quit. I really haven't even heard who he's working for yet. I guess DC; I have no idea. I called in the editors, and I said, "If Doug is going to leave, is that going to put anyone in a bind?" No, no one was in a bind. Everyone had lots of people and writers assigned to the book to pick up where Doug was leaving. It's probably one of those deals when it's the best for all involved. I felt the same way about Gene Colan. He was having trouble here working with a number of the writers. It's a shame for a man as talented as Gene Colan, as brilliant as Gene Colan, who has been doing this for thirty years, to not be able to produce the kind of work the writers he's working with can accept. I'd rather have Gene Colan be someplace else and be a star because Gene Colan ought to be a star. DC should have a good artist. That's fine. We should have good artists. Everybody should have good artists. I don't want to trap people. Look, it's really better for everybody. It's better for everybody if everyone is where they feel best. So, with Gene, with Doug, if they really felt they had to be someplace else, that's good. They should prosper.

(The publishers of *Comics Feature* also publish a companion title, *Comics News*. We contacted Jim Shooter to do a brief interview about the creation of *US 1* for the first issue of *CN*. During the course of that interview, he told us some very interesting details about how he approaches a book and about what he feels makes for good comics. Most of this material was beyond the scope of the article which ran in *CN*. Feeling the material too good not to print it appears here for the first time, deleting those sections immediately relevant only to *US 1*.)

SHOOTER: Everything we've done has gone well. Marvel hasn't had a comic book which lost money in about four years. We're in the very comfortable position of being able to try things without many worries. Basically my editor-in-chief posture here is that there's nothing too outrageous. One of the criticisms that has been leveled at Marvel, and at comics in general, is that there tends to be an awful lot of superheroes and not a lot of anything else. If somebody comes along with something different, even if I suspect it may not be the most popular thing to ever come along, I feel we should try it because it's different. If it is something that catches on and takes off, great, but if it isn't, that's okay, too. It's something we should have tried anyway.

CF: Has Marvel found a problem with vehicle-oriented books such as *Team America* or *Ghost Rider*?
SHOOTER: I think the really big factor is trying to get stories that are well executed. The problem with *Team America* had nothing to do with motorcycles or lack of motorcycles or anything else, but it simply was not a well-executed book. It wasn't good. If it had turned out to be what it was intended to be, I think it would have been very good.

CF: Didn't you have a hand in the writing of the earlier issues of *Team America*?
SHOOTER: They asked me if I would come up with some sort of book involving a motorcycle team. Why? Because Ideal Toys had a set of motorcycle toys and they wanted us to do a story or a series of books about motorcycles that they would tie into their advertising. People come to us all the time with all kinds of outrageous ideas. For instance, the Smurfs: They came to us with the Smurfs four times before we finally took it. Each time they came to us, we said, "Oh, no, we really can't do it." After the Smurfs were on television and were very popular, we finally said, "Okay, we'll do it. We'll do it as a whole separate thing for the younger market," because at that time we had Marvel Books. We used to distribute coloring books and stuff like that, so we actually had somewhere to sell the *Smurf* books. Like the Smurfs, we have people come to us all the time with things they want us to do or they'd like us to try or whatever. You guys out there never hear about the ones I turn down. I've never been overruled. No one has ever said, "We're going to do it anyway," because the people here respect my opinion. So, how do I make a decision? Some toy company

calls up and says, "Hey, we've got these motorcycle things. You want to do a deal together?" We've walked away from a hell of a lot of those deals because we don't need them. We don't need them at all. We make our money publishing. We don't need to make deals with outsiders. The way you make money in publishing is you publish something good that people want to read and they want to buy. *Team America* had an audience that it reached that just loved it to death. I got letters from people that said, "This is my favorite book." I get a lot of letters from kids of Spanish American descent who like the character Wolf; therefore, it's their favorite book. Who'd have believed it? It didn't deserve to be their favorite book. I think it shows the opposite. I think the vehicle thing is possibly an asset, but I don't care about that stuff. I know that if *Ghost Rider* had been done well for a long time it would have been a hit. Just like *Daredevil*. People used to think of *Daredevil* and *Ghost Rider* as one and the same. They were second class books. That was the wisdom of the previous administration here: "There are first class books, and there are second class books." Horse shit. They're all first class books. If they would stop thinking of it as a second class book . . . they had just decided that this would always be sort of a second stringer. Frank [Miller] started really putting himself into it, and, my God, it took off. Now it's one of the top selling books.

CF: As the largest comic book publisher, why doesn't Marvel try to break new ground?

SHOOTER: I think we've done that quite a bit. I've heard people say, "Oh, yeah, Marvel, all they do is superheroes." Look at our line.

The thing is that people write off our books as being superhero books. I look at our books and none of them seem to be superhero books. There's some guy, and lightning strikes him. He has powers, and he immediately feels that he has to go out and patrol the city. We don't do any of that stuff. All of our characters have some kind of motivation . . .

CF: But they're still superhero books just with little better motivated protagonists in them.

SHOOTER: I guess it depends on your point of view. I mean, I look at Ka-Zar and . . .

CF: And still Ka-Zar is not a typical person involved in a romantic situation.

SHOOTER: This is another book I perceive as being different, and if they fail, no problem . . .

CF: By romance books, I mean straight forward . . .

SHOOTER: I agree. At the moment we're not doing any straight forward romance titles. I also say that we have made many attempts to be different. I look around, and I don't see any two the same.

CF: I agree with you to a point. Your books aren't all stamped out of a cookie cutter. I'm glad to see that there is going to be a Kid Colt miniseries.

SHOOTER: Oh, yeah.

CF: When are you bringing back Nick Fury and S.H.I.E.L.D.?

SHOOTER: It would be very easy for me to get a bunch of guys and say I'm going to do S.H.I.E.L.D., I'm going to do romance, and off they go. But that's terrible; that's not good. The way to do it is the way I did in *US 1* and the way I did *Team America* and that isn't to get a guy and say, "Say, are you interested, can you come up with something?" The guy says yeah, and he comes back. Then we say, "Fine, we don't want to do it. Here's your money. Thank you very much." The way to do it is when the guy comes in here on his own. When someone comes into me with fire in their eyes, and they say, "I've got it!" They explain it to me, and they convince me that it's great. That's what we're going to go with. That's how it should be. My door is open right now. My door is always open. When somebody comes in here and says, "Jim, I want to do a war issue," and he's all excited about it and it's something I can get excited about and get interested in, we're going to do it. I want to wait 'til the right one comes along. We've got a responsibility to try outrageous things.

CF: Do the tastes of the fans change?

SHOOTER: I always feel that a lot of that is really not very well considered. I've seen it happen that really incredible artists, artists that you know are going to be the fans' favorites—artists like [José Luis] García-López—and he doesn't make it to the top. I've seen it happen where someone sort of gets discovered. Yesterday they were nobody, and now they're big news. I think the key to it is that it's good stuff. It's almost sincerity; it's almost caring, when they see the kind of detail, the kind of attention to what's going on and a real—back in the old days, the thing that made Ditko my favorite artist was that the physics worked. When Spider-Man spun a web, it looked the way it would look. I thought, "If somebody did that, that's what it would look like." It really doesn't matter who they are, if they're doing a good job people are going to realize it. You can't really make any kind of generalization. What I'm saying is, I refuse to make decisions on anything except whether or not the stuff is good. I admit that some things don't work out. Generally it's not that the people aren't talented. Generally it's not even because the people don't care. It's because something didn't match up right or something just isn't cooking or you've got the wrong inker with the wrong penciller or you've got the wrong penciller with the wrong writer. That happens. We had one thing recently which I think had superb artwork and had a very good writer, and they just weren't . . . The artist was saying, "I don't know, I'm not getting enough visual stuff to draw," and the writer was saying, "Gee, this is visual stuff, and I'm getting back pictures that aren't quite right." All these guys are good. The thing was, what the writer was telling the artist was wrong; he apparently wasn't making clear to him, "These were supposed to be visually exciting pictures; pay attention." And the artist, by the same token, would not read the writer right, or the writer was failing to get it across to the artist. The artist would take the weakest point of view every time because the writer hadn't made it clear to him that this was supposed to be . . .

CF: Very often the very best work seems to come out of writer-artists.
SHOOTER: Writer-artists occasionally are a very good solution. It's often the best solution if you've got a guy who's really good. But there are a lot of writers who can't draw and a lot of artists who can't write. That's what editors do; they take artists and writers and make combinations that work. If it works it works real well. If it doesn't it looks like we're totally . . . fans out there, all they see is that the product isn't working, and they say, "How come you do this?" It's not as easy as it looks. We're trying. We'll get it better next time. Not that they should forgive us for that. They should not pay for it, and they should write us angry letters. All that stuff is good. But what they shouldn't do is presume that we don't know any better. If they don't like it, we probably didn't either. The way I judge the success of a book—I don't look at the sales figures—I look at them, but that's not how I make my judgments. The comics are passed out around here and I watch. If everybody's pulling out *Daredevil* to read it first, I don't have to look at the sales figures, that's a hit. Even if it isn't, we should publish it anyway because if it's that good that the guys here have to see what's happening this month, then it must be wonderful. I've never seen it fail because if it's a book that we like, then the world likes it.

Top Dog: An Interview with Jim Shooter

SPEAKEASY / 1986

Originally published in *Speakeasy* #71 (1986).

SPEAKEASY: It seems to me that during the sixties there was quite a coherent concept of the Marvel Universe, which during the seventies became far more diversified. The emphasis in the eighties seems to be returning to a more unified universe, concentrating on continuity. Would you agree with that assessment?

JIM SHOOTER: Nothing could be further from the truth. No, the reason that the Marvel Universe had a more unified look in the sixties was because so much of that early material was done by the same people—Stan Lee, Jack Kirby, Steve Ditko. And Stan's writing was functionally literate, in that a person who had never read a comic book could understand it and follow it and enjoy it. What happened was that after Stan left, in the seventies, he left behind a bunch of kids in charge, and yeah, you are right, a lot of strange stuff started to emerge from Marvel then. Do not get me wrong, a lot of those kids were very talented, but very few of them were professionally trained. The fault with their work was not that there was anything stylistically wrong with it or that they didn't have ideas, the problem was that they didn't know what they were doing. They were not craftsmen. They were not writers and artists; they were not storytellers.

What I have tried to [do] is bring up the level of craft at Marvel. In all those things we publish I don't ever discuss style, and I do not feel at all interested in getting everyone to march in a row. I am, however, interested in the craft of storytelling, in both art and writing, and that's what I've been trying to teach people.

I think what happens when you have the rather anarchistic situation that we had in the early seventies is that a few people will know what to do and use the freedom to advantage and come up with something brilliant, and about 98 percent of them will not be qualified to do anything decent with their freedom and will produce utter garbage. What I am trying to do is acquire good editors and teach them to understand what is already good and what they should leave alone, so we still have the 2 percent that's brilliant. And those who are bad will receive the help they need to polish their skills as storytellers.

I feel funny defending my stance on style and diversity because I can't imagine how anyone could think otherwise. I am the guy who created *Epic* magazine and the Epic Comics line. I am the guy who has thrown house style out of the window and encouraged people to do everything from *Savage Tales* to *Power Pack*.

SPEAKEASY: It wasn't a house style in the sense of a sameness about the Marvel line, but rather reestablishing a coherent view of the Marvel Universe. This seemed to be reflected in the problems artists and writers were having with their deadlines in the seventies, which you appeared to iron out when you took over as editor-in-chief.

SHOOTER: That's just basic professionalism. When I first came in I realized that before we really could do anything creative and constructive, we had to get out of the deadline crunch. The first month that I was editor-in-chief, we were supposed to publish forty-five comic books. We in fact published twenty-six, and there were comic books that were still in the house that should have been on sale two months earlier. It took me four months to begin shipping the right number of comic books, and a year before we were on time. It was only after that I felt I could spend more of my time trying to get new things started, like *Epic* magazine.

I think it is an editor's job to deliver absolutely great material, but he has also got to deliver the goods on time. I don't ever want the material compromised because of the schedule, and I don't think that the schedule ever needs to be compromised. I will give you a good example: When *X-Men* artist John Romita Jr. was having trouble keeping up with the schedule, Ann Nocenti, a very professional lady, anticipated the need and worked with Barry Windsor-Smith to do an issue of the *X-Men*. Nothing was lost. The fact that you are conscious of deadlines doesn't mean that at the last minute you have to shove in reprehensible filler. If you are truly professional people then you can make certain that even if you have to use another artist or another writer, it doesn't hurt your ongoing continuity.

I would like to look back and say that my record at Marvel has been perfect, but frankly we have published an awful lot of stuff that I don't like and an awful lot of stuff that I don't think is good enough. So while I think that over the ten years that I have been at Marvel I have dragged us a little bit in the direction of being professional and understanding our storytelling craft, I think that we are nowhere near the standard I feel we ought to be. However, I do think that overall we are the best in the business.

SPEAKEASY: What is your role as editor-in-chief?

SHOOTER: What I try to do is oversee as little as possible. I try to get everyone to agree on what the goal is, and then I try to give everyone what they need to fulfill the goal. Then I try to stay out of their way. For most of the things we publish the goal is telling the story. We are, fundamentally, in the same business that Homer was in, telling good stories. What I try to do is teach the basics and the nuances of comic book storytelling, but the basics are essential to understanding the craft.

Overall, Marvel publishes titles where the story is the primary concern. I discuss the goal with the editors and the creative people, and then I try to stay out of their way. For a long time I didn't even read the books until they were in print because I really wanted the editor to feel like he had the last word. That meant there were some books which went out of here that were nowhere near good enough. The benefit was that the editor and the creative people I think were in a better position to learn by making the mistakes, and then later I could go to them and say, "Look, don't do this again because this is why it doesn't work."

Occasionally the goal is not telling a story. Sometimes we publish posters, portfolios, or we publish *Epic* magazine, where storytelling may not be the principal objective, and we may be more interested in the story's graphic impact. We are now publishing a magazine called *Savage Tales,* and I don't really think that storytelling is paramount. The action is probably more important in that book.

Over the last year I've been trying to read most of the books before they go out, mainly because I felt that people were not learning fast enough and that perhaps another approach would be a good idea. Perhaps if I went back to the editor with the actual boards in my hand . . . and we talked about them it might be more immediate. Also that way I could stop the worst mistakes before they were in print. All in all I think that our editors and our creative people are the best in the world, and I think that it sounds very self-important for me to sit here and say, "Well, I could teach them all this stuff, and I can catch their mistakes."

However, being in a position to make a second opinion gives you a huge advantage. The other thing I would like to say is that I actually do have some training which is not usual in this business. I spent a long time working very closely with Mort Weisinger and learned an awful lot from him, and then I spent about five years working very closely with Stan Lee. Amazingly those two guys agree on everything. The only real difference I could see was that Mort deliberately aimed his books at a younger audience, which I hated, and that Stan really tried to write for himself, tried to write for adults. I feel that I do know a lot about comic book storytelling not because I am so brilliant, but because I am the only one you can find that had ten years working with these old timers who virtually invented the business. I feel that I have something to offer, or I would not be in this job.

All I can say is that I think our general approach must be working. Since I have been here we have grown bigger and faster than ever before in our history. When I came here we were kind of neck and neck with DC, and we now outsell them better than three to one. I am a lot happier with what we do. I just managed to pull us in that direction by making us a little more conscious of our craft. Guys like Chris Claremont don't need me telling them how to write. What they need is for us to agree on what we are doing, and, once they understand that, they can accomplish it. I think that if you follow Chris's stuff in the middle seventies it had just as many ideas and was just as creative and well written in many ways, yet you will find that it is very hard to follow, scattered—a thousand things going on at once. Characters were not always introduced and brought on stage. There is not always a clear conflict, and even Chris would lose track of story lines. I don't know that I told Chris something that he did not already know, but I think that I made it clear to him that the fundamental principles of writing are not so different in this medium. I think that if Chris were writing a novel even back in the mid-seventies he would have done everything that I always told him to do, but the fact that those things should be applied to comics was news to him. I think that he is happier with his work now that we have established what we are trying to do.

SPEAKEASY: Speaking of Marvel's success, it appears to have gone hand-in-hand with the rise of the *X-Men*, consistently a top seller. Obviously it is very hard to pinpoint why something does succeed. Have you any ideas why Marvel has been so successful since you took over, and why in particular a book like *X-Men* has succeeded so well?

SHOOTER: Well, it's a lot easier to figure out why things fail, but I really believe that the way to succeed is to do good work, to tell good stories. Okay, what's a good story? Well, a good story is something that has some theme, some power, some conflicts, some statement about the human condition. It has characterization and has action and has things to interest the reader. Okay, we know what a good story is and telling it well means making it accessible. We have done that better since I have been here, and I think that accounts for Marvel's success.

As far as the success of the *X-Men* goes, I think that Chris and the various artists who have worked on the book have done what I am talking about better than most people have, number one. And number two, I think that this last ten years has been a good time for the teen books, especially the young teens. These have done appreciably better than the other books. As to why it seems to be a time for young teens I don't know, but there is no point worrying about something that is outside your control. I have never seen a situation where there was a book that we at Marvel liked that didn't succeed. I mean, when we knew it was good it did fine, and as far as I am concerned if there ever is a book that we all think is great and it goes out there and dies on the newsstand, then I am proud to have done it anyway. Being a successful company, it's great to have the luxury of doing it anyway and still be able to pay your electric bill.

SPEAKEASY: What is the process of editorial liaison and decision-making at Marvel?

SHOOTER: Well, generally, creative people, and that includes editors, come up with an idea. If it's an artist, he will first go to an editor and talk it over with him, and either the editor and the artist and possibly the writer will come to me and talk about what they want to do. I am really the only one they have to convince. I have never had a case of a book that I wanted to do that we didn't do.

SPEAKEASY: You said that what you looked for in the continuing series was good storytelling. What do you look for in a character when it has been presented to you?

SHOOTER: I look for the potential for good stories. I look for the character's potential for conflict. A lot of times I will try and explain this to people, and they won't understand what I am saying. They think, well, he has got to have a quest. No, that's not it. The character has just got to show potential for stories. For instance, *Power Pack* was brought to me by Louise Jones and, I think, Carl Potts, and they pitched it to me. It was unlike anything that I ever heard before because for the first time we were going to do very young superheroes, who are not "superbabies," who are not just adults who talked baby talk. Louise has a kid of her own and has a great memory of her own childhood, and when she was telling me about this it was clear that she was going to really explore, say, what happens when you have a five year old who can disintegrate North America. I mean, that's a scary concept, and she was going to address it. As we sat there and talked, I kept thinking of story after story. I saw that opened doors to all kinds of things that have never been touched before, to all sorts of insight into the human condition that I thought was really great. I think that Louise has done a fairly good job. I think she has really managed to find a lot of that insight, to have a lot of substance, sort of, value to her work, and I am really very proud of it.

Power Pack has not sold well by Marvel's standards, although by anyone else's it would be a big hit. If we just played by the numbers we would probably say, "Well, why should we continue with this? Let's go on and see if we can publish another Spider-Man or X-Men title or something." But fortunately we have the luxury to ignore the numbers. We have been doing that with *Dr. Strange* for a while. *Dr. Strange* has always been a very good book. It's always been kind of a cult favorite.

SPEAKEASY: What then is the criterion for cancelling titles?

SHOOTER: Well, once again, it's mostly up to me to keep track of what's selling and what's not and then talk to the publisher, Mike Hobson. Generally speaking I will discuss these things with Mike, and, somewhere short of the point of insanity, he will go along with things I want to keep and things that I don't have any faith in. There are several factors that are discussed. Sales are a factor, of course, and at least an equal factor is our editorial faith in our books. Editorial faith has sustained *Dr. Strange* for years, and it will sustain *Power Pack*. Recently, however, in order to clear the decks a little bit for some of the twenty-fifth anniversary publishing that we want to do next year, we wanted to cancel some books. So we looked over our list on what was selling and what wasn't, and we cancelled a number of books. We cancelled *The Thing* and *ROM*, but they leap to mind because both of them sell substantially more than *Dr. Strange* or *Power Pack* or several other books. Both of them were up in the 160,000-copy-a-month range, while *Superman* would sell about 100,000 or something like that. And that's very good sales in this country at this time, but I didn't like how *The Thing* was going. I didn't think it was a good book, and the people who were on it were talented, and maybe we could find things that they could do that we would have faith in. That's the ideal we want to come up with: things that we are proud of, that sell, and occasionally have something that we are proud of that does not sell. That's our publishing philosophy.

Another title I will mention, by the way, is Epic Comics. Even though I am technically in charge of the Epic department, Archie Goodwin doesn't need me

Jim Shooter and editor Steve Saffel at Marvel convention booth, 1984. Photo by Jackie Estrada. © Jackie Estrada.

looking over his shoulder, and mostly when Archie wants to do a new Epic title we don't question it. Archie has pretty much the final say on the Epic Comics. The only thing that I do is look through them once before they go out.

SPEAKEASY: I was going to ask about the formation of the Star and Epic lines. What was the rationale behind setting these up? Was it to widen the Marvel range or to actually establish independent companies within a larger parent company?

SHOOTER: Well, they're not really independent companies. We felt it would be good, just as book companies have several imprints, to distinguish the types of material we publish. Since the Epic material is predominantly outside the Marvel Universe, we thought it ought to have its own imprint. We had *Epic Illustrated* magazine at that point. We liked the idea of drawing a connection between *Epic Illustrated* and this new line of comics, so I picked the name Epic Comics. I went to Archie as the editor on *Epic Illustrated* and said, "Archie, I have got a great idea. I know you are doing *Epic Illustrated*, but I would like you to start doing a comic line called the Epic Comic Group." He just rolled his eyes at me as if to say, "Oh god, where am I going to find the time to do this," and just sort of slumped down in his chair. I thought that meant no. So I said okay and walked out, and I went back to publisher Mike Hobson and told him the idea and how I wanted to run it. He said, "Okay," and I then went to Al Milgrom and asked him to start working on the first Epic Comic which had been proposed by Jim Starlin. Then Archie came to me and said, "What's Milgrom doing? I thought this was mine to do." I said, "I thought you said no." So, anyway, Al was cool about it, and although he really liked working with Starlin, he cheerfully gave it over to Archie. It was so funny because I was convinced that Archie had told me he couldn't handle it. Well, we hired people for him, and it worked out fine.

SPEAKEASY: Are there any plans to introduce new imprints, then?

SHOOTER: Yes. We have, as you noted, the Star line, which came about because pretty much all the comic book companies since the sixties started to produce comics for teenagers up, and it got to the point where there were no comics for the younger readers. So a few years ago we decided there's a place for comics for younger readers, and with the help of Sid Jacobson and Tom DeFalco, we came up with the Star line. This is our twenty-fifth anniversary year coming up, and we intend to introduce a fourth imprint, about which I don't know how much I am supposed to talk. It involves a new Marvel Universe, but I am not supposed to talk about it. It's going to be a part of our twenty-fifth anniversary celebration and will be launched next summer. I think it's going to be good.

SPEAKEASY: At present there seems to be a lot of thought going into presenting a more defined and coherent picture of the Marvel Universe. Is that part of the lead-in to the twenty-fifth anniversary?

SHOOTER: Those things don't come about through any master plan. The *Marvel Universe Handbook* was suggested to me by Mark Gruenwald years and years earlier. Then I came up with the idea again and was so happy with it and worked with Mark on the origins of the characters, which I have always enjoyed. I was happy listing the specifications of the characters, but in the end Mark made it more like an encyclopedia. I was interested in that kind of background material, and I thought that readers would also be interested. I was right. It sold incredibly well, and I guess that DC is doing pretty well with their version of it, *Who's Who*. It worked for us; it worked for them, and that's great. Even our updated edition, which cost more than the original edition, is outselling the original edition. It wasn't done to codify the universe. It was done because I thought people would like it, and the *Marvel Saga* is another thing that I always thought people would like: taking all the Marvel comics and placing the highlights in order, explaining when the Fantastic Four's rocket went off, that at the same time in Canada the Guardian was getting his suit. When I was a kid reading Marvel comics, I would have given my left arm for that sort of information. Danny Fingeroth and Peter Sanderson are doing a very good job of it. It's a lot of work. It just happened to come at the time of our twenty-fifth anniversary, so it looks like it was designed that way.

SPEAKEASY: There has been a lot of experimentation with paper stock and printing processes over the last few years. Will that be ongoing? Marvel doesn't mention [in] its press announcements about what you are doing, whereas DC made quite a deal of their going over to Mando for their seventy-five cent comics.

SHOOTER: Well, the only thing I can say about that is that we are concerned with what is on the paper a lot more than what the quality of the paper is. I think that when fans and readers start talking about the paper and the staples you have lost them.

SPEAKEASY: What I am talking about is the experimentation without explanation. Readers have now been introduced to the higher-grade papers and new printing processes, and it does show the tremendous effect it has on the final product. I mean, it has got to the state where the colorist really has to understand a variety of printing techniques and production possibilities. The result in some cases can be garish and awful. The reader who only sees the final product will put it down to bad artwork or, if they are more sophisticated, poor paper or printing. Is Marvel going to continue to experiment to find the best level of quality, technically speaking, which will then be standardized?

SHOOTER: Well, you are correct. We did experiment, and, like I said, I was always less concerned with making announcements about the paper, as something like that seemed odd to me. Anyway, here is how it seemed to settle out after experimenting. First of all I wanted to keep the door wide open for us. Marvel did the first Baxter paper book, which was our *Star Wars* special. Marvel did the first Hudson stock book, *Marvel Fanfare*. We certainly had people who had done graphic albums before, but we really introduced the current graphic album format, which has become all the rage. We have been doing black-and-white books for years, and I wanted to continue that. I wanted to keep trying new formats and new types of presentation for new packages, and we have done that right up to and including Bernie Wrightson's *Frankenstein,* which was something we had never done before. So, I definitely want to keep doing new packages and formats. I don't think there is anything wrong with the old newsprint comic.

I think that there will always be a market for the least expensive package that is acceptable, that is readable, that we can put together. Currently this means using the newsprint paper letterpress. Now the trouble with letterpress is that the only presses in the world that we know of that are big enough to print the kind of print runs that we want are the World Color Press. These presses are very, very old, and they are falling apart to the extent that they are cannibalizing one press to keep another one running. They cannot go on forever, and, if we do not start trying to find alternatives now, then some day we are just going to be in deep water. So, we are starting to experiment with Flexograph.

As you say, sometimes you open a comic book, and it's just hideous. Well, that has happened a couple of times, but I think it has happened less frequently with our comics than it has with other people's.

Another thing that we have done is gone to the 70 percent screens, which has helped a lot, enabling us not only to get more colors, but to mute down the yellow when we want it muted down. However, I have discovered something interesting, which has kept us experimenting when a few people have kept telling us that we ought to give up the experiments. If you go out and you find a hundred people, either newsstand readers or casual readers, who have never seen a comic book, and you hand them a letterpress comic book and a Flexograph one, they will invariably, I mean 1 to 99, prefer the latter because the colors are brighter. That seems to register with them more than anything else. What I find is that it's people who have been reading comics a long time that know what a comic book is supposed to look like and want it to look that way [who] are really interested in keeping it on letterpress.

I think that *X-Men / Alpha Flight* #1, which is Flexograph, is beautiful. What we have done is we have dabbled with it enough so that we finally have a sense of how to do it, and we think it is very good for Star comics. Since the problem with it seems to be the brightness, we find that Flexographed comics look better on newsprint, so we have quietly (you are the first to hear it) started a policy of Flexograph books being printed on newsprint. Letterpress books will be printed on Mando stock. In that way you get Mando paper which gives letterpress a nice finish, and the Flexograph is muted by the newsprint.

His Name Is . . . Jim Shooter

JOE MARTIN / 1992

Originally published in *Comics Arena* (1992). Reprinted by permission.

JM: You're a big supporter of creator-owned rights and making sure that everyone who works on a project is well taken care of. Any comment on that?
JS: I think that being on the other side of the desk has helped me. I had no idea that you got only so many pennies per copy. When my first check came it had this little paragraph on the back that said, "This is it. This is your flat rate. We now own your story and everything in it. Thanks." That . . . was a little disappointing.

JM: Which is still thought today by most people.
JS: Yeah. What I ended up making on my first assignment averaged out to about $4.50 a page. It went up quickly after that once I became a regular, but still that's kind of disappointing. So, I took the job at Marvel on the condition that I could change the way we did business. One of my conditions was to institute a royalty plan. It was December 1975 when I extracted that commitment from the president of the company who, at that time, was Jim Galton. He was fairly new with the company, and when I asked that of him his exact words were, "You mean we don't (pay royalties)?" He had come out of book publishing where royalties were normal.

JM: You got the idea for royalties from book publishing?
JS: Yeah, sure. I had had some experience with the real world by that time and had gotten the drift on how things were going, and as we got those programs into place I really tried to make it something that would be fair. I did some reading and studied business administration to determine just what is fair compensation to the people that do the creative work. I came up with a

formula that was good enough for the company but fairly compensated the creative people, I think. I've refined that myself since then, and Marvel's kind of stuck on my first generation plan. Now, at DEFIANT, we have an even better plan. That's on the "universe" stuff. You almost have to have a company own the "universe" so that you have a sort of "central fire control." That doesn't mean you can't make the creators your partners. The main thing you have to watch is that if you have a universe with characters that interact then you can't just have one of the creators dancing off with one of the characters and going to Dark Horse or something. So, the way it works is that these people trade some measure of control for some very good rewards.

And, as you asked, I'm also interested in just publishing some creator-owned material and making a fair deal. I think Dark Horse has been somewhat of an industry leader in that regard. Our deal is going to be just as good as Mike Richardson's—maybe better—but he really deserves a lot of credit for kind of expanding the envelope. We did creator-owned stuff at Marvel in the form of Epic but nothing like Mike does. He has a much better deal.

JM: Dark Horse was a real pioneer in that field, and now it has evolved into something of a market.
JS: Yes, that's why Mike and I get along so well. We think very similarly.

JM: You're responsible for forms of cover enhancements that seem to have become a catalyst for selling multiple copies. How do you feel about that now?
JS: Actually, I think Marvel did a platinum edition of *Spider-Man* #1 that was one of the first cover enhancements. We (at VALIANT) thought that was a cool idea. I never wanted to do multiple versions of a book, but we thought that was a cool idea. It was a Marvel idea. They printed these special versions of the book and gave it to the retailers—they were giving them away! Now, it's sort of mushroomed into this business all by itself. Retailers ended up selling the copies, and it sort of turned into a monster. That wasn't by any means the first cover enhancement. I think there had been a *Ghost Rider* glow-in-the-dark cover and some other things. I think that the idea that we (VALIANT) had taken some bits and pieces of things that had come before and popularized it.

JM: It now has developed into this monstrous side market . . .
JS: I like the cover enhancements. My current philosophy is that if we do an enhancement it will be on every single copy. I don't want to put people in the position of having to buy two versions.

JM: What about the jacking up of prices because of enhancements?

JS: To me, it's really a question of value added. If you come up with something that's a good idea and it's editorially driven, it makes sense. People will say, "Oh, that's cool," and will be willing to pay an extra quarter for it. My best example I can give you is the black cover on *Solar, Man of the Atom* #10. (Barry) Windsor-Smith and I were talking about it one day on the phone, and we faxed a couple sketches back and forth to one another. In those days I usually did a sketch and then Windsor-Smith would make it into real art. We started thinking about what happened in this issue, and Solar falls into a black hole so Barry jokes, "Let's just make it black!" We laughed at first but then I thought, "Hey! That's great!" So many good ideas start as jokes. I wanted to do it all black, even the logo, which we embossed. Everybody tried to shout me down. They were like, "Jim, no, you can't do that!" Jon Hartz and Steve Massarsky hated the idea. In the end I insisted that we do it, and we did. It worked really well. Editorially, it made sense. The embossing costs a bit extra, so we had to charge a bit more, although it was a bigger book—like forty-eight pages or something—but it wasn't an outrageous price to pay.

JM: It's not a secret what you basically think of companies like Marvel, VALIANT, and DC, and how business politics have somewhat corrupted the end product that they produce, but it seems you have a more positive view of Image Comics and Dark Horse. What is it exactly that you feel they're doing right?

JS: First of all, I have mostly good things to say about everybody. A lot of interviewers ask questions like, "Do you think Marvel has lost their creative strength?" That kind of leads you into talking about who has left there, but Marvel still has some very good talent. Marvel is so big that you can almost pick which part of it you want to talk about. They have some very good resources besides the deep pockets. They've gone off in some bad directions but there are good things to say about them, too. I don't have a blanket condemnation of any of them. That's the same with DC. They've done some really good stuff, and then they've done some things that I just can't figure out. As for VALIANT, I find that I honestly just haven't been able to look at those books since I left there. Someone gave me one to read just the other day, and I just couldn't do it. I tried to read it but . . .

JM: Does it leave you with a bad taste in your mouth because of what was done?

JS: The company was stolen from me. I've had people ask, "Don't you get good royalties from them?" They don't pay me a dime. I actually lost money in my experience with VALIANT. It cost me money to make my ex-partners millionaires. People talk about Jack Kirby getting ripped off but at least Jack Kirby got paid—I don't.

JM: What a bummer.
JS: Yeah. I feel like I created those characters, and they don't even give me credit for that.

JM: Especially isn't there something about *Harbinger*?
JS: *Harbinger* was actually created a year before there was a VALIANT. Originally it was a treatment that I was discussing with Paramount. Later, I wrote it into a comic book, but, anyway, I look at that stuff and feel like there are these characters that I created. It's funny. When I worked at Marvel I talked to Steve Ditko, who certainly has enough grudges against Marvel, but we got along real well and had a mutual respect for one another, so it came to the point where I was saying, "Steve, c'mon, draw a Spider-Man!" And he was like, "No! I won't do it!" He wouldn't draw Spider-Man, and he wouldn't draw Doctor Strange. I couldn't understand why. Now, I understand exactly why: he created it. He made it what it is. Now he's got to struggle for his next job, and these people are multimillionaires! I don't care what the law gets away with, there are some things that are just not right.

JM: I suppose it's made you somewhat paranoid.
JS: Absolutely. Basically I went through the same naive curve that everyone goes through, it seems. I started out as a writer and thought that was really cool. Then I discovered that you couldn't do what you really wanted to do and that you really are under the editor's thumb and have to abide by all these rules and regulations. In order to get your ideas realized you actually have to be higher up the chain, so I took a job as an editor. Then I became editor-in-chief, and I found eventually that it doesn't matter what your title is. If you're an employee, especially if you have any principles, then sooner or later you're going to come into conflict with your employers. At that point, you're still hamstrung. I thought, "Alright, I've got to start my own company to be the president and the CEO and a partner; that way, I'm the boss." I did that and started up VALIANT. I was a partner. I was the boss. I owned a part of it, but then I found out that being a partner isn't enough. If you have principles, then sooner or later, you're going to come into conflict with your other partners. And if there's more of them, which in this case there were—there was Steve Massarsky and his wife—then they could outvote me.

So, that didn't work either. This time I set out with the money and the conditions that I had ownership and control. The investors here are silent partners and my real partners here are that everybody owns shares of DEFIANT; that can never be taken away from them. These people cannot have their stock taken away from them ever. Anyway, I got off track a little here. The original question was something like I've said more positive things about Image and Dark Horse?

JM: Exactly.

JS: I also have a fairly positive view of Malibu Comics. I think that a lot of people have wondered if Dark Horse and Malibu were going to perform, and they have. I think they've really done a commendable job, and I understand that they're both doing pretty well. Image Comics is hard to lump together because they're really a bunch of smaller companies. There are some really great things about Image Comics, and they're almost not in the same business that I'm in. I'm in the business of telling stories and being an entertainer, and Image is doing more like what I call "rocket rides." A lot of people want to get on a Todd McFarlane rocket and just go. It may not go anywhere, but it's a fun ride. I read *Spawn* #1, and I said, "Wow! That's great! I wonder what it's about." But it really was great. I could see especially where a younger reader would really get off on it. My first impression of *Spawn* was, "Nobody who paid two bucks for this book is going to want their money back!" Each guy (at Image) has different strengths, some stronger than others, but one thing that you can't argue with them is that, by chance or design, they really have marketed themselves. They've really done a great job of capturing the imagination of the buying public and holding it. They've been the first group of guys to do it like rock stars.

JM: They've been tagged, at times, the "rock 'n'roll stars of comics."

JS: You can't take that away from them. But one of the things I've said is that I'm especially impressed with the stuff that's come out of Dark Horse. The quality is excellent.

JM: So far. They're going to spin some titles off from their Comics Greatest World stuff, but I'm really looking forward to the Legend imprint stuff.

JS: Yeah, that should be good.

JM: We'll see what happens. After reading the first couple of issues of *Warriors of Plasm*, I must say I very much enjoyed them. I'm looking forward to *Dark*

Dominion and *The Good Guys*, and I see that you eventually plan to publish as many as fourteen titles out of DEFIANT and perhaps some creator-owned titles.
JS: What we're trying to do here is make the universe as big as it can be and still be good—not get out of control. I think that if you try to manage more titles than that it becomes difficult to keep it in close continuity and all working together. I want to keep it like the early Marvels were, where you had to have them all, and you could.

JM: Yeah, there was only, like, ten of them at a dime a copy, so you could follow the whole Marvel Universe every month for a buck.
JS: Exactly. Cost is a bit more now, but that's the approach we're taking. Of course I'm wanting to do some creator-owned stuff, too, and we've been approached by several creators . . . Alan Weiss, who is doing some of our universe stuff, has some very good ideas, and whenever you're approached by Chris Claremont you're tempted to listen. I want to do something with him. Jim Steranko called me up. I think there's a lot of good stuff out there, and I believe that Mike Richardson doesn't have to be the only one to do books like that. He may have a little friendly competition here soon.

JM: VALIANT was referred to in one of DEFIANT's press releases as "the rough draft" and with DEFIANT it's "this time for sure." You aimed high and it appears that you've hit.
JS: Our goal is to be a leader in the industry. We really think that we can become a force for good in this business. I want to do it right. The name DEFIANT applies to more than my refusing to just collapse after going through what I did with VALIANT. It refers to all of us like Chris Claremont, who had an ugly parting with Marvel, and Alan Weiss, who has had a lot of bad things happen to him in his life, like Steve Ditko and all people who have run into these problems. What's common among all of these people is that none of them have lost the fire. None of them have lost the desire, and they're all still DEFIANT. Now we know what not to do. We're old enough to know how, and we're all still young and strong enough to do it. David Lapham is still a young guy, but he's the most mature twenty-three year old I know.

JM: Wow, I had no idea he was that young.
JS: Isn't he great? For twenty-three, isn't he great? Can you believe it?

JM: Really good. It seems you want DEFIANT to be more than just a publisher—a participator—thus the Good Guys contest where actual readers will be

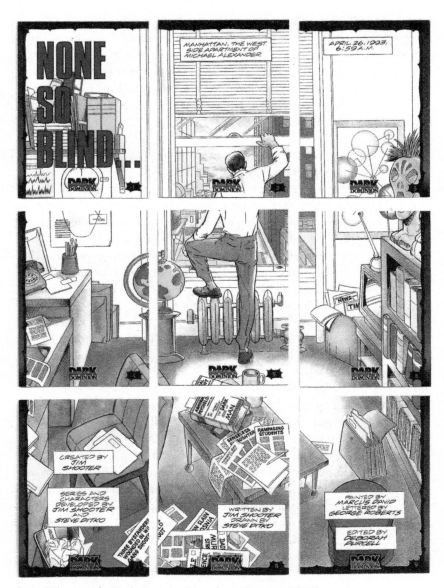

Steve Ditko page for *Dark Dominion* #0 card set. © 1993 DEFIANT.

featured in the book. I even heard about a "Bad Guys for Good Guys" contest for retailers, and you've been doing your "How to Create Comics" seminars. How are all these things doing?

JS: We're going to keep thinking of things like this to do because it's really interactive. I said in my first editorial that we're the most reader-responsive company because we answer more mail, and we do more reader-oriented stuff. The seminars came out of the fact that I realized so many people who come to comic book stores would love to be artists or writers or would even just love to draw their own comics, not necessarily to be a full-time professional but for themselves. There's a need for information. I felt that I was one of the guys that had been around long enough to provide that information. The question that people would ask me sometimes was, "Who rules the lines around the panel?" The letterer does that.

JM: I can understand where many people may actually not know that, but professionals regard it as an almost ridiculous question.

JS: Yes. But when you get questions like that you have to realize that it's one thing to go to the Kubert School to teach you to draw, but it's another thing to just have fundamental knowledge. Basically, in the seminar, what I do is give a broad overview course on writing and all aspects of art, and I talk about lettering a little bit. What I try to do is take all these great tidbits that I've compiled in twenty years of learning from guys like Stan Lee and Jack Kirby and Mort Weisinger and people I've worked with and simply share those important high points. Obviously, I can't teach a guy to write in an hour, but hopefully I can give him some really good guidelines and generalities. This isn't the "How to do it the DEFIANT way," but this is all stuff that applies no matter where you go. Another reason I came up with the seminar is because everybody was wanting us to do these tours, but tours basically consist of going store-to-store and signing books. I sort of refer to those as the "greed tour."

JM: The "greed tour"?

JS: It really is because basically everybody makes money. It's not bad for the fans. It's nice to go get your book signed and all. That's cool.

JM: But doesn't that depend a bit on who's making the tour? Some companies—smaller companies—tour primarily to promote their books and not to make bucks.

JS: But to promote themselves what are they doing? They're trying to sell more books. If they don't sell enough books to pay for the tour then they're probably going to stop. I felt that we'd make enough money selling comic books the normal way. What can we do to give back? What kind of tour could we do that's not money-oriented? I mean, sure we do that, too. We'll go to a store or two and sign some comic books, but what can we do so we can give something back to people? The response to the seminar has been incredible so far, and people are serious. They come in, and everybody sits there and takes notes.

JM: Where do these things take place?
JS: The pilot program was done in a store in Anaheim, California, and we fit about a hundred and twenty people in comfortably. That was good. The second one was in Nashville, and we seated about four hundred people in a hotel ballroom. The third was in San Diego, and, again, we sat about four hundred people in one of the convention rooms. The last one I did was at a theater here in New York, and we had a bit over two hundred people there.

JM: So you've already spoken to close to twelve hundred people?
JS: Yeah. We've been lucky enough to get some guest speakers to give my voice a rest. I drone on about writing for fifty minutes and . . . at one of the shows Len Wein was in the audience, so he came up and joined me.

JM: "Hey, Len, come on down!"
JS: I asked him first, of course. One time we had Mike Witherby come up and talk a little bit about inking, and Alan Weiss and David Lapham talk a bit about penciling. One of these days I'd like to get something like this together with several big names to chip in their two cents. I believe we all should do this. We should get everybody who's been around for a while and get them out there to . . .

JM: To tutor people. To educate them.
JS: It's fun. I guess we're going to keep doing it until people get tired of it. I'm also thinking of having it transcribed and published in some form. The thing is, I do it in three hours. I could spend a week on each discipline, easily, just from all the stuff I've built up over the years. I suppose if we keep going on with it, it'll expand or be divided into installments. It'll be like three hours of writing and then three hours on art and so forth.

JM: If that were made into a book it would be the size of a bible! For someone who wants to be a comic book writer, what's your advice? I mean, do you have a standard format that you follow for telling good stories?

JS: I think that a lot of people sit down and they've read a lot of comics, but they try to write before they really learn how. I don't think it would occur to anybody who didn't have knowledge of anatomy and perspective to just sit down someday and decide that they could draw a comic book. Since we all use language for other reasons—writing letters or whatever—people don't realize that there's anatomy and perspective and structure involved in writing a story that you have to learn. It's not enough to have a ream of paper and a typewriter. My first advice to people is to learn to write, and in order to do that you need to do what you would do if you wanted to learn to draw: you study and take courses and attend seminars.

JM: The Jim Shooter seminar . . .
JS: The seminar, by the way, is all donated. We provide materials to aid the seminar, and we pay for them. Usually we get a cosponsor who pays for the hall. All the admission money that is paid is entirely donated to a charity. No cost deduction is involved whatsoever.

JM: Very good. You've been heard to say that you feel you have a "physical communication problem" and that you'd like to be "a little more gentle and understanding" at times. Do you think that these things hinge on the fact that some people who don't know you have said, "Oh, Jim Shooter? Yeah. What a jerk."
JS: First of all, I'm six foot seven and the way I look when I'm just being normal is a natural scowl, and I sometimes have people come up to me and ask, "What's wrong?" And I'm like, "Uh, nothing. I'm fine."

JM: You'd have made a good pirate.
JS: Yeah, I probably would have. But, anyway, I'm probably not the most natural warm-and-fuzzy type. I also think that perhaps since I've been in this business for a long time that I sometimes move too fast for people. I've been given advice like if an artist is doing three things wrong, maybe just tell him two of them and save one for later. That's a good theory and it works sometimes, but sometimes it's like, "You're on stage tonight!" I just feel like it's not fair to the reader. The reader expects it to be right.

I run into the problem where people feel like I'm pushing too hard. But we're performers, and we've got to perform. I wish my delivery was more graceful. Stan (Lee) can tell you you're doing something wrong, and you walk out feeling like a million dollars.

JM: Constructive criticism is an art form in itself.

JS: Absolutely, and Stan Lee had mastered it long ago. I struggle. People tell me, "First, you tell 'em something nice, and then you kind of ease into what they're doing wrong." That's so hard for me. I'm like, "Oh, uh, well . . . you do great eyebrows, but let's talk about these ugly noses . . ." I don't know. I feel . . . hypocritical or like I'm trying to con these people, and I don't want to do that. I'd rather be direct. Some people actually take my directness wonderfully well and have no problem with it, but there are some who take it as more confrontational. Communication is a major human problem, and I'm probably not the best in the world at it. I feel like if you check with the people who work with me and the people who really know me, then you'll see we get along. If I was a real problem to work with, then Claremont wouldn't be back here. Weiss and Lapham wouldn't be here.

I started in the sixties in comics, and back then editors were editors. They were the boss. You did what they said . . . Mort Weisinger, Julie Schwartz, and even Stan; people did what Stan wanted. He had a gentle way with them, but they did it. I remember Gene Colan telling me one time that he had to redraw pages, and there was a stack that looked to be a whole ream of Jack Kirby pages in the office that never saw print. They were all rejected pages.

JM: Wow.

JS: Yeah, so editors were editors in those days, and something happened in the late sixties or early seventies because when I came back (to Marvel), having been off doing commercial comics for a while, anarchy had set in. At Marvel, for instance, the first time anybody saw a book was when it was all finished! Writers were sending scripts directly to pencillers, and pencillers were sending directly to the writers to script. Then it went to the letterers!

JM: The editor's job was just to proofread the stuff.

JS: Yeah, to just sort of process the stuff through. So, I came in and was given the responsibility of running Marvel Comics. First of all, the company was losing two and a half million bucks a year, and I felt I had to do something. Most of the books were four months late! It was a nightmare. First thing I said is "We've got to get these books out on time." When you call up a guy who's been drawing Potato-Man for a while and you say, "Look, you're three months late with Potato-Man, so I'm going to get another artist to do a fill-in issue . . . ," he hits the ceiling. He goes off and tells the fans that you're taking his book away from him. Then, there's a worse-case scenario where you have to call a guy and say, "Your Potato-Man isn't good enough. Look, let me help you" or "Why don't you just do the penciling for a while?" They don't like that either. If you're going to be an editor then eventually you're going to have to say "no" to somebody, and as soon as that happens then you're the bad guy.

When you come in and you're attempting to establish order and improve some quality and change some bad practices and you're following a period of anarchy, then you come across looking like Mussolini no matter how gentle you are. But I think now that if you take a look at the early eighties comics, which was when I had finally gotten a lot of things and programs in place and we were paying people some decent rates, that was when Marvel was doing perhaps its best stuff ever. John Byrne and Claremont were rocketing high with *Uncanny X-Men*. There was Frank Miller doing his thing, and Bill Sienkiewicz was taking off. It was like a mini-golden era in comics. Everything was doing great, and Marvel was making a huge amount of money—I think my unit made something like seventeen million dollars a year. We were on time, and we were doing all this great new stuff!

JM: It was a good time.
JS: It was a great time. Comics had entered a new age. In the early seventies you would have been hard pressed to find somebody to say bad things about me, but after I turned things around . . .

JM: Things turned around suddenly and wickedly.
JS: Sure.

JM: For the record, do you think we'll see the day when Marvel is not number one?
JS: It's already happened. There was one month where DC was number one—the month that Superman died. It was the first time in an age, but I think that that is going to happen with greater and greater frequency. I think if you look around the comic business at the end of next summer then it will be a far different picture.

JM: Do you have any predictions as to the top five companies at that time?
JS: Marvel will be among the top five. DC will still have pretty good odds, but that's not quite as sure. I think DEFIANT will be there. I think Dark Horse and Malibu will be there. The ones I'm really not sure about are Image and VALIANT, either of which could be in there or not. It's hard to tell with Image.

JM: They may not even be around then.

JS: It's not a true company, so it's difficult to predict what that loose kind of confederation is going to do. VALIANT has come to a crossroads. They've got some good talent, but after I left they kind of went way in a wrong direction. If they can come back to succeeding with the stuff between the covers then they should be in there. They've become a bit too gimmick-oriented and . . .

JM: Maybe it was your dealings with VALIANT that left a constant scowl on your face.

JS: Actually I don't think about it that much. I'm not going to lie about it or sugarcoat it. I'm more angry about how David Lapham and Debbie Fix and Janet Jackson got ripped off. They counted on me and got ripped off. What happened is that my partner, Steve Massarsky, got married to a lady who was the investor, and with that they controlled more of the company than I did. After we really started doing well their first plan was to sell the company to her brother. I would've become an employee, and her brother would then become the president and CEO.

JM: It would have been time for you to leave anyway.

JS: Yeah. Did I want to stay and sign a ten-year employment contract to work for my partner's brother-in-law? Or do I want to leave? It came down to when I refused to sign the contract they simply fired me.

JM: That had to be a stunning moment.

JS: It was amazing. The fact that the laws in this country permit somebody who has created something to be literally ripped off on little technicalities . . . There was a clause in my contract that enabled them to just take away some of my stock and the terms of what they had to pay me—they actually paid me less than my lawyer cost me, and the bottom line is that if you look over in Europe this kind of thing can't happen. There's something over there stating that if you're a creator then what happened to me can never happen to you. But here? Ah, it's just a commodity. It can be taken from you just like that.

JM: That's the true advantage of living in a capitalistic society.

JS: I suppose. But this time everything is set, and I've made sure to have a lot of good people with me on the DEFIANT launch. We're going to give the readers the best we can.

Interview: Jim Shooter

MARTY GROSSER/ 1993

MG: Okay, Jim, I'll start out with an easy one: Are you really as difficult to work with as some people have claimed?

JS: No, I don't think so. But, I think the real answer is that in this business, for a long time, there were essentially no editors. In the seventies when I showed up at Marvel, I showed up at a place where writers and artists just simply delivered complete books—I mean, no one had seen them before they were delivered.

There was what you might call "complete anarchy." The company (the people who hired me) wanted an editor, someone who would be reviewing stuff. When you have a situation like this, some people will take advantage of the freedom, and they will do wonderful things—like Starlin's *Warlock*. And some people will take advantage of the fact that nobody's looking, and they'll hack. Some people need a little help. They need somebody to work with, and I'm not just talking about beginners. I think a lot of guys—long-term, established professionals—prefer to work with some [outside] creative input. I think, for instance, that Chris Claremont does his best work when he's got a good team around him that gives him support.

In the first four or five years I was at Marvel, I don't think anybody had a problem with me, except for the people who were hacking and that I didn't let them get away with it anymore. In the last three years I was at Marvel, the people who owned it were selling it, and that kind of put me at odds with the upper management because I was sort of the highest-ranking officer who was not an owner. That creates a situation that makes you sort of a "labor

99

leader" because you're the one trying to protect the interests of the people in the company who are not owners. During that period of time, the people upstairs did just about everything they could do to damage my position with the creative people so that when push came to shove, if they had to get rid of me, everybody wouldn't leave with me! During those last couple of years, Marvel was actually trying to sabotage my reputation.

I think that if you're an editor and you do what's right, you occasionally have to say "no" to people. To the good people, the professionals, that's fine. But the people who are hacks, they won't like that. I had a guy come into my office one time and say, "I want to do a story where Spider-Man fathers an illegitimate child." I said, "We've licensed Spider-Man to people who make fuzzy toys for infants. We can't do that. By licensing that character, we've made a commitment to observe certain standards with Spider-Man. What if it's a slow news week and we get on 60 *Minutes*, and for one solid week, nobody has anything better to talk about than Spider-Man's morals? And the guy who makes the fuzzy dolls starts getting them back from Toys "R" Us by the container load? We can't do that to him; that's not fair. We have a debt of honor to this person, and we have to observe it." So I told the writer, "Do the same story—even make a character that everybody really knows is Spider-Man, but call him something else, and we'll do it for Epic Comics." He stormed out in a huff: "Jim Shooter—can't work with him! He's denying me my creative freedom!" I know I will again. I will do it every time without fail. But I think if you take a look around here [at DEFIANT], and you see the kind of people we have—Chris Claremont works here . . . and he worked for me for years at Marvel. Mike Barr is working here. Roger Stern says he wants to write for us as soon as he unburies himself a little bit . . . Alan Weiss, Ken Hooper, David Klein. Steve Leialoha is back. A lot of people from Voyager—Janet Jackson is here; the office manager, Debbie Fix, is with me. If I'm such a tough guy, why are these people here? These are people who can work anywhere. Marvel kind of did the hatchet job on me, that's the easiest way to attack me. Anybody who wants to attack me, they just trot out that old thing and go at me again. But the people who have actually worked with me know better, and I can say confidently that in all my years at Marvel—and all my years since—there is no decision I ever made out of malice, spite, greed, or self-interest. I did the right thing. I did the right thing when it meant taking heat. I think there are very, very few people who can say that in this industry.

MG: What have you been up to since leaving VALIANT and before the formation of DEFIANT?

JS: My last day . . . I was fired on June 30, but there was a clause in my contract that kept me from doing any work in the comic book industry until October 18, 1992. So, between June 30 and October 18, I did things for myself. I mean, they can't keep me from listening to people, and I'd talk to anyone about any deals. But a lot of people called me up, made me offers . . . there's nothing wrong with listening. The people at Malibu flew me out, spent a couple of days with me, kind of trying to see if they could work out a deal with me. I went to see the people at Dark Horse; they flew me out and talked about a deal. The people at Innovation [Publishing, a comics company backed by venture capital; it existed from 1988–1994] flew me out and talked about a deal. I sort of did a tour of the country, and I kept telling everyone—and you can ask them—during that period often I wouldn't say a word! But I was content to listen to what they had to say. I did my own thinking about what I wanted to do—they can't keep you from thinking! Mostly, I made plans for what I wanted to do and how I wanted to do it.

I was introduced to some people—investment bankers—and talked about how, after the October deadline, I'd like to raise money and do it again. I also spent much of my time defending myself from Voyager. Voyager sued me, a motion for summary on a guarantee (that I didn't owe them), and that took up a lot of time. I was out 100,000 bucks to defend [myself], but eventually their motion was denied and was thrown out of court. Also there were other legal matters having to do with Voyager. They exercised their right to recapture my stock, so there was a lot of legal stuff going on, arbitrations and so forth. So that pretty much filled my summer! After October 18, I started actively working on DEFIANT. It took maybe a couple of months to get all of the pieces in place, and by February 18, we closed the deal with an investment group called DCS Partners.

MG: How did you get people like David Lapham, Janet Jackson, all these people you used to work with, to come back with you on this new venture?
JS: The day I was fired by the bad guys at Voyager, they also fired Janet and the office manager, Debbie Fix. Sometime later they basically gave David the ultimatum to either sign an exclusive contract or get out. I think his crime was he had been seen with me at San Diego [Comicon], and he was too close to me. He said no, he wasn't going to sign an exclusive contract, so he was forced out. Each of those people went and got other jobs and did whatever they had to do, I guess. Then when they heard I was starting again, they came to me. I mean, this is what we do. I know that our office manager, Debbie Fix, got an extremely good job at a major bank working for their corporate counsel—very

well-paid, very fancy offices, all that stuff—and when she heard we were start-ing, she called and said, "When should I give my notice?" I said, "Are you sure you want to do this again?" But, she's here. If we didn't have her . . . she's the one who bought all the furniture and arranged all of the space and did all of the administrative tasks that somebody has to do to make a business work. And Janet: I think she's the best designer in comics, and I think she's the best colorist in comics. She's also our printing expert. I was very glad to have those people [back]. Of course, I think David is the best new artist I've seen in a decade.

MG: Even Steve Ditko came along with you, too . . .

JS: Yeah, he was working for us at VALIANT, and after I left there they pretty much cut him loose. I was very glad to have him. He's working with Steve Leialoha on *Dark Dominion*. I have to tell you, the stuff just looks great! Ditko builds you a great foundation. He's a brilliant, creative man. Steve Leialoha, as you know, is a fantastic artist, and he really makes everything look terrific. They've got me writing—and I'm doing the best I can to keep up with them. It's good looking stuff!

MG: How will DEFIANT, as a company, differ from others?

JS: I think we're the leaders. When I started VALIANT, it had been decades since a superhero company had started up and succeeded in any significant fashion. A lot of them had just crashed and burned along the way. People liter-ally laughed at us. We were doing story-oriented stuff, trying to do continuity, and do all of the things that I liked when I was a kid reading. I had people, even the distributors, saying, "Where are your holograms?" "What do you mean they're 'readable'?" "So what?" "Who cares?!" I got that a lot, and it took us a while to just get people's attention. But once we did, as you know, it took off like a rocket. It's the same people again, and I think we'll do it again. Now you look around, Dark Horse is doing a very story-oriented/continuity-oriented universe. Malibu is doing a very story-oriented/continuity-oriented universe. That's become the new rage. We started it. I think we're still the leaders, and we're the people who showed them how. The way I look at it is: There's going to be an awful lot of good stuff coming out of many places this year, but I still think we're the team to beat because we're the ones who started the trend.

MG: With such a massive influx of new superhero series and universes crop-ping up all around, do you feel that now is the right time to launch? Don't you feel you might get lost in it, perhaps?

Jim Shooter accepting a lifetime achievement award from the Kansas City Comic Book Club, 1993.

JS: Not at all. I think that what I'm seeing now in the marketplace, although there are a lot [of] things out there, there's a shortage of good things. I think to myself, "Do we really need more superheroes?" The answer is we need more good superheroes. We probably don't need another hyper-steroid case that goes around smashing things. But if you have some insight, something interesting, some new take on it, I think that we need that as an industry. I think that what's going to happen this summer is that the good stuff will succeed and the mediocre stuff will fail. There's really plenty of room. It could happen that Dark Horse, Malibu, and our new titles succeed fine—*all* of them—and the other stuff which isn't as good and doesn't deserve to sell what it may be currently selling, will start to crumble. I think we're already seeing that in the marketplace. A lot of people are not buying some of the titles they used to. People were buying titles on momentum. They bought it because they bought it every month—and that's going to change this summer. People are buying what's good.

There was an era where there really were Marvel Zombies who bought everything—if it had "Marvel" on it, they bought it! Now there's, what—a hundred and fifty Marvel titles every month? It's beyond the means of almost everybody. A lot of it just isn't as good as some of the stuff from some of the other companies. I'm not singling out Marvel here; that goes for everybody. I think that this is going to be a year of major shakeup. The way I feel is: It's a level playing field, and the best teams will win.

MG: I'm sure you try to keep up with what everyone else is doing. Tell me your first impressions or feelings when I name off some of the other comics publishers . . . if you feel comfortable with that.
JS: Okay.

MG: Marvel.
JS: Marvel is extremely vulnerable. Marvel, I think, has proven to the world that they can no longer win creatively. When I was at Marvel, the expression we always used was, "We beat 'em between the covers," meaning that DC would out-promote us, their ads looked better, their production was often better, and they certainly out-publicized us. They had the marquee names—Superman and Batman—and we outsold them four or five to one! The reason we did was, we beat them creatively, we were better creators—and "We beat 'em between the covers."

Marvel's so big, they've obviously got some good books and creators. There are some real shining lights, but, in general, Marvel has lost its creative strength. They're not going to beat anybody between the covers anymore. They've got a lot of money and a lot of power and the ability to market and crowd the shelves. They get a lot of exposure and publicity, but it's almost like DC used to be, as far as I'm concerned. When I was at Marvel, that's sort of what our opinion of DC was. Now, unless they do something very smart and very fast, I think they're headed for a major nosedive.

MG: How about DC?
JS: DC is a strange place right now. DC has some things that are really the best of the best, some really outstanding stuff, really wonderfully creative stuff. Then they seem to have a lot of things that I cannot fathom—they're just kind of at the bottom—and I don't think they have much in the middle. It's like somebody said, "Do you think DC will be hurt by all this competition

this summer?" And my answer to them was, "DC's best books won't be touched. DC's worst books are already so far down that they can't go any lower." That's very weird, but that's my honest assessment of it. I think that what DC really lacks is a strong creative leader. They have little places where they do very well, and the rest is just chaos that would benefit from a vision. It doesn't have to be an individual or a confining vision. I hope that my vision is not confining! I've had people say, "You only like to do a certain kind of book!" Where did you get that idea? Wait a minute; let's go to the videotape here, pal. Let's look at what we did at Marvel. We did everything from Smurfs through Bill Sienkiewicz's stuff in Epic—I'm the guy that hired Sienkiewicz, think about that. I'm the guy that had to talk Archie Goodwin into doing *Moonshadow* and *Elektra: Assassin*. I like weird. I like cutting edge. I like variety. I like all that stuff, and I do my best to encourage it. But when you're starting out, starting a superhero universe, you do need to have consistency among the titles. As you grow, then you have the ability to experiment and introduce eclectic, creator-owned stuff.

MG: Dark Horse?

JS: Dark Horse, I think, is . . . interesting. I think that Mike Richardson is brilliant. I think he's just one of the bright stars in this industry. But I think that they've probably come to a point where they're not going to be carried along by licenses anymore, and they're going to have to start succeeding on their own creative strength. Doing licensed books is, to me, kind of a short-term thing because you're not really building any equity. Eventually the license wears out, and what do you own? You own nothing. You haven't built any momentum that remains with your company or that remains to the benefit of your creators. Dark Horse relied on licenses for a long time, but they're doing the right thing by getting into creative things of their own. Mike, of course, is extremely fair and generous with the kind of deals [he offers], so he'll get very good talent. It's interesting: I really see them in a real transition phase, and any time you're in a transition phase, it can be a little spooky. A lot of things can go wrong. But they're doing the right thing, making the right moves. They've got a burden of proof—they've got to prove they can do it. I would bet on Mike; he's very smart. The other thing is, Mike will always do a lot of creator-owned, eclectic stuff. He even does it when it doesn't make money just because "It ought to be done!" So, he's always going to do a lot of that, and, of course, it could be that some of that stuff eventually will also take off to the point where it really becomes a mainstay, a pillar of Dark Horse. To me, it's hard to put that into a business plan: "I'm going to find the next *Sin City* tomorrow." How do you know that? I think he's entering the real creative phase as opposed to depending on licensing.

MG: Image?

JS: Image really seems to me to be a whole bunch of different little companies. It's hard to talk about it as a group. I think that the Image guys really deserve to be where they are. They've earned the notoriety they have. Todd McFarlane was being criticized at San Diego because of his writing, and I told him, "Todd, the guys who are criticizing you: 1) they're jealous because their books don't sell like yours, and 2) they don't really understand that you're in a different business than they are. You give 'rocket rides,' and these other guys, I don't know what they're trying to do. They're trying to convey their philosophies or whatever, but there's a big market for 'rocket rides.' There's nothing wrong with selling 'rocket rides.' That's fine. It's perfectly okay!"

To Todd's credit, when he felt like he wanted to get some help writing, he went to the best! [In response to criticism of his writing, McFarlane brought in guest writers Alan Moore, Neil Gaiman, Dave Sim, and Frank Miller, for issues 8–11 of *Spawn*, and then Grant Morrison for issues 16–18.] That's a smart guy, and he'll continue to sell "rocket rides" and continue to get friends like Alan Moore and Neil Gaiman to do some story stuff for him once in a while to create new impetus, new fodder for his mill. I think he's doing a lot of things right—most of them are doing a lot of things right. I think it's great that such a thing could happen, that this industry has gotten to the point where we can have these rock-star personalities who get this kind of attention and get this kind of media. Although there's not a whole lot of story in some of those things, I never insisted that there had to be. In mine there is because that's what I do. In Alan Moore's there always will be, and [in] Neil Gaiman's there will be. But it's not a rule to me. What they're doing is using their talents the best way they can, and they're doing fine. So God bless 'em!

MG: VALIANT?

JS: I haven't really looked at much VALIANT since I left there. It's sort of hard for me to even look at that stuff.

I think that VALIANT, just from what I hear in the marketplace, has probably become way over-dependent on speculators, and I think that that's a bubble that is easily burst. Will it happen to them or not? I don't know. I think that publishing comics is a lot like piloting a balloon. When you pilot a hot air balloon, if you see a hill coming, you turn up the heat at that moment because it takes a while for the balloon to rise. If you want to go down, you cut off the heat because it takes a couple of minutes for everything to cool down. And I think what happens with comic book companies something will change or you make an adjustment or whatever, and it takes a while for that to really set in. I think, for instance, that Marvel has been going on momentum for a couple of years now, and it's just now that they're paying the piper for mistakes that they made eighteen months ago. Similarly, I look at something like VALIANT and I wonder [if], a year from now, some of this dependency on speculation isn't going to come home to roost.

MG: Okay, back to DEFIANT. What will DEFIANT's attitudes be towards readers and collectors?

JS: I think we are reader friendly. We are entertainers first. We probably answer more letters and make a greater effort to get out and meet people and listen to what they have to say than anybody else in this business. I've always done that, wherever I've been. That's one of our things. I see comics as the most collaborative medium on Earth. If you go to a movie and you don't 1ike it, if you write Spielberg a letter, I guarantee you, he's never going to read your letter. If you want to go up to him and give him your opinion, you won't get past the bodyguards. But, if you don't like *Sin City*, you can go to San Diego and look up Miller, and you can give him a piece of your mind. You can find Terry Stewart [then-president of Marvel]. At the conventions, you can find me. You can find Paul Levitz [then-president of DC]. You can get right to them. The point is, we're always influencing each other, and even those few in this business who pretend not to care what the readers think, it gets back to them and influences their work. They read other people's work, and it influences their work. Acknowledging the fact that it's one big party here is one of the keys to success.

Listen to people. Our attitude is very, very friendly towards the readers. By the way, I want to clarify something: I've had people say, "You're against collectors and speculators, aren't you?" No. I think collecting's fine. I think that it's great. But I think when you're tricking them . . . I'm against that. I'd like to have people collect my work. I'd wanna have people think DEFIANT is worth collecting and preserving, but I want my books to be collectible the way *Amazing Spider-Man* #1 is collectible—it's just accepted and people collect it because it's good and because it means something to them, as opposed to wanting to buy a bunch of them and dump them in two weeks and make a profit.

MG: What about DEFIANT's attitudes towards retailers?

JS: I think there again, it's all very collaborative. I think we're all on the same team. This is the only business I know of where there really are no adversarial relationships. If everybody does his job well, then everybody wins. If we create a good product, then the readers are happy. Then the retailers are happy, and if the retailers are happy then the distributors have sold a lot of books. If the distributors sold a lot of books, then the publishers have sold a lot of books—everybody makes money, and we're all happy.

Compare that to the newsstand business, where there is a definite adversarial relationship between the publishers and the ID [independent distributor] wholesalers. The ID wholesalers are in business to rip you off, okay? You have an agent, a national wholesaler, who's supposed to be your representative. But think about it—who sends those guys checks? Do you? No. ID wholesalers send them the checks. That's who they work for. So, you need in-house staff to protect you against your agent, and basically it's this whole game of trying to catch the people ripping you off and make them play fair. The national wholesaler is the guy who bumps you so that someone else can pick your pocket. It's a dirty, ugly game, and too many businesses are like that. This is the only business that I've ever seen where we're really all on the same team—all the way from consumer to creator—and when we all do our jobs well, everybody's thrilled.

MG: Will DEFIANT be aggressively searching for new talents?

JS: That's another thing I've always done. I got my first job by sending in an unsolicited submission to DC Comics, so I have a special place in my heart for unsolicited submissions. We get behind sometimes. We're behind right now because I've been scrambling to get so much work done in a short period of time, but we answer everybody, every time. We occasionally find people out of the submissions that come in and the portfolios that people show at conventions and so forth. Dave Lapham, for instance—when I was at Marvel it was like a "Who's Who in Comics"—Miller, Michael Golden, Bill Sienkiewicz, Marc Silvestri, Rick Leonardi—it's an endless list of people. Not all [found by] me, but it was something that I kind of impressed upon my crew there. Allen Milgrom discovered a lot of these guys—Paul Smith . . . he gave Ron Frenz his first work although I met Ron in a comics shop in Pittsburgh and introduced him to Al. Basically, that was a part of our corporate culture when I was Marvel, and it's certainly going to be something that we do a lot here. I've already picked a few people out of the submissions that I think we're going to try to work with and see if we can get them up to the speed where they can compete with the Weisses and the Leialohas.

MG: Will you be writing all of the series?

JS: Oh, no, no, no, no! Like I said, I have Chris Claremont, Mike Barr, and eventually Roger Stern. I'm going to do a lot of the writing, but this time I want to have a lot of other good writers working with me. At VALIANT, we basically didn't have enough money, so I ended up writing just about everything. Also at VALIANT, early on it was very difficult to get commitments from experienced guys because, in the beginning, everybody looked at us and said, "Here's a little comic book company" and "These things come and go." If a guy had a regular gig at Marvel, he wasn't going to give it up to go work for a little company that might not be there in six months. Also, little companies are famous for paying slowly or not paying at all. My reputation is very good for paying people, and that helped us get a few people. One thing I did at VALIANT for the first year and a half was whenever somebody handed me any pages or anything, I handed them a check—as I accepted their work I handed them a check. Here at DEFIANT, we're going to pay people instantly their royalties. We pay people on the spot quite frequently, although at this point, my credibility is enough that most actually prefer to wait 'til the end of the week—they don't want to be paid for each job along the way; they want it all gathered up at the end of the week. As I said, having had the success of VALIANT, now I'm getting these guys who are big name creators showing up and looking for work and content to work here and believing in what we're doing. It's a much better situation: instead of writing all of the books, I can give my attention to coordinating among the writers of the books. All of these guys I've mentioned, by the way, are people who work well coordinating with other writers . . . I mean, that's a skill all by itself! Look at what Claremont did with Louise Simonson at Marvel on the X-books, for a long time making that little segment of the universe airtight. That's the kind of thing that Roger Stern loves to do. That's the kind of thing Mike Barr loves to do. These guys like to do that. Roger likes to help keep the continuity going in general. He used to pick up mistakes of mine back at Voyager and call me up and say, "Hey, I read this, and this isn't quite right. But here's how you can fix it."

MG: Tell us a little about your debut series, *Plasm*, and its origins . . .
JS: Plasm is an extradimensional place; a place where life has gone wild. The ecosystem has been maxed out, and every atom of the world of Plasm is involved in living matter. If you think about the Earth as a very thin biosphere on top of a basically inorganic mass, in Plasm, the biosphere has consumed the entire planet. Furthermore, Plasm is an empire that is spreading out through the stars of its dimension, constantly incorporating resources, incorporating biomass into the Org because they think of their world as one organism and think of themselves as cells in the organism. On Plasm, because the ecosystem is maxed out, in order for there to be growth or in order for someone to have

a child, they have to bring in new resources because there aren't any resources to support any new beings. On Plasm, they are masters of genetic engineering. If you think of yourself as a very complex machine, if you could engineer genetically on that level, you could engineer yourself a fax machine or a vehicle because a car is a much simpler machine than you are. So on Plasm, everything is alive. They don't build buildings; they grow them. Therefore, in a society like that, there are a lot of ramifications. Since people think of themselves as cells in a larger organism, there's less of a premium placed on individual life. It's less of a crime to kill your neighbor—that's a misdemeanor. If you don't recycle the remains, that's a capital crime.

Imagine if we could genetically engineer things here. For about two weeks, everyone would look like Schwarzenegger and Cheryl Tiegs or somebody. Then everybody would get tired of looking the same, and before you knew it there would be more variety than there is now. Someone would decide to be the tall guy or the short guy or the fat guy or whatever. On Plasm, there's just endless diversity, and fads sweep the nation. One week everybody wants to have twigs instead of hair; the next week they all want horns. There's a whole industry of cosmetic mutation on Plasm.

Also on Plasm, they have a kind of Roman Empire–style conquest machine, always trying to incorporate new resources because they are, in fact, this incredible military/industrial complex. There are some people on Plasm who don't believe in this "cells of the body" thing, who actually believe in the sanctity of individual life. One of these is Lorca, a high-ranking officer in the military who has kept his cover because if that was found out it would certainly ruin his career. He's kept his cover because he intends, at some point, to pull a coup and to overthrow what he sees as a corrupt and evil regime. His role is target acquisition, and through his research he discovers this place called Earth, which is right in the same space as Plasm but a dimension away. He doesn't tell anybody because he sees an opportunity. Here is a world full of individuals who will fight desperately to remain alive, who do value their lives. So he decides he's going to bring in ten thousand of them, genetically reengineer them into a superhuman army, and use them as the spearhead of his revolution. He brings in ten thousand—but only five survive the mutation process. Five is not exactly enough to overthrow an empire, he thinks, so he tries to get rid of them and do a cover-up. But he has made a miscalculation because he's right about these people. They don't die easily. They're not just ready to curl up and die. So, that starts the adventure of *Plasm*: Five ordinary humans [who] are thrust into this wild and strange environment and find

Barry Windsor-Smith
promotional artwork for
Unity. © 1993 VALIANT.

themselves at odds with the empire and at odds with the man who brought them there and, in a war, way over their heads.

Plasm, in terms of strategy, is like my *Unity*. With VALIANT, I started with individual titles and built towards *Unity*. With DEFIANT, I'm starting with my "Unity"—my outrageous extradimensional, visually spectacular adventure—and from it, just like in Unity, I'm going to bring things back from Earth. From *Unity*, we brought back Turok and dinosaurs; we brought back some technology. *Plasm* will serve the same role, and all other DEFIANT series are set on Earth. We have ten of them in development right now, which we will roll out slowly. But *Plasm* is sort of an ongoing *Unity*—that really is the foundation of our universe. Also, as we go along (we've already planned out the first fifteen months of stories), people will slowly see what the relationship between Plasm and Earth is—why there is a Plasm, why it is what it is—and understand how it fits in the conceptual base of this universe, which is a quantum physics base. I don't know how much you know about quantum physics, but it's pretty weird stuff! You don't need much magic when you've got quantum physics on your side.

MG: How much of a role will Lorca play in the series or at least after the first story arc? He seems to be kind of caught between a heroic role and that of a villain.

JS: Exactly. Lorca will remain a very important character for the foreseeable future. You're exactly right. Here's a guy who is heroic—he wants to overthrow what he sees as an evil empire—but on the other hand, if it takes killing some people along the way, that seems okay with him.

MG: He uses the exact mind-frame that the empire uses, in just using ten thousand people out of the blue . . .

JS: But to me that rings true, because if you grow up and spend your whole life living in that environment, even if you start to think differently, there are going to be a lot of ways that you are still conditioned. I grew up in the fifties, and between the 1950s and the 1990s, this whole society has changed. When I was a little kid, little girls were supposed to grow up to be nurses and teachers and housewives. That was just a given. No one debated it. It was just sort of like, "grass is green and sky is blue"; it was a fact. Since then, the world in general has wised up quite a bit, and fortunately, little Jimmy wised up with it. My point is, is that during that transition, you would still find yourself kind of lapsing—I'm talking about 1961 now, I'm not talking about last year—but back when this was news: "Oh, I see. Girls can be rocket scientists. Well, gee, nobody told me that!" During those years, there were all kinds of things you didn't realize you thought or did—like in a crowded elevator, kind of scrunching up to let ladies off first. Why the hell shouldn't the person nearest the door get off first? You have to go through all your actions one at a time and sort through them and question them. That's the same situation he's in. And believe me, someone's going to point out to him, "Hey! Isn't this just like they do?"

Absolutely. I really try to live this stuff through in my brain and try to make it as real as I can make it. That's why it's good to have guys like Chris and Roger and Mike around because you do that by yourself and you do the best you can. I mostly did it by myself at VALIANT . . . I had some help from Bob, and a lot of help from JJ and other people, but I wrote fifty-three of the first sixty issues. A lot of that was me alone in the middle of the night trying to reason things out. It's much better when you've got somebody like Chris you can call and say, "What do you think of this?" And he's gives you a point of view that maybe you hadn't thought of, and you can bounce things back and forth. That's a great luxury!

MG: How big a role will the existence of Plasm play in the month-to-month existence within the DEFIANT Universe of Earth?

JS: I think it's going to be an important title, but it's one of what will eventually be twelve to fourteen titles. It's sort of our Unity, starting things off, but this is not going to be the Plasm Universe. This is the DEFIANT Universe. Almost all of it [will take place] in the here and now, on Earth, in real time . . . real dates . . . and real settings.

MG: What can you tell us about some of the other new series coming from DEFIANT in 1993? How about *Dark Dominion*?

JS: *Dark Dominion* is about a man in New York who learns, through concentration and decades of research, to see a greater degree of the spectrum than you or I can see. He starts to realize that there are things that cannot be explained, that we are blind—we can only see certain electromagnetic, chemical, and physical information—and there's a lot more in this world than we know about. When he learns to see what I call the "Quantum World," then he realizes there are things around we know nothing about—some of which are not good, they're dangerous and bad. *Dark Dominion* is the story of a guy named Michael Alexander, who becomes aware of what's really going on in the world, and the fact that New York is a "Dark Dominion," and he's the only one that has a chance of preventing it from becoming . . . worse.

MG: *The Good Guys*?

JS: I've been doing young kid superheroes since 1965, and I'm going to keep on doing it 'til I get it right! *Good Guys* was an idea we had—again, all sort of based on quantum physics, going back to Plasm . . . I don't even want to tell it because it gives things away as to where we're building this, but basically because of events in Plasm, there are seven young kids ranging in age from seven to sixteen. They are all at a comic book convention, and at this comic book convention their wishes become real. They become like the characters that they dream about. Other people at this convention also have some wishes become real. Let's face it, at any given moment, there may be a few people there wishing for a Big Mac, and they just suddenly get the urge to run across to McDonalds. There may be a few people wishing for Todd McFarlane's autograph, and suddenly Todd would walk up and volunteer it for them. Somebody might be wishing for *Harbinger* #1 at cover price, and some dealer would sell it to them. But there [are] a few people there who would have dangerous wishes, and that's what *Good Guys* is about: It's about seven kids who become the superheroes that they dream about.

MG: *Charlemagne?*

JS: *Charlemagne* is . . . best explained in the context of a character called War Dancer, so I'll explain War Dancer first. War Dancer, created by myself and Alan Weiss, is actually from *Plasm*. The nearest example I can give you is War Dancer is probably akin to Solar, Man of the Atom, in a sense that this is an individual who has discovered that he can become one with the quantum field, with energy. This happened a long time ago on Plasm, before it had become the organic nightmare it is. When he returns, he discovers what's happened to Plasm, discovers the Earth, and slowly through the series, the relationship between Plasm and the Earth unfolds. He, in a way, is the keystone of the continuity, which will lead to our first crossover in the summer of '94. He fulfills the same role as Solar filled at VALIANT—the only way he can set right what is going wrong between Earth and Plasm is maybe to destroy the whole thing. That gives you context for Charlemagne.

Charlemagne is a character who, like the Good Guys, has his desires actualized due to events that take place in the Plasm book. Charlemagne is basically the adversary, the nemesis, of War Dancer. His backstory is, as a child, when his brother didn't come home from 'Nam, he went looking for him. His name is Charles Smith, and through determination, courage, and relentless never-say-die effort, he finds his brother's body. But he's a person of indomitable will; therefore, when his needs and desires become actualized, he becomes, more or less, the champion of life on Earth. He's not at all happy that there's somebody here who thinks it's a good idea to just erase the whole thing. I think this is probably the first time I know of where there are two characters that are basically at odds, each [starring] in their own monthly series. It's sort of a crossover every month . . . a very parallel continuity.

MG: How about *Glory?*

JS: Glory's one of the five people who survives the genetic reengineering on Plasm. I think the nearest example I can give you to *Glory* is probably the Fleischer Superman—leap ⅛ of a mile and that kind of thing. Glory is in her early fifties and is recently a grandmother and is a woman who grew up before the fifties—grew up in the forties—a little bit like my mother and ladies of her generation, who came along at a time where it was the rule that women grew up to be housewives, school teachers, and so forth, and a lot of them did. Whether they did it because they were conditioned to or pushed into it, or whatever, they went along with that. This is such a woman. But like many women, especially older women of my mother's generation who went through that and fulfilled their prescribed roles, it doesn't mean they're not great people. My mother, for instance, is one tough lady. But the thing is, unless some need were thrust upon them, you'd never know that this was a person who could have won the Medal of Honor. So here's this woman who's done the prescribed thing all her life and been what she was supposed to be, and now she is thrust into a situation of great power and great responsibility. *Glory*'s the story of her rising to the challenge. I find it very interesting . . . my father was in World War II, and if they hadn't had a war he wouldn't have been a war hero! You never would have known; he just would have been another steel worker. But they had a war and he went (because he had to), and he did great things. You need to be tested in order to be proven, and it's a shame that people have to get tested. But I think things like that are fascinating. I've always been fascinated by Sgt. York and things like that. People who just rose to the challenge.

MG: *Prudence & Caution*?
JS: *Prudence & Caution* is the first one from Chris Claremont, based on an idea by me, but anything Chris gets involved in, you know he's going to contribute to it heavily and make it his own. *Prudence & Caution* involves a female character (that's Prudence) from Plasm, and one of our original five humans who was brought to Plasm—his name is . . . actually, in the book we are calling him "Ironhead"—he's a fellow who lost an arm in a factory accident, and things like *that* tend to make you careful, hence the name Caution.

MG: Where would you like to see DEFIANT at this time next year?
JS: I think at this time next year we'll have six or seven titles out. I think the industry will have changed significantly, and we will be a leader in the industry with only these six or seven titles. We'll be at or near the top.

MG: After all you've been through, what keeps bringing you back to comics? Bottom line.
JS: This is what I do. This is it. I've spent a long time learning to do this, and I think I have a rather unique set of skills. Most other people who have the background I have, where we really had a chance to work with some of the all-time greats, working with [Mort] Weisinger, Stan Lee (I worked with him closely for about eight years), with Neal [Adams], Carmine [Infantino], and Julie [Schwartz] . . . most people who have that kind of background and that kind of education have gone off to be freelance creators—writers or artists. I think I'm probably the only one who stayed in editorial and management, so I have sort of a unique situation. I don't think there's anybody else in this

business who does what I do, and I feel like a lot of what I went through was a learning curve maybe I almost had to go through. I was a freelance writer, and unless you're discovered as a freelance writer you can't get to do what you really want to do. I was an employee at a large corporation and soon discovered that if you have principles, sooner or later, those principles will put you at odds with the people who own that corporation. I couldn't really do what I wanted to do. I became a partner in a company and discovered that if you have principles . . . Sooner or later you're going to be at odds with your partners. This time—I've gone through all that, had all of those experiences, and I learned all of those things—I've created a situation where I don't have anyone else I have to satisfy in terms of what we do and how we do it. I have partners—lots of them—they are the creators. But I have a situation in which I'm secure; they can't get rid of me. No one can steal it from me, and if it goes down there's no one else to blame. It's me. I feel at this time I've learned all of those things, and I have a chance to do it right. I'm the same age as Stan was when he started Marvel. Also, I feel like this time, because of the success of VALIANT, everybody's looking. Last time, at VALIANT, I had to struggle to get people's attention. I had to fight to get people to look at the books. I had to fight to get anybody to help me . . . to get creators to come in. I have lots of friends in this business, but in those days it was tough because we were a little start-up company and nobody wanted to jump on board.

This time, lots of creative people are showing up. This time, everybody's looking. I don't have to struggle to get people's attention this time. Everybody is going to look at what we do. Everybody is going to at least pick it up and give it a look. All I've got to do is be good. There's not an athlete or a performer or an entertainer worth his salt, that wouldn't take that challenge. The stands are full; they're all looking. All you've got to do is catch the ball. Then if you drop it, you had your chance. But to me, this is the opportunity I have been waiting forty-two years for—and here it is! We're not going to drop the ball.

MG: One final question, Jim. How do you feel?
JS: I feel great! I tell you, I've never had this much fun in my life. This is the best time of my life.

The Kid Who Wrote Comic Books Speaks Out

RICHARD ARNDT/ 2015

This interview was conducted via phone on February 14, 2015. Printed by permission.

RA: Thank you for agreeing to this interview. I know you're originally from Pittsburgh, but I don't know much more about your early life beyond that. Would you like to start with that?

JS: Sure. I grew up in a suburb of Pittsburgh. I needed to make money for the family. I read comics when I was a little kid, but I grew bored with them when I was about eight. Then, when I was twelve, in 1963, I was in the hospital for a week. Back then, in the kids' ward, hospitals had stacks of old comic books. When I was a kid, all kids read comics. It wasn't a little cult thing, like it is today. I discovered these new-fangled Marvel comics there. I got interested in those Marvel comics and started picking them up when I could.

I've had a conversation with Roy Thomas, who told me he'd started to work at DC for Mort Weisinger. He told me that Mort was going around the office showing off this comic that a kid sent in. So Mort wrote me a letter and told me that he thought my comic was pretty good, and he mentioned that he thought I could draw features for them someday, based on my layouts. He told me to send him another story, so I sent him a two-part story, which was kind of rare for DC at the time. I was taking a chance there. I turned that in to him in September of that year, when I turned fourteen.

On Feb. 10, 1966, I got a call from Mort. He said he wanted to buy those Legion stories that I'd sent in and that he wanted me to write a Supergirl story. He wanted twelve pages, and he wanted it in a week. So I wrote a Supergirl story called "Brainiac's Blitz!" that appeared in *Action Comics* #339 (July 1966). It was a back-up story, which was fairly common for titles in those days. Later that month that first "Legion" story appeared in *Adventure Comics* #346. That issue also introduced four new Legionnaires—Ferro Lad, Nemesis Kid, Princess Projectra, and Karate Kid—which I created.

After that I became a regular writer at DC. Every time I finished a story, Mort wanted me to do another one. He bought them all. He saw problems in some of them. One thing he said to me was "You need to learn to spell"—things like that. But basically I never had to do any rewrites or corrections. I became the regular scripter on the "Legion of Super-Heroes." It was about that time that he found out I was fourteen.

He told me, "I want you to fly up to New York and spend a few days here." I hemmed and hawed, and he asked me, "How old are you?" I said that I was fourteen. He said, "Put your mother on the phone!" So I had to wait until school was over, early in June, and I had to bring my mother with me on my first business trip to New York, which was maybe a little weird.

DC put us up at the Lafayette Hotel, wined us and dined us, and took us to see the Broadway musical *It's a Bird, It's a Plane, It's Superman!* Mort had apparently arranged the license for Superman to the Hal Prince organization for that play. The theater people knew Mort, and he was kind of a big shot there. So after the play we went to the stage door, and they saw it was Mort and let us in. We met all the people in the cast. They showed us how they made Superman fly. I got the show's star, Bob Holiday's autograph on a picture. It was pretty great! It was like a dream experience.

RA: You mentioned earlier that you had to earn a living at a very early age for a kid. Was there any particular reason that you yourself needed to do that, besides the fact that you and your family were poor?

JS: My father was a steelworker. The steelworkers were the last big union to get a good contract. In those days, the steel industry was in a boom-and-bust cycle. The contract between the union and the management came up every two years. Because the people who were buying the steel were afraid that there would be a strike, they would stockpile steel. The mills would be busy as hell right up until the time for either a contract renewal or a strike. So, even if the steelworkers signed a contract and there was no strike, because so much steel had been stockpiled, the price of steel would drop and suddenly there was no work! People were laid off, sometimes for months. It was bad for the steel industry but also bad for the steelworkers. It was just a repeating cycle. Eventually, the army, the manufacturers, and other big steel purchasers would buy steel from Japan and Germany, who were selling below cost because they were trying to capture market share. The steel industry went into a tremendous decline. There were more and more layouts, more and more times when you were not called back to work.

My father, who was a hell of a man, got jobs where he could when there was a strike or no steel work. He would mow people's lawns and do what he could to make money. There just wasn't enough work like that to make *enough* money for a family. We didn't live fancy. We lived in a tiny house, but it was still very hard to get by. We were, most of the time, pretty desperate.

So I figured that I should help bring in some money. That would solve the problem! That doesn't usually work. Kids' first jobs are mowing lawns or something like that, but I did my best. It helped a little. There were times, though, that it was too little, too late. Still I worked my way through high school. I'd go to school all day. I was trying to earn a scholarship because I knew that was the only way I'd be going to college. I'd work late into the night on the comics because if you missed a deadline with Mort—oh, my God, he would just kill you.

This will crack you up: I would be getting down to the wire on a deadline. I'd finish the script and layouts late at night. I'd walk down to the trolley station, which was about a mile away, and catch a trolley into Pittsburgh. I'd go to the main post office, which was open 24/7 and mail the package airmail special delivery, which was fifty-five cents, to New York. I thought that price was outrageous! It usually got there the next day. This was way before Federal Express or anything like that.

Then I got even worse than that. Mort and I would go over everything I did, and he would always yell at me. Yet, he paid me and used it all. He almost never touched a word, but it got to the point where I was afraid to put anything on the paper because I knew that whatever I put down there Mort would consider wrong. Then the fear of missing the deadline would eclipse the fear of putting something on paper. The last few days before the deadline I would be working like a madman. I would take days off from school, stay up all night. I would do whatever I had to do to get that story done. I would drink a lot of coffee. I found out about this stuff called No-Doze, which was pure caffeine, and would pop them just to stay awake all night. It got to the point where, on the due date, I would be up all night, finish the thing, drive my brother's car to the airport, and then get on an airplane to New York. I'd go to the DC offices and hand the receptionist the package, then run away before anybody, especially Mort, could see me, and go right back to the airport to fly home.

If that sounds extravagant to fly to New York, well, at the time the airlines had this thing called student standby, which cost twenty-five dollars round trip from Pittsburgh to New York.

RA: Boy, I wish there was something like that now!

JS: When they raised the price to twenty-eight dollars a trip, I was outraged. The bus from Newark Airport to New York cost, just like the post office, fifty-five cents. Sometimes, when the deadline was the next day, I even resorted to traveling to the airport, finding a passenger who was going to New York and asking them, "Would you drop this in the post office in New York for me?" They always did. Those were exciting times!

I used to go up to New York fairly frequently and spend a couple of days in a hotel because Mort wanted to yell at me in person. Today, if a fifteen-year-old kid gets on a plane by himself, flies to New York by himself, and checks into a hotel by himself, the parents would be arrested. Such a thing is just impossible nowadays. But in those days, nobody batted an eye. Fifteen-year-old kid checking into a hotel room—that's fine.

RA: If you had cash, that was all they cared about. Nowadays that wouldn't be legal because you need a driver's license to check into most hotels and a fifteen year old wouldn't have one—not a legal one anyway.

JS: Yeah, today the authorities would be all over something like that. Back then, nobody seemed to care about that. So I did that fairly frequently.

One time I sent in this cover sketch and my story had a thing that would turn people into glass [*Adventure Comics* #372 (Sept. 1968)], and Superboy had been turned into glass. This guy wearing a hood like an executioner was shattering Superboy with a sledge hammer. On my cover sketch I'd colored Superboy like glass. Whites and blues. Mort objected to that on the grounds that up until that point Superboy or Superman had never appeared on a cover in anything but their super-costumes' color—in this case, red, blue and yellow. If Superman was at the center of the earth or at the center of the sun he appeared in his costume's natural color. But Carmine Infantino, who wasn't the publisher yet but was the DC art director, loved the idea and overruled Mort. When I was up at the office the next time Carmine gushed over that cover.

RA: Do you remember the pay for doing layouts?

JS: There was no pay for layouts. I got paid for writing. Nothing for the cover designs either.

RA: I don't think cover layouts were paid for until the early 1970s. I recall Rich Buckler mentioning a run-in he'd had with Julie Schwartz about that.

JS: Could be. I don't know.

RA: Every writer and artist I've ever interviewed has that moment when they realized that they don't have to simply admire the artists or writers that they've been reading. They come to realize that "I can do that!" Clearly that realization came at a very early age for you.

MORT WEISINGER Editor,
Superman magazines

Dear Jim:

Here's our check for your latest Legion story.
You can tell your mother I've made reservations
for both of you at the Hotel Summit..you can
arrive there any time after 1pm on Thursday,
June 16th. The Summit is half a block away
from our office, and we've got you a really
elegant room, with large twin beds.

It would be best for you folks to make plane
reservations now. I'd suggest you take the
family plan trip, which will allow you to
leave on Thursday and fly back on the following
Monday.

I will arrange for our company car to pick you
up at the airport and drive you to the hotel.
So let me know what flight you'll be taking and
what time the plane will land and at which
airport, Kennedy or LaGuardia.

Bestest,

Mort W.

Letter from Mort Weisinger
inviting Shooter and his
mother to New York.

JS: In my case it was just youthful stupidity. I was a kid. It wasn't a big ego thing. The "I can do this" was just my not knowing any better.

RA: I don't mean that it took a big ego to believe that but just the realization that you had the skills to actually do that.

JS: Well, I thought I could do a reasonable job based on what I'd learned and what I liked in reading Stan's comics. I really did analyze his work. Some kids would read a comic and throw it down. I actually sat there and studied it. Once I got an idea of what I thought he was doing, that's when I thought that I could do this thing. I actually tried to figure out what Stan was doing and why he was doing it. When I wrote that first "Legion" story, what I found out was that what most people who sent in submissions, back in the day, would write in their first story was something that would change the direction of the book, like kill Aunt May.

Now, you can't do that. You have to write really good stories that don't have the forced drama of killing Aunt May. What an editor wanted was a writer who could write a good story without killing Aunt May. Then maybe they'd be interested. So the first story I did—I admit I thought the Legion Clubhouse thing was stupid! Did I change it? No. I wanted to sell my story. I wanted to fit in with what was going on in that book—maybe bring a little bit of hip sensitivity to it.

My first thought was these other writers, Otto Binder and Edmond Hamilton, were terrible. Their stuff felt so outdated. But the more I got into it, I realized that these guys were geniuses! They were great! They *were* older guys, and they weren't real hip or in touch with teenage wants or whatever. I wanted to be more contemporary. At DC they used to call me their Marvel writer. DC did not like Marvel! So that was really an insult.

The DC guys would discuss Marvel comics and dismiss them as ugly. "Why would anybody buy this? Look at the color. It's terrible!" They actually started thinking that if they had worse art the books would sell better. I remember thinking, "What was wrong with these guys?" One picture they looked at featured the X-Men's Angel flying, and he's taking such joy in flight. Their opinion was that Superman flies all the time. That Marvel page was stupid! Why waste a whole page on something like that?

But that sort of thing is *not* stupid. That was both the difference and the source of the trouble between DC and Marvel. Superman flies all the time, and nobody thinks anything about it! No reaction from readers. But wouldn't it be wonderful to fly? That's what Stan and the Marvel artists were doing. They were showing readers that sense of how wonderful it would be to fly! Of course, I couldn't say that because I was a kid. I learned to keep my mouth shut around Mort.

They hated things like, in a *Spider-Man* comic, there would be two pages of Peter Parker talking to Aunt May. Their thoughts on that were that kids would be bored out of their minds! The reality was that that sort of thing made the characters real. The DC editors had all the wrong sensibilities for the 1960s.

Around the time that Steranko started they started believing that maybe the appeal was all those slanted panels. So they started telling Curt Swan, who was a great storyteller, to start doing the crazy, slanted panel pages. Slanted panels may have worked for Steranko or Adams or Gene Colan, but it was the wrong approach for Curt Swan. I didn't say anything to the contrary. You just didn't say anything to Mort.

They then thought that Marvel's coloring, which to their eyes was garish, was it, so they actually started running color in the gutter! Colored the gutters. Go-Go checks. Really?

RA: I spoke to Stan Goldberg once, and he told me that Stan liked colors on the cover that would really pop out.

JS: Here's my Stan Lee–cover story. Before I was editor-in-chief, what happened was whoever was editor or probably John Verpoorten, the production manager, would look at the pen and ink art, then have the art photostatted, and have the stat sent to the house colorist, George Roussos. George had been an artist almost since the beginning of comics. He remembered Stan when Stan was just starting out. He was a great man. So George got this cover and sometimes, without context, he didn't know what was going on in the cover. He'd color it anyway, and then it would go out.

When I became editor I went to George and said, "George, from now on when you get a cover to color, come to me and we'll discuss it." George was annoyed at that and asked, "What for?" I said that I might be able to tell him some things that he would otherwise not know. I told him, "I'm not complaining about your color, but sometimes you may not understand what the artist's intent was. I do because I'm involved with the entire production line." So he grudgingly does this, and the first couple of times, it went OK. Then a *Master of Kung Fu* cover comes in, and George brings it over to me. It was a very artsy cover. So I said I wanted Shang-Chi all golden and red, his colors, and the background a vivid green and make the logo yellow. George says, "We can't make the cover green." I said, "What do you mean?" "We can't make the cover green. Stan says no green covers." I said, "George, don't worry about it. It's on me. Make the background green." He storms away.

A few minutes later Marie Severin comes in and says, "What are you doing to George?" I said, "What do you mean? I told him what to do on a cover." She says, "You told him to make the cover *green!* You can never make a cover green!" I said, "This is my job. If Stan fires me, that's fine. I'm not laying George out to fry." She replies, "You're just crazy!" She storms off. George comes back and says, "I'm not going to do this. I can't do this." I say, "George, make the cover green or go home." Off he goes.

The cover came out just like I imagined it. It looked great. George is going, "Stan's going to hate this. He's going to throw a fit." Well, first of all, Stan wasn't the boss anymore by then. Second, the cover looked great, and Stan was going to love it. I told George, "Come with me." We both walked to Stan's office. The door was open as it always was. George wouldn't come into the office. He was afraid. I asked Stan's opinion of the cover and showed it to him. He says, "Great!" I walked back out and handed the cover to George, who says, "But he hates green!" I said, "Let me tell you what he hates. What he hates is when a colorist uses a kind of medium color, like green or brown, and nothing in the cover pops against that color. The yellow logo on this pops against that green background, and the gold and red of Shang-Chi pops against this green."

After that, George and I were a lot closer. He started coming in and explaining some unusual cover effects that he would like to try out. They were great ideas! George was a good man, and we were friends until he passed away. That's my Stan Lee–cover story.

Stan learned his color schemes from Martin Goodman. You make the background dark, or you make the background light. If the background's light the logo color is dark. If it's dark the logo is light. If it was a yellow logo, the shadow in the background might be red, against a dark background. When you do a medium color, and, when I say medium, we're talking about the value here—the medium value on the color scale. It can be tricky. You have to make certain you've got hue contrast. Such as red and gold against green. Stan made his green rule because people didn't understand the logic that the logo has to be on the top and the color has to be able to register on the rack. That can happen all kinds of ways, but because somewhere he had a hard time getting that done with the green and the brown he made these rules to not use those colors.

So back to my life through high school at DC. About the time I graduated from high school, I decided that I'd had about enough from Mort. One thing I will say for Mort and that's that he taught me comic-book logic. If you worked for Mort Weisinger you understood the logic! I will never take that away from Mort. He wasn't nice, but he taught me *so* much. It was unbelievable. Not only did he teach me a lot about writing, but, when I went to the office, he would sit me down with this guy, DC's production manager and a wonderful man, and they would teach me about production. All the steps right up to printing. Mort would sit me down next to George Klein, and he would teach me all about inking. I'd write to Curt Swan, and we'd talk about storytelling.

I was getting all these lessons from Mort. He'd talk to me about licensing, about merchandising. He'd talk about media. Nelson Bridwell said he was grooming me to become his successor. The good news was that I walked out of there knowing about the whole process of comics—more than most writers bothered to learn.

What I did next, though, was actually kind of stupid, perhaps the stupidest thing I've ever done.

I had a scholarship to NYU, a full scholarship that even gave me two hundred dollars a year to see Broadway plays—a cultural stipend. I was one of two university scholars. So I was going to go to NYU. But I was eighteen years old, and I had all kinds of debt. My mother never paid my taxes on the comic work, so I was in hock to the government and elsewhere. So, even though I had the scholarship and school was paid for, I still had to work. After working my way through high school I wasn't sure I could easily work my way through college, at least doing writing. I asked Mort if there was some kind of half-time thing that I could do in the office, assistant editor or something, and he said, "No! I need you to write!"

I thought, "You've been yelling at me for four years about what a terrible writer I am, but you need me to write!" Then comes the stupid part. I decided that I was going to try Marvel, and I flew to New York. Then I call Marvel, who knew nothing about me, and I say, "Hi, this is Jim Shooter. I'd like to talk to Stan Lee." For some reason they put me through. I don't think anybody got to talk to Stan that way, but, for some reason, I got through. I guess I sounded adult or something.

Stan asks me what he could do for me. I told him I'd been writing for DC Comics for four-and-a-half years and that I'd really rather write for Stan. Stan's reply was "We don't really need a DC Comics writer." I said, "Look, just let me come and talk to you for a minute." He said, "I'll give you fifteen minutes." So I went up to Marvel and started talking to Stan. He explained, "We don't *like* DC Comics. We don't like the writers that work there." So I told him, "At DC Comics they make fun of me. They call me the Marvel writer because I write stories differently from them. It's not that I'm as good as you, but I learned to write from reading your stories." So we start talking about story and character and how to make a story more real or compelling. My fifteen minutes turned into two hours, and he hired me on staff.

The trouble with that was that it was a full-time position. There was no part-time to it. There was nothing I could do part-time during the day, so I turned down NYU and a full scholarship to start work at Marvel. That was in 1969. My job there lasted about three weeks—not because I couldn't do the work. I was doing fine with the work. My trouble was I couldn't find a place to live. I had no money. I went for a couple of weeks with very little food. I just had no money. It got to the point where I just couldn't go on. There were only five or six people who worked in the Marvel offices at the time. Stan, Marie Severin, a secretary whose name I think was Holly, Morrie Kuramoto, and maybe somebody else. This was before John Romita. It might have been Herb Trimpe. Anyway, it was a very small crew. Oh, Allyn Brodsky, who was no relation to Sol Brodsky, was also there.

I worked there three weeks, and they put me in a room with Morrie, who was shooting photostats and doing paste-up. Morrie was the one who taught me to do paste-ups. At Marvel everybody was doing everything, and it had to be done *quick!* When a character would overlap the logo on a cover Morrie would cut the actual artwork and overlap the logo on it. It was amazing! It was like what they used to say on the *M*A*S*H*. TV show. It was a form of meatball surgery! I was doing proofreading. The first story I proofread was a *Millie the Model* that Stan had written. I found a giant mistake.

He had this whole shaggy dog story leading up to a punchline. But, by the time he got to the punchline, he'd forgotten what the set-up was. He was writing about twelve books a month, and he was writing them in pieces—a little bit on this title, a little bit on that one. So I knocked on Stan's door and said, "You said the moon here. Don't you mean Mars?" He goes, "Oh, my God!" Some guys might have got upset about that but he liked me. It was OK. I was doing everything there, even a little art correction. Whatever they needed.

But I just couldn't survive with no place to live, with no wherewithal. I finally had to just give it up. I had to go back to Pittsburgh, where I could at least get a meal. I thought I'd really burned my bridges at both places.

Actually, the first day I showed up at Marvel to work—I guess the rumor mill had been going around—that first day I got a phone call. It was Mort, and he was screaming at me. How dare I betray him after all he did for me? Well, whatever.

Unfortunately, I could last at Marvel, but I couldn't last in New York—not on my own at eighteen years old, anyways. It just wasn't happening.

I went home to Pittsburgh and got some work in advertising. Out of the blue I got a call from this company named Lando-Bishopric. See, all through my high school years the local papers would do a lot of write-ups on teenagers who were doing interesting things, and I became sort of known locally as the kid who wrote comic books. On a slow news day they would do an interview with me on that topic. I even appeared in a national article in *This Week* magazine, which was a weekly magazine stuffed in the Sunday newspapers. I also did interviews on local TV and radio. I wouldn't say I was well-known, but I got some exposure in Pittsburgh.

RA: Well, for a kid you were well-known.
JS: I guess so. Lando-Bishopric called me up and asked if I was the kid who did comic books. I said, "Yeah, that's me." They said they had a job for me, and I started working for them. The jobs were all comic book–related. Advertising done in comic book form. I did a number of projects, but the work wasn't steady. There'd be a job, or even a number of jobs close together, and then there'd be a space where there would be nothing. I had to have a day job. Although working for two weeks for Lando-Bishopric was like working six months at Joseph Horn Company, which was a local department store. I made so much money working in advertising compared to working at a paint

company. I did a bunch of stuff for them and was technically involved in comics, one way or the other.

Then in 1974 or so, I got a call from a guy named Harry Broertjes, who was a journalist and a member of *CAPA-Alpha*, an APA, which helped fans who did monthly or bimonthly or whatever fanzines. They'd send their fanzines all to a central spot mailer, and then the mailer would compile them all and send them back to everybody who was on the APA contact list [this organization was created fifty years ago by Jerry Bails and is still in existence today—RT]. Broertjes was what we used to call a big-name fan.

He kept calling my mother's home, where I didn't live anymore, but that was the only address he had. My mother kept telling me this guy kept calling her about me. So, finally, I was visiting Mother one time when he called, and my mother, being who she was, insisted I talk to him. What he wanted to do was come to me and do an interview. I thought, "alright," and gave him directions to a local landmark. I drove up on my motorcycle and gave him directions on how to get to my mother's house.

He did his interview, and when it was over he asked me why I wasn't working in comics any longer. I told him that I felt I'd burned my bridges. I'd left DC under bad terms. I'd worked at Marvel for only three weeks and bailed out—where was I going to go? He said people, both fans and guys in the business, talked about me all the time—wondering where I was and why they couldn't get work from me. I told him they could find me. I wasn't hiding. I was still on DC's comp list. I wasn't on Marvel's, but I was on DC's and had been for years. Every month DC would send me a big box of their most recent comics. I told him they knew where I was, and he replied that he didn't think that they did. He didn't think the comp list people were telling editorial that I was still around and could be located.

Apparently he went and called someone he knew at Marvel, Duffy Vohland, who was some kind of assistant in the British department at Marvel, but he represented himself to me as an editor at Marvel Comics. I hadn't read a Marvel comic in a while, so I didn't know one way or the other. He asked me how soon I could get up to New York because he wanted to take me in and talk to Roy [Thomas]. He thought they could really use my help. I said, "OK," and told him that I'd be there the next day.

I still had my student standby card and flew into New York the next day, and Duffy walked me around Marvel. I met Roy and talked to him. Roy said he could use me and that I could write Man-Wolf. I had no idea who that was. I said, "OK," and I got some back issues to read. Reading it was like watching a Swedish movie with no subtitles.

I went out to lunch with some guys, and they said I should go to DC, too. In my day, you didn't go across the street. You worked for Marvel or you worked for DC, but not for both. The few guys who actually did that and got away with it used pseudonyms. Gene Colan was Adam Austin. Frank Giacoia was Frankie Ray. Both were guys who "cheated" on the company where they used their real name. They got away with it because they used those pseudonyms and because they were so good that people turned a blind eye. Except for Wally Wood—Wally Wood could get away with anything because he was, well, Wally Wood.

I walked over to DC. I knew Mort was retired, and I was trying to think who could still be there who I'd know. Then I thought, "I bet E. Nelson Bridwell is still there." I was right; he was. He came out to see me and was glad to see me. We'd always gotten along. The only complements I got when I worked for Mort were from Nelson. He was Mort's assistant, and he would, on rare occasions, be the one calling me and not Mort. Nelson would say, "Boy, this is really nice. I think you did a great job." Anyway, Nelson was glad to see me, and he walked me directly to Carmine Infantino's office because Carmine had taken over the publisher's position since I'd been there. When I'd been at DC previously, he'd been the art director.

Nelson marched me into Carmine's office, and Carmine had fond, if vague, memories of me from my previous work at DC. Carmine yells, "You! You're the guy who invented the Legion of Super-Heroes!" Well, no, not quite. I'd written it for a while, but I didn't invent them. Carmine asked me if I wanted work, and I said, "Yeah, sure." He walked me down to Murray Boltinoff's office. He was the current editor of the Legion. Cary Bates was writing most of the Superman stuff at the time, but, according to Murray, Cary didn't want to write it all anymore so he said I could write some of it. Then Carmine walks me into Julie Schwartz's office and says, "Julie, this is Jim Shooter. I want him writing some Superman stuff." Julie goes, "Well, you wrote for Mort, so you can write for me." I didn't realize it at the time but Julie and Carmine did not get along. Julie's thinking that I'm Carmine's kid. Julie hated me. We had a stormy couple of years. It was kind of weird. It was really all a misunderstanding. He thought my being there was nepotism of some sort. I really didn't even know what was going on at first. For a couple of years I wrote some *Superman,* some "Legion of Super-Heroes."

Murray was great. He challenged you. He never accepted anything that was boilerplate or full of dull ideas. He wanted new all the time. For one story, I'd envisioned a sort of futurist monorail thing which Superboy rescued somebody from, and Murray said, "Monorails are old! Get rid of that." I invented a magnetic canal. You didn't get away with anything with Murray! On the other hand, he was getting older, and he would forget the characters' powers. Once he sent a story back to me and rejected it on the grounds that "Well, that's Phantom Girl! They couldn't see her!" I had to explain to him that people could see her; she could just go through walls. That's all. It was kind of an adventure at DC for a couple of years. Julie hating me, and Murray kind of forgetting who the characters were. I took that job over the Marvel job because I knew who the characters were, and I had no idea who Man-Wolf was.

Sometime in the middle of it I got a call from somebody at Marvel. It might have been Len Wein. They needed somebody to do a fill-in job on *Iron Man*, or something, overnight. I said, "Sure." Now I had never written Marvel-style. I didn't really know what Marvel-style was. I got this plot and now there's art coming. I didn't really understand why I was looking at penciled pages. At DC I had always done full scripts. I got hold of a guy who was a fan and asked what I was supposed to do with this. I should have called Marv, who was the editor by then, but every time I called Marv, the receptionist connected me with Dan Adkins. I guess the two of them had exchanged extensions or something. I'd call the receptionist and I'd explain that I need to speak to Marv Wolfman, and she kept connecting me to Dan Adkins. I'd call back again and explain who I wanted again to her. She'd say, "OK," and then connect me to Dan Adkins again! After the fifth or sixth time Dan yelled, "I'm not Marv Wolfman!," and slammed the phone down! Finally I realized that I had to go somewhere else for this information.

I bluffed my way through it. The guy I talked to did enough for me to get through it. I did a couple more jobs that way for Marvel. I was really kind of at sea with that, but I needed the money. Then in late 1975 I got a call from Marv, and he said they needed someone in editorial. There wasn't a title for it yet, but he asked if I was interested. I was supposed to meet Marv at 9:00 a.m. I walk into the editorial office, and there's, like, twelve guys there—Roger Slifer, Roger Stern, Scott Edelman, some others, and the lady who eventually married Chris Claremont. I don't remember her name. Nice lady. [Editor's note: Claremont married and eventually divorced Bonnie Wilford.]

As soon as I walked in there they yelled, "The new guy's here!" They ran over to me and said they needed an issue of *Captain Marvel* proofread right now! I said, "I don't work here yet but sure." I'm sitting there marking up this issue of *Captain Marvel*, and people kept coming over to me and asking questions like I was the boss. It felt really weird. I did this for a couple of hours or more, and about 11:30 Marv comes in, goes into his office, and closes the door. Then Len Wein comes in, and they get ready to go to lunch. Marv said, "I'll see you after lunch." I went to lunch with the editorial people. It was interesting, but I admit I was thinking to myself, "What a zoo!"

Still, it was really different from DC. At DC you were not allowed in the office unless you had a jacket and tie. DC looked like an insurance office. Marvel was way more relaxed. We get back from lunch. Marv gets back and we finally go into his office. He explained to me that at one time Stan wrote everything and oversaw all the production. But since then the company had expanded to dozens of titles and that basically every writer was working as his own editor. It was chaos.

Besides which, these poor people in the editorial office were always playing catch-up. They're reading stuff where the costumes are wrong. This guy's dead. This story doesn't make any sense. One guy was a Christian, and he was writing Christian comics instead of super-hero comics. All kinds of little stuff—it was chaos because each book or each set of books by one writer would be its own little company. Marv said he'd come up with the idea of having somebody read the stuff as it went through the production process. Chris Claremont was my predecessor, and his title was pre-proofer . . . as in proofreader.

I said to Marv, "What you're basically saying is that I would be the editor." Marv said, "No, I'm the editor." My reply was, "No, you're the editor-in-chief. What you're asking me to do is read the plots, approve the plots, send them to the artists, get the pencils back, check them against the plot, send the pencils back to the writer for the script, script comes back, and I read it, and if it's good I send it on to the editor. That's the editor." Marv said he didn't like the idea of me being an editor. I asked him what he did want. He suggested the title of associate editor. I said I didn't care. Just pay me. I was the associate editor, but it was kind of like being second-in-command. The proofreaders in editorial would come to me with questions and stuff. It was like being the general's chief of staff. The need that Marv had was so great that he hired me on a Thursday, and he needed me to start work that following Monday. My first day at Marvel was the first working day in 1976.

I did that for a while. Needless to say, when there's anarchy and you try to establish order, the anarchists are not going to be too happy. I quickly became the Great Satan. I'd call writers and say, "Here's what I found here in this plot and let's talk about it. This can't take place because, for example, this guy's dead!" They'd be all mad at me. Some of them would swear at me and hang up. They'd tell me to fix it myself.

There were guys who were bulletproof, and then there were guys who needed a little help. I understand that. You'd be writing three or four books a month. It was just like with Stan. You can get confused switching back and forth with the books. You lose track of something. I was the backstop. That went on for a couple of years.

At some point, Roy was actually going to come back as editor-in-chief. Marv was only my boss for about three months. Then he left, as he put it. Marv is a great guy. I love him. The guy is an idea genius. His mind is like a machine gun with ideas. But like a lot of writers, I don't think he was really interested in the administrative part of being an editor. He liked the creative side.

He was followed by Gerry Conway. Gerry ended up firing guys like Steve Gerber, Don McGregor, and, I think, even Steve Englehart. He tried to keep Englehart, but there'd been some dispute. Englehart was not going to be told anything about anything. Englehart went to DC. Gerry only lasted a few weeks, though. Roy was supposed to come back in, I think, after Marv left, but he changed his mind. That's when they got Gerry.

When Roy was still intending to return as editor-in-chief, he came into the office and was having meetings with several people. I sat down with him and told him that when I worked in the advertising business, if a new boss came in, you offered your resignation in case he wanted to staff the place with his own people. You hope, as a result of that, that you'd get freelance work or whatever. But Roy said no, I was OK, and he'd keep me. He changed his mind about coming back. I think he was planning to move to California or something like that. That's when Marvel got Gerry.

After Gerry's very brief tenure, Archie Goodwin was hired as editor-in-chief. Roy lasted about two-and-a-half years as editor-in-chief. Len lasted eight months. Marv lasted a year. Gerry lasted three weeks, and Archie lasted nineteen months.

Everybody knew Archie was a creative genius, but it was soon apparent that he wasn't much of a businessman. He hated the administrative side of the editorial office. He had a superb work ethic. He'd spend all his time in his office, working on cover design—doing all the creative stuff, which is what he wanted to do. Doing a budget or something like that, his eyes just glazed over. He hated stuff like that. The way I got the job was that I continued on after Marv left as Archie's assistant. That created a bit of conflict because these writers were not cooperating, and I was having to shore up the bottom, as it were. You had to ignore what the best guys were doing because they weren't causing problems. It was simply impossible for one guy, or even two, to edit forty-five titles a month, which Marvel was doing at the time.

So I was always having to deal with the worst. During the time I was associate editor, from 1976–1978, was also the time Stan stopped being a magazine publisher and came back to the comics. He'd been out of touch for a while with the day-to-day operations. Stan started reading these make-readies, and he started calling Archie into his office and saying, "Archie, look at what's happening on this page. How could you let this happen? It's so stupid, etc., etc." Archie, of course, knew what it was supposed to look like. He was one of the all-time geniuses in editing. He'd say, "Uh, Stan, I've got stuff to do." Finally, he sticks it on me. "Jim is the guy who actually deals with this stuff. You should talk to him." So he escaped, and I'm called into Stan's office every week.

Stan would be there with these make-readies all marked up and asked me, "Why is this guy saying this? It's idiotic. Where is this word balloon pointed to? I'm looking at this panel, and I cannot tell what these people are doing. This guy has no expression!" I knew what they were supposed to look like. I knew what a comic book page looked like. After a while, Stan starts explaining this stuff to me as if I were a kindergartener and didn't understand anything.

Anyway, they'd just started the *Spider-Man* newspaper strip, around 1977, and Stan was going to write the dialogue for the strip and edit it, but he wanted to get somebody to do the plot for him because he didn't want to spend that much time on it.

Stan asked Archie who Marvel's number one writer was, and Archie, politically correctly, said Len Wein, which was probably close to right. Archie was actually the best, but Len was good. So Stan offers Len the job of plotting the *Spider-Man* strip. This was a fairly prestigious assignment. It was like a big deal. Len did, I don't know how many, weeks of plot but Stan hated it. And he fired him. Not from the company, just from the strip.

Now everybody's afraid of doing the plot for the strip because Stan might fire them, and their star will fall. So Stan went back to Archie and asked him for a list of all of Marvel's writers, from best to worst. Archie left himself off the list. Archie had done some great newspaper strips. He knew how to do that sort of thing, but he left himself off the list. The list was thirty-three names. Guess who was number thirty-three.

Stan called thirty-two people to his office, and thirty-two people all turned him down. So I was the last one left. He called me into his office, and he's pinching his nose—it looked like he had a terrible headache. He started trying to explain to me how a newspaper strip was different from a comic book. I'd never actually written a newspaper strip, but I knew the process was different. He explained, in that very slow tone of voice he used when explaining the obvious, that everyday something had to happen, but you couldn't have too much happen in the daily because some people only read the Sunday version of the strip. You have to make sure that it's all interesting during the week but that if the reader didn't read any of that he wouldn't lose anything on Sunday.

There has to be lots of action, romance, and pretty girls. Like I said, he was talking to me like I was a kindergartner because, in his mind, I'd already proven to him that I was an idiot. I was just the lowest dregs of the writer pool. He really talked to me like it's the most futile thing in the world to try to explain anything to me. I told him I got it, and I'd do it. So I went in with my first plot a couple days later, and he read it. He said, "This is good." I said, "I know." "No," he said, "this is really good!" I said, "Yes, I know." He said, "How come this is good?" I said, "Because I know what I'm doing."

Stan told me to keep going, and I said, "OK." Then he gave the day-by-day plot to John Romita, who was off-staff at the time and was doing the strip exclusively. They still gave him a room in the bullpen. John would sort of follow the plot, but he would correct things. Then Stan would call me in. By then he'd forgotten the plot, and he'd tell me that this sequence wouldn't work at all. I'd tell him that John hadn't done what I said. Stan would go, "We have to change this!" So now I'm writing every plot twice. Once for John to ignore some of it, then again to make the plot work with whatever John drew.

I love John. I think he is one of the all-time great, hall of fame artists, but he was a little bit of a choirboy. For instance, when I would tell him to do a shot of Mary Jane from the waist up, John would draw her from the neck up because he didn't want to pander to anybody. So the next batch of plots that I brought in, I did layouts for them, just like I'd done in the Legion days. Stan would go, "This is great!" So Stan would write the dialogue right on my plot sketch/layouts. Then he would give the plot to John with the dialogue already in place, and John couldn't mess with it. The plot was now bulletproof. I think John hated me. John would still draw Mary Jane without her bust, but Stan said he didn't care. It was fun. John and I got along, but we had different perspectives on things sometimes. Usually, we just got along.

The only time Stan had a problem with my plots was when I would put notes in the margin to kind of explain things to the scripter. I'd do that and, every once in a while, I wrote a little line of dialogue rather than go into some lengthy explanation of what Spidey was doing. Stan got pissed off at this. "I'm writing this. I can't use your words because I'm writing this. You wrote that stuff, and now I can't use those words! And those are the words I was going to use! Never put any dialogue down! It has to be *all* mine!" I liked that about Stan. He really had integrity. He didn't want to use anybody's words but his own. He didn't care if you wrote the plot, but the words had to be his. I would carefully avoid doing anything that suggested dialogue. I did that for a while. I don't remember how long, but, during the course of that time, I think Stan started to realize that I actually did know what I was doing.

I think it was then that it really occurred to him that when I said I had forty-five titles and couldn't proof them all by myself that it didn't mean I was an idiot who couldn't do it, but that maybe *nobody* could do it. I think he was also starting to realize that Archie wasn't getting tough with the writers, so it wasn't that long after that when Stan proposed to me that he wanted to make Archie a creative director with a big raise and make me editor-in-chief.

I said OK. Marvel had used up everyone else. There really was no one left. I think, and I don't know for sure, but I think that Archie felt like I'd been cuddling up to Stan and had stabbed Archie in the back, which I didn't. I suspect he also felt he was being kicked upstairs. so he said he'd rather not; he'd rather leave. Marvel was just to give him a contract and make him a writer. That was what they did. He got a contract to write three books a month. I became editor-in-chief.

All of the artists and writers who'd been afraid of me before, boy, they were more so now. They suspected that I would make the trains run on time. That's basically what happened. I took over on January 3, 1978, and started doing what I had to do. That month, the month of January 1978, Marvel was supposed to ship forty-five color comics. We shipped twenty-six—some of which were more than four months late. They should have been on the stands two months earlier, and they were still in house! Unbelievable! It took me until April to get the right number of comic books going out every month.

At the end of the year, I got a letter from Bob . . . I can't remember his last name, but he worked at World Press. He said, "Congratulations! For the first time in its history, Marvel Comics is on time." That sort of thing tends to *not* make you popular because it means you're bringing in other writers. You're telling a guy who has four books a month—but actually only delivers two books a month—that he only gets to keep two, and if he does an extra issue of, say, *Captain Marvel* that would be great. Get ahead on your two books a month, and you can do four books, as long as they're on time. I didn't want to take books away, but, if you can deliver two books a month and if you can do an extra one or two for that title, then do two *Iron Man*s or two *Ghost Rider*s a month. Don't do those two titles plus *Avengers* and *Fantastic Four* and have them all be late. Give the other two titles to somebody else. This was before royalties, so the pay would be the same. And all four titles could come out on time.

That idea was still unpopular. If a writer felt like he was entitled to four books he still wanted four books, even if he couldn't write all four books on time. Taking a book away from someone is traumatic. For some writers, if it's late—so what?

To be honest, it's a big so what. We stood to lose our 2nd-class-mailing privileges, and there were consequences beyond that.

I made good on my promises. The head of Marvel Comics [Jim Galton] was the guy who hired me. Stan, by that time, was a figurehead. He really didn't have any responsibilities, except for the *Spider-Man* strip. There was nobody between me and the head of the company. If I got a professional review he gave me the review. Before I took the job I told him that I wanted to change the creator situation. I understood that we had to do work for hire, but it didn't have to be *bad* work for hire. I wanted to pay the creators better. I wanted royalties. You know what he said when I mentioned I wanted people to have royalties? He said, "You mean we don't?" He came out of the book publishing business, and the idea of no royalties was insane to him.

It was on that condition that I took the job. I kept telling guys that I was going to make it better. Stick with me. Neal Adams and I had been buddies forever, but he was doing the Guild [an abortive attempt to create a union, the Comics Creators Guild]—and I was in management at Marvel. Guess what? He still invited me to his parties. We were always arguing about work for hire, and I kept telling him they won't change that. I was just going to make the situation better. And I did.

I started increasing pay rates, adding standard benefits. I was able to get away with that because once the books were on time, we started selling better. Isn't that amazing? Plus, we were the only shop in town that was kind of thriving. We started getting better people and were able to pay them more. I doubled the rates and was able to double them again.

For example, Don Perlin was getting almost nothing. He'd been in the business for thirty-something years, yet he was the lowest paid guy at Marvel. It was because Don wasn't pushy. He wouldn't come in and demand anything. I kept giving him raises. I got him up where he ought to be, up in the Buscema range. Don had been in the business forever and he'd earned it. There were guys like Frank Miller, who earned it because they were geniuses. But Don, guys like him, they're the reason that comic books have lasted.

I tried to get management to realize that if it had to be work for hire, we had to provide everything. You can't expect a cobbler to come to work at the factory and bring the leather, make the shoes, and then you own them. We had to provide *everything*. We'd always provided paper, but I made sure we provided ink; Windsor-Newton brushes, which are damned expensive; erasers; pencils; postage; and, when it came around, FedEx. Phone bills: The business calls you make? Send us your phone bill, and we'll pay the parts that are ours. Travel:

If you have to come into the office, bring us your train ticket. If it's got to be work for hire, it's going to be good work for hire.

The first major incentive was for continuity. If you did so many issues in a row on a book, you got a bonus. Some folks would come in and say they wanted to do one issue of a character. To a reader, that kind of sucks. My goal was to try to keep people on the same book. Then, after a lot of legal issues, I finally got royalties established. All of a sudden, guys like Claremont were making huge money because *X-Men* sold so well.

Every single Marvel book paid royalties. DC had the same plan, except ours was better because ours went up to 8 percent and theirs only went to 4 percent. There were only three or four books at DC that made the royalties threshold. You had to sell a hundred thousand books a month to get the royalties. *Every* Marvel book made the threshold. At DC, *Superman* was dead even at a hundred thousand. The others were the *Titans,* maybe even the *Legion of Super-Heroes,* but there weren't many others. Vince Colletta came in, and he had been doing some work for DC. He showed me three royalty checks from DC for work he'd done, and all of them together did not total a dollar. Here's so and so's check from Marvel, and it amounted to $40,000—for one month!

The royalty incentive really changed the situation at Marvel. Suddenly all these major, talented guys were coming out of the woodwork to work for us. Walt Simonson, David Michelinie, Michael Golden, Marc Silvestri, and more. Archie! Archie came back, and Archie was the best you could do. All these great creators! One time Roger Stern and I and a couple of others were sitting around and wondering which of the big names Marvel didn't have working for them at that time that we really wanted. We came up with only two names. George Pérez had gone to DC. We wanted George back, but he was in love with the *Justice League* and the *Titans.* It just wasn't going to happen. The other was José Luis García-López, whom you couldn't pry out of DC. He's a great guy. He's a genius artist. He's one of the few artists that John Buscema, who wasn't overawed easily, would see his work and say, "Wow!" John was not impressed by anybody. But "Wow!"

You mentioned layout pay earlier. At Marvel I broke it down. There would be layouts—or what we would call breakdowns, simplified pencils—then there'd be full pencils, then inks. If a book had breakdowns from one artist, then you had a finisher, then the inker came in. The finisher had to do part of the pencil drawing. I did that sort of thing at Marvel because when I worked for DC there was so much that I did for which I was not paid. My first rule at Marvel was that nobody works for free. If you do something we pay you.

Sol Brodsky had been the production manager in the 1960s. He went away for Skywald, a publishing venture that failed. He came back to Marvel because he needed a job but there really wasn't a job for him. John Verpoorten was now the production manager. Stan, for his friend, kind of went out on a limb and hired Sol for administrative stuff that Stan didn't want to do. He really just created a job for Sol. Sol was there and they called him the UK operation head, or something like that. He'd do administrative stuff, but he was also going around. Sol was filling the vacuum there and taking care of stuff that nobody else was willing to do. Sol took over things that the editor-in-chief should have been doing.

What he was doing was fine, but when I started my job I didn't want to have that situation. I asked what Sol's job was. He didn't even seem to be on the organizational chart. No one seemed to exactly know. He seemed to assert that he was in charge of stuff, but what he seemed to do was handle Stan's affairs. Everything that was legal, financial, technical, or complicated Stan would hand off to Sol. What did Sol do with legal matters? He'd call house counsel, same as I would do. He'd make a financial call to the financial VP. I could do that. I didn't need a middleman.

The president asked if there was anything Sol could do. I replied that what was eating me alive, what was actually a royal pain, was doing presentation stuff that Stan needed to take to Hollywood, advertising projects, all of that stuff—I hated to call it that because it sounds like the kiss of death—but it was special products. I said if it was okay with the Marvel president, we could give that to Sol. That way I could just work on the comics. The president said great, so I basically created a title and job for Sol, who really didn't have one.

Sol would handle all this peripheral stuff, pretty much on his own. Let's say they wanted a new corner symbol for the *Conan* covers. That would be Sol's operation. If they needed a stand-up Spider-Man display for Stan to take to LA—tuff like that. The pay rates for that stuff was phenomenal! When I came in, if you created a logo, a title logo for a book, the price was $22.00. The coloring rates were pathetic. Previously, my predecessors had left that up to Sol. They didn't want to deal with that. But how do you get a guy to do a title logo that you're going to use forever and not pay him well? Granted it's work for hire, but you pay him twenty-two bucks? I started to pay people who did that a thousand, two thousand, as much as I could pay them and get away with. They were happier with that than the other way.

Mind you, I don't have anything against Sol. He was one of the cornerstones of Marvel in the 1950s and 1960s. Sol did that Special Products job brilliantly.

He was so happy to have his own little production department. He did fine. Sol took over Archie's old office. I was supposed to move in there when I became editor-in-chief, but I didn't have time. I decided to stay in my little office, which was closest to the bullpen, and told them to give that office to Sol. It gave him a place, and Sol was really good at the special products materials.

The whole time I was there I was in the tiny office until we moved to 387 Park, where it was all built out for us. There I had this enormous office with a couch that went on for seven or eight feet. Fancy stuff.

At Marvel, after being in the business since 1966, I could talk intelligently to the printer, the colorist, the penciller, the inker—of course, none of them would admit that. I had a good background, and I understood business. Up to that point, I was the only editor-in-chief who was ever taken out to a board meeting with Cadence Industries, Marvel's owners. One reason was that I dressed presentably; I didn't come into work in sneakers and jeans. Second was that Jim Galton, who was also on the Cadence board, knew I wouldn't embarrass him. He knew I wouldn't say stupid things. I knew enough about the business, especially the financial part of the business, that I was both presentable and credible. I'm not guessing this. Galton *told* me this. But I'd been learning this stuff since my time with Mort. I had more editorial training than nearly everyone who'd come before me.

Since the early 1960s, or maybe even the late 1950s, I can't name one person who was trained in everything you needed to do as an editor-in-chief. Even in those days those guys who understood that part of the business were getting older. Comics hit their peak in 1951–1952, when Fawcett's *Captain Marvel* was selling two million copies a month. It hit a peak and then the Kefauver Committee came about in 1954—the hearings about comics causing juvenile delinquency—plus all that stuff in *Seduction of the Innocent* by [Fredric] Wertham. When all that hit the fan the comics went into decline. When comics are in decline you don't have to develop new artists. There are a hundred unemployed ones just walking around the streets carrying their portfolios. It's easy to get someone to work for you.

You can count on one hand the significant figures that came into comics from 1955–1966: Buscema, perhaps . . . a few others . . . not very many. So many guys left comics to do advertising because the jobs just weren't there. Or maybe they got tired of Mort, too.

RA: After the Comics Code started, around 50 percent of the comic book companies went out of business.

JS: Exactly! The streets were awash with unemployed artists and writers. There was a fellow, I think his name was Alvin Schwartz, he used to write *Superman* in the 1940s and early 1950s. I met him when he was about a million years old. He ended up in Canada, working on industrial films or something like that. I met him at a convention one time. He told me he used to write *Superman*, and I told him, "Me, too." He asked who I worked for. I said Mort Weisinger. He said, "Me, too! He's why I quit comics!" I replied, "Me, too!" He said, "I like you!"

The point here is, in those years, there was no reason to develop new talent. But by the mid-1960s, enough of the writers and artists had died, retired, or found other employment that all of a sudden they needed people. This new wave came in. I can't put them in order but among this new wave was Archie Goodwin, Denny O'Neil, Roy Thomas, me, Neal Adams, Cary Bates, Marv Wolfman, Len Wein . . .

RA: Mike Friedrich and Gary Friedrich (no relation) came in around that time.
JS: Yeah, somewhere in there. There's this large generation gap between old and new. When I started working everyone was fifty years old or older. I was thirteen. Archie and Roy were older but only by about ten years. Those guys were really the bridge. Neal is also ten years older than me. Most of them were older than me but not as much as the old-timers. I was a kid and fairly suddenly all those old guys were dying or retiring, and the kids are running the ship. Most of them hadn't had any training whatsoever. Roy, I think, was an exception because he worked with Stan for a few years—although I don't think working with Stan gave you much preparation for business or production work.

All these guys, with very little to no training, were running the ship. In a lot of ways, they just didn't know what they were doing—even with the best of intentions, even though some of them were brilliant writers and none of them were bad ones. I think that's why between Stan and me, even counting Roy, the editor-in-chief of Marvel Comics was really the head writer because he didn't do a lot of editing. During that period of time Roy wrote some incredible stories. But Marvel went from a few titles, eighteen or so, to forty-five titles overnight.

The reason for that was that for many years they were suppressed by their distributor, which was Independent News who also distributed DC Comics. Martin Goodman was forced into that deal in the 1950s when his distributor collapsed just after they signed with it. He had to go begging to Independent News, and they took him on but limited how many comics he could publish because they already had DC Comics. In the 1960s, while Marvel's sales were growing, they were limited from real expansion by the distributor deal. When Marvel was sold by Martin Goodman to the company that became Cadence Industries, Cadence had their own distributor, Curtis Circulation. Marvel moved to Curtis Circulation, and all of a sudden Marvel could publish all the comics they wanted to. And they did. There was a giant explosion of Marvel Comics heading to the newsstands. Some of the stuff was just inexplicable: They tried an underground book called *Comix Book,* that Man-Wolf thing, for Christ's sake, all kinds of stuff.

At first that worked well but, as the 1970s moved on, the newsstands started to dry up. Marvel started losing money. Marvel was losing two-and-a-half-million dollars a year when I came in. Comics were just so newsstand reliant. Getting better people to do the comics made a dent, but it wasn't stopping the slide.

I suppose I'd get 14.6 percent credit for the turnaround in Marvel's fortune, but the rest was the advent of the direct market. When I started, DC had about 30 percent of the market, and by the end of the year it was almost dead. Marvel was doing about 30–35 percent. At one point in the early 1980s, in a growing market where everybody was rising, we got to 70 percent. DC was 18 percent.

RA: I can believe that because I remember when the direct market began to be a big deal. In 1981 and 1982 there was an explosion of titles appearing from independent companies, and both Marvel and DC started paying attention to that as well.

JS: Marvel was the first major company to make a move. We published trade terms and, all of a sudden, instead of one distributor there were something like eighteen overnight. That really made the direct market take off. Marvel sponsored meetings with all the direct market distributors. We flew them down to Florida, let them stay in a hotel, listened to their gripes, and got their suggestions. We also did a presentation of what we had coming up. We financed that for years. Carol Kalish started this cash register program. I had my issues with Carol Kalish, but that was a genius idea. A lot of these guys at the comic stores were working out of shoe boxes. We helped them get cash registers. We started doing a promotion of the market. Every year we would have a professional convention before a regular convention. The dealers and retailers would be there. Certainly not all of those things were my ideas, but Marvel started doing a lot of that sort of thing.

It was my idea that we should have a booth at the conventions. Nobody had a booth at that time. The next year DC had a booth. We worked out with Shel

Dorf of the San Diego Comic-Con that we'd fly the entire *X-Men* team—this was right after the Dark Phoenix storyline—to San Diego at Marvel's expense. The only stipulation was that they had to be on the program and appear on panels. No company had ever paid for the creative team of a book to go to a convention and promote their stuff. We took that convention by storm! It was riotous. The next year DC sent people, and it became kind of commonplace . . . not so much now since everybody's pulled in their horns. I don't know if they still do that sort of thing, but for years they did.

We did whatever we could to help the direct market. Sometimes the upstairs people would complain that we were helping the competition thrive. I said, "These independent companies aren't our competition. They're the farm teams. Some of these people are brilliant. We're growing the market, and, eventually, the good people working for the independents will be working for us. If they don't come to work for us, and they make money then God bless 'em."

If we consider the industry first, if we foster the industry, we win. If we get protective and defensive we've lost. The biggest battle I lost, when the direct market really took off, was when the circulation manager and Carol Kalish, who was the sales manager, and others at Marvel really began fighting for going direct market exclusively. I was against that. I said, "If you lose the newsstand, then you lose the reach." With seventy thousand newsstand outlets, some kid who's never heard of *Iron Man* will walk into some store, see a comic called *G.I. Joe*, and buy it. That first book is impulse, but once you get them hooked then eventually they will find their way to a comic shop because you can't always find what you want on a spinner rack. Then you have another direct market customer.

I kept saying that but the newsstand became less and less important to Marvel, and the direct market became more important. We'd done direct market exclusive comics. The first one was *Dazzler*, and it sold four hundred and twenty-eight thousand copies. I suggested we do a newsstand exclusive. Everybody said that wouldn't work. The direct market was the place for that. I said we had to support the newsstands because if we just let it die we too will die. That really is what happened. We pulled out of the newsstands completely, relied entirely on the direct market, and now we're right back where we started when the newsstands started to dry up. Nowadays *Superman* sells twenty-five thousand copies.

The speculator market of the early 1990s was a disaster for the industry. The crash in 1993, which I predicted and I can prove it, caused the market to drop 80 percent. It's taken a long time to recover. I hear the market seems to be growing again, but it's growing from a tiny base. It's not anywhere near where it was. I think moving away from the newsstands was part of the downfall, and I couldn't stop it. I was gone from comics at the time it happened. I wonder if Roy would agree with me on that.

Original Jim Shooter Interview

JASON SACKS, ERIC HOFFMAN, AND DOMINICK GRACE / 2016

Previously unpublished interview. Printed by permission of the authors.

Jim Shooter (JS): Before I ever went to grade school, I learned to read. The way I learned to read was that my mother read me comic books: *Superman*, *Donald Duck*. She'd point at the words. She'd read them real slowly and point at the words. After a while, I didn't need Mommy anymore. I started at one school; then I moved to another school in the middle of the year. The teacher didn't know me from any other kids. She didn't know if I could read or not. We were playing this game. Every kid had to come up with a word. If you could spell the other kid's word, but he couldn't spell yours, you would get a point. This is first grade. People are coming up with *cat* and *dog* and *door*. So I say *bouillabaisse*. The teacher says, "You don't even know what that is." I said, "It's fish soup." She said, "You can't spell that." I said, "Sure I can." She said, "Come up here." She made me write it down on her paper. She had to look it up. She said, "Okay class, the word's *bouillabaisse*." Needless to say, I won. I was ready to go again. I had *teletype* and *invulnerable*. I had all these great words. I got that from a comic, actually a Carl Barks comic book, although I didn't remember that origin for years.

Years pass. I'd told that story here and there. I started thinking it was apocryphal. I started thinking I must have made that up. One time, a bunch of us were sitting around the office at Marvel. I told the story, and, at this point, I wasn't even convinced that it really happened. I say, "It was in this *Donald Duck* comic book. There was this word *bouillabaisse*." Walt Simonson says, "No—Uncle Scrooge." I said, "Really?" He says, "Yes, because Uncle Scrooge sent Donald and the nephews to Africa to get the secret recipe for crocodile bouillabaisse." As he said "crocodile bouillabaisse," I said it with him because he brought it back. I said, "Crocodile bouillabaisse."

To me, that validated the story. If Walt remembered *bouillabaisse*, then . . . I got to tell Carl Barks that story at his ninetieth birthday party. He said, "Young man, I don't remember that story, but I'm glad you enjoyed it."

Again and again, month after month, he created great comics. Brilliant guy. He doesn't often get listed among the great comic book creators, but he should be right up there.

Jason: One of the things that you preached was attention to storytelling fundamentals. Did you call on learnings from Barks as part of that?

JS: I had a million Carl Barks books as a kid, and I guess I picked up something from him. I also read Kirby books and Ditko books and anything that . . . The thing is that when I was a kid, I read comics. I stopped when I was about eight because they all seemed pretty much the same. In the fifties, that was true. Every issue of *Superman* was like Lois is trying to discover his secret identity, and there was no action. They started to get tedious, so I gave them up.

Then when I was twelve, I was in the hospital for a minor operation. If you're in a kids' ward in a hospital in 1962, or whatever it was, there were comics everywhere. So I'm looking at these comics. There were lots of DC comics. They were all in good shape. There were all these ratty, dog-eared, other comic books. Those were Marvel comics, which had been read to death. Hardly anybody touched the DC comics.

I was familiar with DC comics, so I picked up a couple of those. I read them. They were exactly the same as when I was eight years old. Nothing had changed.

I thought, let me try some of these other, ratty ones. One of the first ones I read was maybe the second issue of *Spider-Man*. It had the Vulture in it.

I'm like, "Whoa, what happened to comics!?" I thought, "These are really great."

I started scouting around for Marvel comics when I could. In those days, you'd get two cents for every soda bottle that you returned. I'd go walking along the railroad tracks or along the road looking for bottles. Get six bottles, that's a comic book. I was really annoyed when they went from a dime to twelve cents.

I started tracking down Marvel comics. I got *Fantastic Four* #4 in a barber shop. I asked the barber, and he said, "Yeah, you can have it." At that time I needed a job. My family needed money. I thought, "What am I going to do? I've got to make something and sell it. What can I make? I bet I can do this."

I literally spent a year studying, mostly Marvels, trying to figure out what I liked, what I didn't and why. That's when I started analyzing storytelling. I guess I'd always noticed it, but now I started thinking about it. Looking at the ones that I really liked and the ones that I didn't like as well. I was like, "Oh, I see."

For a year, with intent, I studied comics. Then when I was thirteen, I thought, "I'm ready. Okay, here we go." I wrote a comic book story. My theory was that I knew I couldn't write as well as Stan, but I thought I could write well enough to sell to DC. I said, "Those guys need help."

I wrote a comic book, Legion of Super-Heroes, which I thought was one of their more boring ones. It's really funny; I later got to know some of those guys. As I learned more, I got to appreciate what they did. They weren't bad. They were a little old fashioned. I thought I could make a difference there. I wrote a story. My mother helped me. I mailed it off to the editor at DC. He actually sent me a letter that said, "Send me another one." I sent him another two. I sent him a two-part story, which was a little risky because they didn't do a lot of those, but I had what I thought was a good story.

Then, he called me on February 10, 1966. He said, "I want to buy these, and I want you to write a "Supergirl" story." I said, "What do you want?" He said, "Twelve pages next week." I said, "Sure, I'll get right on it."

Then especially once I started working for DC regularly, I was being taught by professionals. I was actively being instructed. I started going back and look-ing at old stuff, even the Carl Barks stuff. Even though it wasn't what I was doing, the fundamentals are the same. That stuff was always some of my fa-vorites. I still have the comics, though they've since crumbled in my hands.

I lived in Pittsburgh, so I'm doing all this by mail and on the phone. I worked for Mort Weisinger. Then he started saying, "Give me a "Supergirl." Give me a *Superman*." No instructions, just to see what I would do. Everything I sent him, he bought. I guess he finally decided, "I'm going to use this guy regularly." He called me up and said, "I'm going to use you as a regular writer. I'll give you a regular series and maybe some other stuff. We want you to do Legion of Super-Heroes, an occasional *Superman*, *Superboy*, 'Supergirl,' *World's Finest*." I said, "Sure, fine." He said, "But I warn you. I'm pretty tough on writers." I said, "It's okay. It's fine."

Eric: Would you say that your naiveté was an asset at that point? Insofar as your lack of awareness of the business end of things.

JS: Yes and no. I was obviously good enough to get in the door. I guess so. I learn pretty quickly. Mort warned me that he was going to be tough. After he found out I was fourteen, he said it again, "I don't care if you're fourteen. I'm going to treat you just like I treat every other writer." I didn't realize that

Jim Shooter in
2016. Photo by
Jason Sacks.

meant he was going to be a monster, and he was evil, nasty. The guy was terrible. He was mean as a snake to everyone.

This is an apocryphal story. The story is that at his funeral they couldn't get anyone to do the eulogy. Finally, they got a guy who had known him all his life to say, "His brother was worse." That's the best thing he could say about Mort, that his brother was worse. That didn't really happen, probably. I wasn't at the funeral, so I don't know. I don't believe it.

He was nasty. He'd call me up swearing at me and screaming. I'm a fourteen-year-old kid, and this big, important man from New York calls me up and tells me I'm an idiot. All the time. That's how editors were in those days. Most not as bad as Mort. They were always yelling at you and chomping on their cigars and screaming. That was to keep me from asking for a raise. He would go through the stuff. Every week, we had a regular phone call on Thursday night, right after the *Batman* TV show. We would go over whatever I had sent him that week, panel by panel, word for word. Screaming at me if I made a spelling error. I used to do little layouts to go with the script. He would say, "What's this guy holding? Is that supposed to be a gun? It looks like a carrot!" I was like, "I'm a kid. I'm just trying to lay it out for the artist. I can't draw."

A lot of this conversation was me saying, "I guess I can't do this" after he screams at me for two hours. "I just can't do this. Maybe you'd better get somebody else." He says, "No, I'll give you another chance. . . ." He'd say, "I know your family needs some money. You're my charity case." Charity case. After a few years of this, I get to be about late sixteen, seventeen-ish, I started to realize he would not keep sending me these checks if I really was that bad. It was like, "Nah, this is just what he does." I did get past that.

Eric: Did he buy every script you sent him?
JS: Every one.

Jason: I'm trying to imagine what you must have felt like as a kid going through that.
JS: He was right. We needed the money. I didn't have any choice. I had to keep doing it. My mother was desperate for money. Like I say, I try to think it through, and I try to have the characters be people who I can relate to. I do have a habit of basing characters on people I know. Everybody does that.

When I was a kid, and I first started writing, I couldn't imagine how these guys could create these characters. A lot of my Legion and other DC characters—I'm stealing the personalities of my high school classmates. Thinking I was cheating. For instance, Bouncing Boy: Before me, they played him straight. Are you kidding me? The guy bounces! You know? I thought I'd play him as the comic relief. He tells everybody he's the self-appointed chief of morale. He's going to make people laugh. He's clever, he's funny, and he's self-effacing. I had fun with him. That was entirely based on a guy I went to school with whose name was Tom Kulaski. His initials were T. K., and he was kind of a chubby guy. They used to call him "tea kettle." I don't think I ripped off anything from him that was too personal or too actionable, but what I did was make Bouncing Boy like him: witty, funny. Everybody loved to have him around. Everybody was happy when he was there. He was quick and smart and funny.

Jason: Bouncing Boy ended up with a beautiful girlfriend.
JS: I wanted to show that it's not always the handsome hero who gets the girl. She sees something in him. In the very first issue I wrote, she had a crush on Superboy, and I wonder if I did that on purpose. I wasn't planning Bouncing Boy at that point, but, as I went along and I had the opportunity, I said, "Yeah. He beats Superboy's style."

I actually was very pleased years later when they did the wedding, mostly because Dave Cockrum drew it. He did such a good job on that issue. In that wedding scene if you look carefully, there's like Marvel characters at the back. The Avengers are there and all these Marvel characters and all these characters that shouldn't be there.

Eric: You were probably the first creator or writer to bring that Marvel sensibility to DC. DC was all archetypes.

JS: On the one hand, Mort and these other guys, Bob Haney, they would get snarky with me, "Aw, you start that Marvel crap." On the other hand, Mort saw that it was doing all right.

For instance, the very first issue I wrote had a postal statement of ownership, and it sold around five hundred thousand copies. The very last issue that I wrote had a postal statement of ownership, and it was selling about five hundred thousand copies. Every other DC title in that period went down. The reason they put the Legion as a backup feature in *Action* was because Mort convinced himself that the Legion was diluting the sales of *Superboy*. If you check that run, you'll find that there's a couple issues in there where he deliberately took Superboy and Supergirl out, just to see what the sales effect would be. Of course the sales went down.

I didn't write those issues. Mort did them himself with another writer. Superboy and Supergirl leave and are replaced by these masked characters Sir Prize and Miss Sterious. Okay. It was an experiment to see what would happen if there were no Super characters in there. He talked himself into believing that *Superman* and *Superboy* would sell better if "Legion" wasn't its own book.

Eric: That speaks to the importance of relatability and character development. Those are the narrative storyline aspects that you adhered to.

JS: And learned from Stan.

When I was working at DC—all right, they had *Batman*, which was selling like a million copies because of the *Batman* TV show. I'm not saying they didn't have any successes, but in general DC comics were on a downward trend. We used to talk about that all the time.

In Mort's office and in his house there were stacks of Marvel comics everywhere because he was trying to figure out, "What the hell is going on here? Why are they winning, and we're losing?" They didn't get it. To this day, they don't get it. They get Marvel guys, and they do an imitation of what Marvel used to do. But Marvel isn't doing it either, so Marvel is doing an imitation of what it used to do. They missed the point entirely.

Jason: Tell us about your experience working for Marvel after you worked for Weisinger.

JS: I worked for Marvel for three weeks in 1969. I couldn't hack it because I had just moved to New York, and I had no money. I didn't eat for two weeks. I couldn't take it. I had to reluctantly leave. While I was there, I said maybe

I would like to be an inker. Stan did everything that he wanted to do, which was creating. Sol Brodsky did anything that was legal, technical, financial, or complicated. I go over, and I ask Marie [Severin]. She says, "Go see Sol."

I go see Sol. Sol says, "I don't know. Here—I can give you a couple pages to ink and show me what you got." He gives me this gigantic stack—more than a ream of pages of rejected pages, all Kirby. In that pile was Kirby's original drawing of Spider-Man. I held it in my hands. I'll never forget it. He had Captain America boots, a belt, and a web gun. That's why they went with the Ditko one. He gave me this page. I inked it as faithfully as I could. I showed it to Marie. She says, "Eh, you got possibilities." I took it to Sol. He said, "It's no good." I said, "Tell me why." He said, "It's cluttered and busy. That's why it was rejected. It's still cluttered and busy." I said, "You told me to ink it. You didn't tell me to fix it." "You just don't understand it," he said. "All right. Forget anything."

Dominick: What did you take away from your experiences with Weisinger in terms of editing? Were there things that you thought that you should do as an editor? Or were there things that you thought, "these are things that I will never put anyone else through"?

JS: Those are the two alternatives you face. There are some people who can't wait till it's their turn. There are some people who say, "I would never do it to anybody." I tried to never do that to anybody. On the other hand, when I was in the position of being an editor, I had anarchy and chaos in front of me. I had to be fairly strict. A lot of people would say that I was—Ann Nocenti once said that I was fascistic. Ann doesn't know what that word means. She meant dictatorial. If you tell a guy nicely ten times or five hundred times that you have to introduce the characters, about the five-hundred-and-first time you tell them, you tell them a little louder. Maybe I was dictatorial. But what I was faced with when I took over at Marvel as editor-in-chief . . . I had learned from Mort. That guy taught me a lot of stuff, and he was good. He believed all comics are read by eight year olds. He tended to aim lower than Stan. He also didn't want anybody experimenting. He wanted you to stick to the formula. I got away with more stuff than anybody, but mostly he would give you rules. He would say, "Always do this, . . . and you never do that."

Sometimes I would think, "Stan does that and it works. I'm not going to do it." Then if it worked, he would never say, "Hey, you didn't do what I said." He could see when it worked.

Jason: That's one of the hallmarks of your time at Marvel. You seemed to care very much about following the goals of Stan's storytelling, but you also had creators like Walt Simonson, John Byrne, and Frank Miller, who were talented enough to break those rules and do work that was still outstanding.

JS: It was like this: I had Mort saying do this, don't do that. Then I'd see Stan violating Mort's rules and coming up with something really good. I thought there must be something deeper. There must be some bedrock that's under this. Here's the bedrock. Here's Mort's formula, and here's Stan freewheeling a little bit.

What I insisted on was the bedrock. Make it clear at a glance. People have to read this stuff. Everything clear, unless as a story point it's not supposed to be clear. If you're going to have a figure in the shadows and you're not supposed to know who it is, fine. Let's not be clear then. But unless there's a story reason for doing something like that, let's tell the damn story. I learned from all that stuff that went on before, and Mort taught me a lot. When I started at Marvel, I ended up working very closely with Stan for five years, more or less. I learned a lot from that.

I also divided it among guys who know what they're doing and guys who are newer or don't know what they're doing. Miller, for instance, when he first started out, I said, "For the first little while, I want you to do the Kirby grid, real straight forward. Don't get cute. I want to go over everything with you."

With Marvel, you got a plot. Then the artist would draw it from the plot. He didn't have a panel-by-panel description of what to draw. He was the cinematographer. Every time Frank would do a job, he would come in. I'd sit there and go over it with him. I would say, "There's two guys here, and now there's three guys. Did this third guy hear what they said? When you establish the scene, show me everyone who's in it. Place the characters in the location. Then you can do your close-ups and stuff." He said, "Hrmm." That was his typical reaction, "hrmm." Frank was very intense. We'd go over stuff like that. Here you got a scene where there's not much background. Here you've got a scene where—have we cut to Mars? You have to make sure we understand transitions. I'd explain that entrances and exits are key to clear storytelling, all kinds of stuff. He'd go "hrmm." Then he comes in one day. He brings me a job. I go, "It's great. It's really nice." He said, "What do you mean?" I said, "It's great; it's fine." He said, "Really? Oh. Okay."

The next day he came in. He sticks his head in my office and says, "I got it. We're telling stories. We know the story, and they don't know the story. We're telling them the story." I said, "You got it. That's it." Then he wanted to start playing around a little bit. That's when he started doing those long, narrow establishing shots in *Daredevil* with the four movie screens down the side. Because I explained to him that you've got two eyes side by side, your standard field of vision is roughly oblong. That's why film screens are shaped that way. That's why TV screens are becoming shaped that way. That's the most comfortable thing because that's what you'd see if you were there. He found a way of fitting more movie screens into the book through those long, narrow establishing shots.

He earned the right to experiment, to bust it open. It's the same with Walt [Simonson] or [Bill] Sienkiewicz. There's a story behind Sienkiewicz. I got a call from Neal [Adams]. He says, "I got a guy here. I don't know if you want his stuff or not." I said, "Why?" He said, "He draws like me." I said, "Send him over." He sent him over. Bill comes in. You would have sworn Neal drew it. I'm like, "Holy cow, this is great." I don't have anything I can give him. I'm not going to let this guy leave here without a job. I don't want him going over to DC or anything. I run around. Nobody has a job for him. I went and I looked through the obsolete inventory drawer. I found something that had been scrapped. I went to him and said, "Oh, this is real important. We need you to do this." It was basically make-work to keep him busy until I could find something real. He went off and did that. He did such a good job on it that we ended up using it.

At first, his storytelling wasn't great, so I'm coaching him. Then he also had a breakthrough. He came in and showed me an issue of *Moon Knight*. He says, "I did it in a different style. I hope you don't hate it." I said, "I don't care. Just be yourself. If you want to draw like Neal, okay, draw like Neal."

It's funny, he showed me his *Moon Knight* story. It was great. It was a totally different style. He really got the storytelling. He was doing it perfectly. He really could do it.

[Chris] Claremont needed an artist on the *New Mutants*. He said, "Bill wants to draw this, but what we want to do is go crazy and do experimental stuff." I said to myself, "We're Marvel Comics. If we can't experiment, who can?" Claremont's good; Bill is a genius. Let them swing for the fences, go ahead. With my blessing, they went, and it was very deliberately planned. They were going to go do crazy stuff, and they did. It was dazzling. It was a little hard to read sometimes, but you've got to try stuff and fail.

Jason: In a way, it's audacious. *X-Men* was selling big numbers at that point. *New Mutants* wasn't selling nearly as well but it still was selling extremely well. If the experiment had failed, you could have seen sales plummet, theoretically across most mutant books.

JS: Yeah, but I also always felt like a lot of people in this business, if they get something that sells, it's like a miracle. They could never do it again. They're afraid to tamper with it. They're afraid to do anything but what they're doing. To me, it's like we can do it again.

I wasn't worried about it at all. In fact, the newsstand sales plummeted. The direct sales quadrupled. It ended up being more successful than it was because the aficionados loved it. The kids who still bought things on the newsstand couldn't make head or tails of it.

Eric: I'm assuming there was a point where the direct market had enough of an effect that you could say we're willing to take a chance on an artist. Was that around the same time?

JS: I was not willing to take a chance on an artist. I wanted good books. I wanted good stories. If I had a Sienkiewicz, who wanted to try something experimental, that's fine. If Walt came to me and said, "I want to do something a little off the wall," fine. If one of the younger kids said, "I want to do this crazy stuff like Bill does," no. Sorry, forget it. Once a guy proved he knew what he was doing, then fine. There's also a theory that I call "big guns you can't aim." Like Walt. Walt's great. Great talent. But he doesn't want to do what you tell him to do. He wants to do what he wants to do. Fortunately, what he wants to do is what I want. We never had any problem that way.

Some guys can take direction; some guys can't. John Romita Jr. is as great as they come. He'll listen to you, and he'll say, "Oh, okay, I can do that. I see." Some guys aren't ready to do that. If it's a younger guy and he's not ready to do that, then goodbye. But if he's somebody who has chops and who wants a chance to show off a bit, that's fine too. But it wasn't about, "Oh I'll get a great artist and that'll sell on the direct market." I just wanted to make good comics. When I was a kid reading those Marvel comics; why did I love them? Because I cared about Spider-Man. I wanted to know what happened next. Whereas the DC books . . . first of all, you could read them in any order. It didn't matter. The characters never changed or wised up. Guys used to say you have to keep developing or progressing the characters. No, you don't. You can develop them inward. You don't have to have Aunt May die. You don't have to come up with a thing like that every issue.

When I first started as editor-in-chief, all of a sudden I'm on the circulation list for all of the stuff from the sales department and getting all this information I didn't have before. I'm getting the print orders and stuff. I notice on the print order there's Curtis, which is the newsstand, there's subscription, the military, there's Whitman, and then there's this thing called Seagate. I go and ask the circulation director, "What's Seagate?" He closes his door. He admitted to me that he had a little cost-plus deal with this guy Phil Seuling. He was selling them out the back door at a ridiculous discount.

I start keeping track of those numbers. I notice that it's going up every issue. The ones that I thought were good books were higher than the ones I didn't think were so good. A pattern begins to emerge. I kept track of that information. Now, I wasn't quite sure what I was going to do with that information. When I'm talking about the sales going up, I'm talking about from 250 to 300. *X-Men* from 975 to almost 1,100. We're not talking huge numbers yet. This is 1978.

A couple of months into my tenure as editor-in-chief, this guy shows up named Chuck Rozanski. He had tried to get a meeting with Jim Galton, who wasn't interested. Chuck came to see me. We sat down, and he said, "Are you aware of the direct market?" I said, "Funny you should mention that because I've been charting this stuff for a couple months now." I went back, and I got the whole previous sales print-orders and charted it for quite a while. I said I see it's going up and up. He was thrilled that I knew what I was talking about. Basically, he told me what was wrong with the direct market and how we were doing it wrong—how we were limiting it by having everything go through Phil and that was illegal anyway. He had this eleven point plan for things that should be done to change the direct market. I called Galton and said we need to talk to this guy. We went upstairs. We sat with Jim Galton. Ten of Chuck's eleven points were enacted on the spot. Then there were lots of other developments in the direct market. There was a lawsuit, and there was all kinds of other crap.

It did get to the point where we did the right thing. We published trade terms, and anybody could be a distributor. It really started to take off. This is in a matter of months. Then, all of a sudden, six months into my term was Kirby's last month. His stuff kept coming out for a few months after that. I'm looking at these numbers, many comics are now up around five thousand or six thousand. Kirby's are selling thirty to thirty-five thousand. I did the math. I said, that's just about enough to break even all by itself. Even with this stupid, ridiculously high discount we give for the direct market. That was actually what led to us publishing the first all-direct one, which was *Dazzler* #1, which sold four hundred and thirty thousand copies.

Eric: Was part of Galton's resistance to hearing this out the idea that seemed to be prevalent at the time that comics as an industry was on its way out?
JS: Oh, yeah. When he hired me, he basically told me that my job was to preside over the death of Marvel Comics. "Try not to lose too much money until I can get us into other businesses." He was interested in getting into children's books and animation. He had been in real world publishing, employed by a place called Popular Library, which then got acquired by CBS Books, which

then fired him. He came to Marvel with no knowledge or experience of comics. He was there the whole time I was there. At the end of it, he didn't have any more knowledge or experience. He didn't care about them. I kept telling him that we could be bigger than Disney.

I took the job on the condition . . . I said, "I only want to have this job if we can start paying our creators royalties." He said, "You mean, we don't?" I said, "No, we don't. I want to pay them better incentives." He said, basically, "You do what you want, as long as it doesn't cost money. If you can make it break even, you can do anything you want."

I had to make everything self-liquidating, but I was able to get all this stuff done and introduce all these royalties and things. It's too bad that the direct market didn't happen earlier because it might have changed the whole thing with Kirby. It would have changed a lot of stuff.

Eric: Did your wanting to implement royalties predate DC's decision to do that?
JS: Oh, by miles.

Eric: The general assumption is that Marvel instituted the royalties program because of DC.
JS: No. When I took the job, as a condition of it, I said we're going to do royalties. Then two things happened. I started working with Barry Kaplan, who was the director of finance, something like that, on how to do this. It dragged on and on and on because he kept saying that the guy who does *Spider-Man* automatically gets more money than the guy who does *Daredevil* or *Ghost Rider*— maybe it should be that we should give them royalties on the increase. I said, "No, no. Just pay them."

There was this big debate about how to do it. He came up with one plan, and we were talking about it. He realized he'd have to hire people to do this. It got complicated. That goes on for six months. Then, as soon as Kirby leaves around June 1978 . . . right away, Kirby starts rattling his legal sabre. I used to say that there was a lawsuit. There really wasn't. They never filed, but we were getting letters from his lawyers every day. I was in a million meetings to talk about what to do about this and what to do about that. He was demanding back royalties and all that. One other thing that I was trying to get done was I was trying to get all the old work returned to the artists because we were returning current artwork but we weren't returning old artwork. He was threatening us about the artwork, too, making claims about the ownership of the characters. The lawyers, when I'm talking about us having a royalties program, are like,

"Hell, no, you're not," because it's like a tacit admission that he's right. You can't do it.

I was fighting for Kirby on the inside. One of the things that I proposed was when I finally did get the royalty plan established was that if you created a book, even if you didn't work on the book anymore, you still get a 1 percent override. For example, [John] Byrne still gets paid for Alpha Flight, at least he still did when I was there. If you create a character, you always own a small part of the character. I knew there was no way we were going to go back to 1939, not Captain America, but I said how about from the date this plan starts, for everyone, we start paying them this little percentage for *Fantastic Four*, for all these things. No, they didn't want to do that. I couldn't win that fight, but I tried.

I'm six months into it. I've been working with this financial guy but can't work out something that suits me that he'll live with. The Kirby situation progressed to a point. I fought that fight again and again and again. I even had to go to the [Cadence] board [of directors] to try to convince them of some of this stuff. I finally made some progress there. But there was still some question about how to go about it. Then DC announces their royalty program. I got a copy of it. Then, to Barry's ever-lasting credit, he looked at it. I guess he felt we obviously have to match this. Then he said, "No, we don't. We can beat that." Their plan was 4 percent divided among the artists and writer. Our plan was start at 4 percent divided among the artists and writer, with a sliding scale going up to 8 percent as sales go up. On top of that, we had a point that went to the creator of the book, if any. I got the editors involved. Editors got a piece of the success of their books.

Jason: Is it true that the royalties on every Marvel book that was presenting new material, including the lowest-selling book at the time, which was *Master of Kung Fu*, were more than the royalty on the highest-selling DC book, which I think was *Teen Titans*?

JS: Yeah, *Teen Titans* sold about a hundred and seventy-five thousand, so it paid some hundreds of dollars in royalties. There was *Teen Titans*, *Warlord*, and *Legion of Super-Heroes*. *Superman* was about break even. It was around a hundred thousand. They had one or two other books that were around a hundred thousand. Everything else was below that. When DC institutes their royalty plan, it costs them nothing. Okay, a couple of books get checks for a couple hundred dollars, big deal. But if they could get Marvel talent to come flooding over to them, as they imagined, all their sales would go up, and everything would be fine. That's how I won the fight at Cadence. I said we do this, or we lose everybody. My point is, they were paying almost nothing. We did the math. If nothing changed, if all the books sold exactly as they had, it was going to cost us three-quarters of a million. Because sales were high, it actually cost us $2 million, and we were happy because sales had gone up.

Jason: Within two years, the company was doing fantastically well. Do you attribute that success to the royalty program and giving creators incentive to do work that really engaged the readers?

JS: You are correct. At that time, every Marvel comic sold over a hundred thousand. I think *Master of Kung Fu* was only at 103,000. Every Marvel comic paid royalties. With the sliding scale, *X-Men* paid fantastic royalties. I remember handing Byrne a check for $30,000. I said, "You know the comic book we paid you all that money to draw? Here! Here's a tip."

But the thing is, when I started there, I started as associate editor. There was no organization whatsoever. There was total anarchy, total chaos. The editors-in-chief before me acted like they were head writers or something like that. Like, "I'm going to do my books. Everyone try to do what I do." Every writer was his own editor. The editors-in-chief, at least the ones I was aware of, left it all to the production manager. You'd think he ran the company—John Verpoorten.

Steve Englehart would write a plot for *The Avengers*. It never saw the office. He would send it directly to the penciller. The penciller would draw it. He would send the pages back to Steve. Steve would write the dialogue. He would sent it directly to the letterer. The letterer would letter it. The letterer would send it directly to the inker. Verpoorten would be on the phone to me saying, "Oh, this guy Klaus [Janson] is open. Send it to him." All of a sudden, this book comes into the office—completely finished! There were no editors. No nothing. We had what they called proofreaders.

These finished books would come in. There'd be stuff in them that was crazy, like "Isn't this guy dead? Wait a minute, we can't have him here; he's over there." Or the costumes are all wrong, or they'd make some other crazy mistake.

How I became associate editor . . . Marv Wolfman called me up. He was trying to cope with the chaos. His theory was that he would get someone to read the plots and maybe even look at the pencils when they came in. He hired Chris Claremont to do that. Chris's title was pre-proofer. We had the proofers who, when the book was finished, would go over it. They were looking for costume mistakes, like Thor's belt is wrong. John Romita is sitting there, fixing Thor's belt. That's like killing a fly with an elephant gun. To lessen the amount of stuff that had to be fixed at the last minute, Marv decided maybe someone should look at it earlier. I'm like, "Geez, that's a brilliant idea."

Marv didn't even know what to call the guy. He decided on associate editor, but basically I became the editor. To everyone's shock and amazement, I started trying to do that job. All these guys who'd never even had anybody even look at a plot—all of a sudden, I'm saying, "Send me the plot." Some of them did not take kindly to that. I started trying to get it under control. If I found something, I was very respectful. I'd call them up and say, "You need to work on this. Maybe we should have something different here. Or this dialogue you wrote; first of all, it's a hundred and twenty words in a ninth of a page panel. That won't fit. Do you want to trim it down?" Half of them would say, "Screw you. I'm busy on the next job." Because it was page rate; you get paid by the page. Having to go back and fix a page that you'd already done—nobody wanted to do that because the faster you turned it out the more money you made.

A lot of these guys said that they didn't want to do it. I ended up doing a lot of the re-writing. Some guys were great. If Archie Goodman wrote something, first off, it was always perfect. The one time I found a spelling error, I was so pleased: "Oh, I found something!" Gerber's stuff was very clean. There were some guys—Claremont, to his ever-lasting credit, he didn't want anybody else's words on there. He wanted his words. I would find stuff with his work. I would say, "Chris, it might be nice if we mentioned the character's name this issue." Stuff like that. He would grumble and go find a typewriter, and he would fix it. The first time I tried to put a little note in the margin, he came to me said, "Don't do this! Don't do this!" I said, "Why not?" He said, "I want to do it myself." I said, "Okay." He said, "Put an X and tell me what's wrong, and I'll fix it." That's what I would do in the scripts, put an X. He would say, "What's this?" I would say, "Chris, this character, you've got this thing here, and it doesn't work because of what you said on the previous page." He'd go, and he'd fix it.

It was really funny, he used to retype the whole page so that his scripts would be clean and pristine. I admired that. One time, I screwed up. It was too complicated to explain, so I wrote a couple words for this caption in the margin. He couldn't think of a way to say it better in that much space. He was really annoyed that he had to use my words.

When I was associate editor, I didn't have the power to hire or fire anybody. I could enforce things and fix things. I did. If a guy was willing to fix it, fine. I'd explain to him what it was and what the problem was, then let him do it himself. A lot of guys weren't willing to do that. I wound up doing a lot of stuff. I tried to raise the level on the bottom stuff as much as I could.

I became editor-in-chief. Now, they're all afraid: Now, he has power. Not only is he an editor, now he's going to make us work. I started having meetings with the writers. The major subject of that first meeting was that you need to mention the character's name in the story someplace. You need to identify these characters—not even introduce them, just tell me who it is. That was one of my first meetings. The next meeting was: something needs to happen in each issue. That sounds pretty simple, right? Kicking and screaming, I dragged these guys toward telling a story better. Some guys didn't need to try. The good ones, they obviously knew better than I did. I started making an improvement in this stuff by getting them to introduce the characters and identify the characters and have stuff happen. I started preaching structure, preaching storytelling, and pushing them as hard as I could without breaking their spirits.

Jason: You said that you studied the Marvel books when you started your first script. You're talking about ten or twelve years later, and you're now in a position to help propagate these rules that you learned. Do you think that this lifelong learning and thinking about comics was paying off?

JS: When I first started at Marvel as associate editor, I was trying to actually do the job. All these guys were like, "Who the hell is this? Is this some DC writer telling us what to do?" That was about the time that Stan started getting back more involved with the comics. He had been out on the lecture circuit. He had been the publisher of the magazines upstairs, all those crummy magazines that Magazine Management did. Those were dying. Those were losing serious money. I think he wanted to dissociate himself from this disaster, to come back. He moved back into his downstairs office. He really didn't have any day-to-day responsibilities. His job was to be Stan. He wasn't even on the organizational chart. He was a little circle off on his own with no sticks going to him.

When I started at Marvel, Marv was editor-in-chief. After three months, Marv Wolfman quit. He will tell you he quit; Galton told me he was fired. I don't know. But, I think what they tried to do was they told him, "You have to leave, and we'll let you leave with dignity. We'll give you a contract to write." Then, Gerry Conway came in. Roy was going to come back and then decided not to. Then Stan was an authority. Anything he told Galton, Galton would do. He said, "Let's get this Conway." They hired Gerry Conway. He was there for about three weeks. That's a long story. Then, after that, they hired Archie Goodwin. This whole time I'm associate editor. I'm sitting there doing these books.

Archie was there for nineteen months. That was about the time that Stan started getting interested in the comics. One of the things he would do was that when the make-readies came in from the printer, Stan would go through them in ballpoint pen and mark things. Then, he would call Archie into his office and go over them with him. Archie didn't need to be told. He had to sit there and listen to Stan. Meanwhile, he's got stuff to do. Finally, Archie tells him, "Stan, Jim is the guy who actually does the hands-on editing. You should do this with him." He was trying to escape and dump it on me. I get called into Stan's office. Stan sits there and goes over all the make-readies with me. We're publishing forty-five comics a month. I'm only one guy; I'm doing the best I can. The first few times Stan's going over this, he says, "Look, don't let them do this. I want nice straight pointers. Look what the colorist did here—it's mud. Tell them not to do this. This guy doesn't understand storytelling. What's this person saying?" He wasn't telling me anything I didn't know. But there's only so many hours in the day. I was shoring up the bottom. I was fixing the worst, most egregious stuff. I couldn't quite get to some of the stuff that needed to be done, but it was better than the stuff that I fixed before I fixed it. We would do this every week. About the tenth week, Stan is talking to me like I'm a kindergarten kid. He says, "See, Jim. You need to explain to these guys they need to get these pointers straight. I don't want these little snaky pointers." I say, "Stan, I know. I'm doing the best I can. I got a lot of books to do, and I'm doing my best." He's telling me the same stuff again and again. It's because there's forty-five books. I'm trying not to get Archie in trouble. I'm trying not to say anything. So many times, I want to say, "I want to fire that guy!" But Archie won't let me. Why? Because he actually delivers stuff on time even though it sucks.

Archie always used to say, "Most of it's going to be crap. A few guys will take the freedom, and they'll do something wonderful. That's the way of the world." Fix what you can, and don't worry about it. But I'm the guy getting yelled at by Stan. I did actually learn some stuff as we were going through these books. I thought, "All right, that's an interesting thought." Or he explained something to me his way that Mort told me was a rule. Then Stan would say it more reasonably. We'd talk about the bedrock. I'm not saying I didn't learn anything, but I already knew most of what he was saying.

Then, all of a sudden, there are all these books that literally had to be written overnight. This is a *Ghost Rider* story, and it was a very stupid story. I wrote it overnight. I worked all day in the office, get home to my little house, and was up all night to write this book. It was just words on paper. It wasn't great. Stan is going through this book, and he says, "No one can save this. What's this? I don't know." It made sense. It was functional. But it wasn't good. He was like, "I don't know about this. This is pretty bland stuff." He finally says, "Who wrote it?" He looks at the credits. It's me. I say, "Yeah, I wrote it in six hours." He thinks I'm a moron. Then we started working on the *Spider-Man* newspaper strip. Len [Wein] did the first six weeks of the strip. I did it from then, from whenever the strip started until I became editor-in-chief. When I was editor-in-chief, I said, "Stan, I don't have time to do this anymore." He said, "I need you." I continued to do it for a while. It was killing me. Then I stopped for a while. I don't know who did it then. He asked me to come back and do it again. I did a little more. Then finally he got his brother, Larry Lieber, to do it because Larry could do the layouts too. That's what he wanted. That worked out. I did maybe three, four, or five storylines.

That was when Stan realized I wasn't an idiot. He was talking to Galton: "We've got to get Jim more involved." He was also starting to realize that Archie—while one of the all-time greats, a genius, a really intelligent guy—was really not a businessman. He did not have any interest whatsoever in all the administrative stuff and all the bureaucratic dealings with the people upstairs. He just wanted to do the creative part. They were trying to engineer something where he would sort of get kicked upstairs. He'd become the vice president in charge of special things and would be doing the editor-in-chief stuff. He felt pushed out. That never came to pass. He knew I was working closely with Stan. I think he thought I ratted him out or something. So he quit. He took a contract.

I became editor in chief on the first working day of January 1978. We wanted to wait until after the first of January to tell everybody. When Stan announced it at the Christmas party, you could have heard a pin drop. Archie and his wife are boring holes in me with their eyes. Everyone else is terrified, thinking, "The monster is in charge. What are we going to do?" The only people who were nice to me were a couple of the old guys like Danny Crespi and John Tartaglione. They came over to congratulate me. Everybody else was like, "Oh, god." The next morning was Saturday. It was 7:00 in the morning. The phone's ringing. I pick up the phone. I say, "Hello," and it's Marv Wolfman. He doesn't say hello. He says, "What are you going to do?" I say, "Go to sleep." All the guys who were writer-editors were worried that I was going to take that away from them, and they might have to actually do their jobs. I said, "I'm not going to do anything for a while. Give me a chance, will you?"

A lot of guys were terrified that I was going to ruin their lives. I started trying to raise the quality of the editorial: get them to tell real stories, trying to explain structure to them. Make sure you introduce the characters. Let's have a significant event. Let's have something go on–here's where the issue starts; here's where it ends. It's a different place. I kept trying to do that. Also, we did get some incentives. Since I couldn't get the royalties going because of all the chaos that was going on there, I got what I called the continuity bonus. You do three issues in a row, you get a bonus. Every six issues after that, you get another bonus. It was substantial. It was like $500 or something, which was nice. It made a difference to people.

The other thing I did was I standardized the benefits and the contracts. I also started introducing benefits for the freelancers. The first working day of January 1978 was the day that the Copyright Law of 1976 took effect. I'm sitting at my little editor-in-chief desk, and the phone rings. It's Alice Donenfeld, who's the house counsel. She says, "What have you done about the Copyright Law of 1976?" I said, "Lady, I've been here fifteen minutes! I haven't done anything. What are you talking about?" The Copyright Law required people to sign a piece of paper in advance of their work. I got that, and nobody wants to sign anything. We can't stop producing. Every month, we're producing stuff that we don't technically own.

Neal Adams decides this is a great time to form a guild and go on strike against Marvel. Now, Neal and I were friends. I'm like, "Neal, give me a chance! I'm going to work on this stuff. I'll get it done. Give me a chance." He had a big meeting. For some reason, though I was management—he was meeting with labor—they wanted me to be there. Paul Levitz was there, too. There were hundreds of people.

When the whole copyright thing started, I ended up spending a lot of time with the lawyers upstairs, and the Cadence people sent me to a three-day legal seminar, trying to learn about copyright. Then the lawyers produced this thick document, this multipage work-for-hire document. They gave it to me, and they said, "Get everybody to sign it." I'm starting to give it to people. It's being torn up. It's being thrown. It's being crumpled up. Everyone was like, "Screw you." I'm reading it, and it's all legalese: *now, therefore, whereas,* blah, blah, blah. I wrote the original Marvel work-for-hire document, one page. I put it in the simplest English I possibly could. Of course, the lawyers had to vet it. But they said, "This'll do." But now it's a one-page thing, and it's less scary.

I started working on getting people to sign it. First of all, we had a bunch of guys under contract. If you're under contract, you've already signed it. It's got this language in it. I asked them if they'd sign this little redundant piece of paper, just so I'd have a little sheet that I could wave around. Some said, "It's fine." Some guys had no problem. Frank Thorne said, "Of course." He says,

"Every farm hand who pulls a teat thinks he owns the cow." That was his approach. Then what happened was that a lot of guys resisted.

Then DC imploded. They cancelled 40 percent of their line in one day. The next morning—I used to get to work around 6:30 or 7:00 in the morning—I had so much to do. When I get there, there's already a line at the door. Everybody there is signing a work-for-hire contract. All the DC guys figured they'd come over, sign the work-for-hire, and get the jobs from the Marvel guys who wouldn't sign it. All the Marvel guys were there because they knew the DC guys would do that. I even had Archie guys; everyone was there to sign the work-for-hire. Sol helped me. The Guild dried up and blew away, too, because everybody was desperate for work.

At this meeting that I went to, three significant things happened. Levitz and I both were trying to convince everybody that DC was losing big money. Marvel was losing relatively smaller money. I said if you make life hard, they'll close. At this meeting that I went to, three significant things happened. Levitz and I were trying to convince everybody that DC was losing money. Marvel was losing relatively smaller money. I said if you make life hard, they'll close or they'll all go reprint like Harvey and Archie. During '78, Charlton went out of business. Harvey was nothing. [In fact, though Charlton briefly went all-reprint in 1976/77, all of these publishers were putting out new material in 1978.]

It was really down to a couple of us. That was one thing at the meeting where Levitz and I really convinced them that we're not making hundreds of millions of dollars. Another thing is, Neal was talking about what the rates should be—about several hundred dollars a page for the colorist and $800 a page for the penciller. "Neal," I said, "Look around you here. All these guys are talented. But if I pay $800 a page, I'll pay you, and I'll pay Leonard Starr. A lot of you guys won't make the cut." Neal was talking about how the union would help get justice for the creators of the past. In particular, he cited Steve Ditko. Neal was talking about doing what he did for [Jerry] Siegel and [Joe] Shuster. Steve happened to be there, and Steve objected. He said, "I'm nobody's poster child." He said, "I was an adult. I knew what the deal was. I will honor it." Because that's Steve. He's an honorable man.

The other thing that happened . . . This was a killer. They started talking about artwork return. Neal's opinion is that the penciller is the artist, the inker is an assistant, and the inker should only get something if the penciller chooses to give it to him. When Neal started talking about the inkers don't get pages and the inkers are only assistants, the inkers walked out. It all crumbled. The whole storm, the implosion, the fact that people started realizing that companies were dropping like flies. Are we really making millions of dollars?

People settled in and realized we're going to do this, and maybe they had to play ball. I started giving these incentives—then amazingly the stories started getting a bit more coherent. We started getting some guys back who had left. All of a sudden, sales start going up. Then *X-Men* took off, which became the bell cow.

Suddenly guys were starting to make more money. More guys show up. Guys that stormed out and left . . . Englehart. Gerry Conway, who was there, left—he comes back. Even Roy eventually came back. All of a sudden guys like Bernie Wrightson are showing up. Kaluta walked in, and here's Starlin back. All these good guys started turning up.

Jason: Your tenure was the beginning of what I think of as Marvel today, this IP juggernaut with these characters that people have grown to love. A lot of what embedded them in people's minds was *Secret Wars*. I speak to my friends who are not big comic fans. That's one of the first things they mention to me. It's ironic in a way because it was intended as a toy tie-in comic, but it sold fantastically well.

JS: I didn't intend for it to be a toy tie-in. The thing is it was in reverse because Kenner licensed DC's superheroes. There were doing a line of superhero toys. DC actually published a book called *Super Powers* that nobody read and nobody cared about, although the art was nice. Mattel, when they found out Kenner was going to do *Super Powers*, didn't want to be the only giant toy company that didn't have superheroes. They came to us like, "What have you got?" Our licensing people said, "We've got Spider-Man. We've got Hulk. We've got Daredevil. We've got . . ." They're like, "We haven't heard of half of these guys."

There was a meeting. One of the troubles at Marvel was that Galton hadn't ever opened a comic and didn't really know much about them. Most of the upstairs executives had not opened a comic book. We had an international licensing person, Gail Munn. She called me up one day all excited because she'd made this fantastic deal for Wonder Woman. I said, "We don't own Wonder Woman." She said, "Why'd they call me?" At this point, we were like 70 percent of the market. If it's comics, they think it's us! I said, "Why don't you call . . ." the licensing lady over at the LCA [Legal and Corporate Affairs]. I said, "Tell her you teed up a deal for her. Make out like you were doing her a favor." She was furious. She says, "I made this great deal!" I say, "Too bad."

The licensing people used to like to include me in all these meetings. Therefore, they never had to open a comic book because I could provide the information. When Mattel started saying, "We don't even know these characters. What are you going to do to help promote this?" The Mattel people said, "What we would we like for you to do is to do some big event—whatever, anything that can get publicity—make a big impact that can help people get to know these characters. If you do that, then we're interested in licensing." I say, "How about we do this twelve-issue story with all the major villains and all the major heroes in one big story? I get fan mail that suggests this every day."

The idea came from fandom. People were writing in all the time, saying, "Why don't you do one big story?" We did that. My intention was to make it a good comic book first. Mattel gave us some little requirements, nothing I couldn't handle. They said, "We'd like Dr. Doom more technological-looking; he looks too medieval." I said, "I can do that. I can work it into the story." They wanted them to have vehicles: "They're on an alien planet. They can have vehicles. Sure." Stuff like that. Mattel said, "We need stuff for playsets." I said, "I'll give them a headquarters." Nothing I couldn't work with. Then they left me alone. I never heard from them again.

Jason: Did they ask for the black costume for Spider-Man?

JS: The black costume was also suggested by a fan. He wrote a plot, and he sent it in. I paid him for the idea. The plot was amateur. It was about Reed Richards making a high-tech costume for Spider-Man. His costume was described as a black costume. Two words. Black costume. I called him up, and I think I paid him $500 for the idea. I said, "We can do a black costume. We don't have to pay anybody. But I don't want you to feel like we ripped you off here." He was thrilled. I said, "This entire story is going to fall between the December books and the January books." It was going to go twelve issues, but it all technically happened right here. We had to plan everything in advance. I told all of the guys, "Get your characters to Central Park in your December issue. Pick them up in Central Park at the start of the January issue. But they're going to be a little bit different. People are going to wonder what happened." We came up with things for each character. Like, the Thing wasn't going to come back at all. She-Hulk was going to be in the Fantastic Four. We came up with all the stuff that was going to go on. Then, I'm like, "What have we got on Spider-Man? There's the black costume—bingo!" I called [Mike] Zeck. I said, "I want you to design a new costume for Spider-Man." He said, "What do you want?" I said, "Black. Black costume." That's the only instructions he got. He did it all from there.

It appeared first in *Spider-Man* because it didn't come out until our eighth issue. As soon as we decide to do that, I go to the licensing people. I said, "Oh, we're going to change Spider-Man's costume." They say, "Uh-huh." No reaction. I go to the PR lady, Pam Rutt. I say, "Pam, we're going to change Spider-Man's costume. Should we do like a press release or something?" She said, "No one will care." I said, "Okay."

That first issue of *Spider-Man* comes out, and the storm happens. First thing that happens is that the licensing people call me, furious. "We have the red-and-blue costume licensed all over the world. What the hell are you doing to us?" I'm like, "Relax, it's going to be okay." I got a complaint from some bigshot upstairs. All this stuff starts happening. Then my phone starts ringing. It's the wire services: it's the *Daily News*, it's the *Times*, it's the *Post*, it's the *Miami Herald*, it's the *Cleveland Plain Dealer*, it's other papers. I go to the PR lady, and I say, "How do you want me to handle this, Pam? You said no one would care." She had to scramble around and put together—pretend—we already had press releases and send them out. We got coverage all over the place. The book sold like mad.

The thing is, at first, all these licensing people were mad at me. Then they started getting calls from Germany, saying, "We want to license the black costume, too." We already had the red-and-blue costume licensed. It doubled the licenses because everybody wanted the black costume. It went from everybody being mad at me for a minute to them printing up business cards for everyone with the black costume. They're printing up stationery with the black costume. I said, "There's no reason he can't have two costumes. I've got more than one set of clothes." It took off. It sold in huge numbers. It boosted the sales of the other books. It got enough publicity, enough attention, that it became one of those things where it got people into it. They'd see this cover with all these characters on it, and they'd be like, "Oh, I've got to have this." Part of my theory was that the direct market was taking off. As the direct market took off, the sales people got less and less interested in the newsstand because the direct market was shooting fish in a barrel. I was like, "No, no, no. That's seventy thousand outlets. That's where people get hooked. Then if they really like something, they'll go find the comic shop to get more." We felt we had to do everything we can to keep the newsstand happy.

Eric: Was part of your drive with your editorial philosophy and pushing story to the forefront and making sure that people paid attention geared towards newsstand sales? Those readers who had spotty distribution, they were able to pick up one issue and make complete sense of it.

JS: To me, it was all about reaching out to build an audience and tell stories. Get people to care the way I used to care about Spider-Man. I couldn't wait to get together with Spider-Man again next month and then see what was going on. We didn't have that feeling in the 1970s. We tried to get that back, and we did. We had our clinkers. But we had a lot of good books.

The black-costumed Spider-Man. Panel detail from *Secret Wars* 8 (1984). Art by Mike Zeck and Bob Layton. © 1984 Marvel Comics.

Eric: So you don't necessarily see art and commerce at odds.

JS: Not at all. The Sistine Chapel—that's commercial art.

Dominick: It's a complex question, though, because, on the one hand, you can see the synergy and the increase in sales. That's an important part of your legacy. But does there come a point where that kind of thing actually becomes counterproductive?

JS: They immediately ran it into the ground. We did *Secret Wars*, and DC right away did *Crisis*. They'd been talking about *Crisis* in one form or another since Jenette Kahn first came. Finally, when we were doing *Secret Wars*, I guess they figured it was time to try something like that.

The first *Crisis* didn't really solve anything. It just made it more complex. Recently, they did that *New 52*, which is more like it. I didn't actually like that.

We did this first crossover. They followed with *Crisis*. Their first issue came out the same week as our last issue. Then, right away, the people upstairs were so happy with all the money that they made from *Secret Wars*, I get this call from the president of the company. He says, "We need the sequel as soon as possible." I said, "Whoa. I need a couple of months off. I've been working all day and all night. This is getting a little old." He said, "No. You don't understand. If you take a couple months, each month is so many hundred thousand dollars off our bottom line. Get on it." I said, "Okay." He didn't ever actually open *Secret Wars*. All he knew was that it made a lot of money.

Dominick: The art-commerce balance—

JS: The art-commerce balance—I had the commerce gun to my head! But nonetheless, I was trying to do it right. I was trying to do it well. I said, "I'm not going to do the same thing again. I can't do the same thing."

The next time, we did it in step with the regular issues and branched the story into the issues. Every time we do this we're going to do it different. I didn't really get a chance to do it. The next time I did it, I had my own company, VALIANT. I did it in the actual, regular books, with a special issue on either end. Basically, I kept trying to come up with new ways to do it.

Jason: You were going to do it with *Schism* for DEFIANT Comics.

JS: We had that all planned to do it differently from the other ones. I kept saying we've got to change it up. Everyone else said, "Easy money!" They would have these stories where they would throw a bunch of characters together. Every summer, everybody was doing it. It devalued pretty quickly. I think it actually had a detrimental effect in the long haul. It's become a joke.

If I ever was in a position to do it again, I'd come up with a new way. I'd dazzle them. I'd make it work along with the continuity and everything.

Eric: Do you feel like the downward trend in comics right now is partially a result of these convoluted narratives being somewhat difficult for a new reader to latch onto?

JS: Oh, absolutely. Individual books are incomprehensible. There are a few guys that seem to have a clue. I think Scott Snyder at DC is pretty good. He has a clue. There are some other guys that are okay. But no one is telling them to introduce the characters. They're not. Stories start in the middle and end in the middle. There's a lot of sound and fury, but what actually happened here?

Even their supposed number one guy, Geoff Johns—for some reason, I had to read some of his stuff. I think it was because they had Legion of Super-Heroes characters. They send me his books. The first one I looked at was *Justice League*. I open the book, and there on the splash page is a whole bunch of characters. They don't all have their costumes on. They're all referring to each other by their first names. I didn't have any idea who some of these characters were. I had a vague idea of who some of them were. Like, this guy didn't really look like the Mr. Terrific I remember, so he's somebody else. They're all calling each other Bruce. "Anybody seen Kal?" Okay, I knew who Bruce was. I knew who Kal must be. Then they're saying something about the Carters. I think, "Who are the Carters?" The thing is, if you ignore the readers having to understand it, you can write kind of glib dialogue. Use a lot of pronouns, and it's fine. But I'm pages into this book, and I have no idea who these people are. Nothing seems to be going on. They talk about stuff that isn't there that might be going on someplace else. There's a very cleverly written scene where somebody gets murdered. I thought, "Okay, that's good," really well written. But it goes nowhere. About two-thirds of the way through, I thought, "Carters—Hawkman. It's Hawkman!" If you're reading a book, and, in the middle, you realize, "Oh, that's Hawkman," it takes you out of the story. When I used to read Ditko or Kirby, I'd get to the end and feel like I'd seen a movie. I hadn't taken my eyes off those pages, and, if somebody asked me about an individual panel, I probably couldn't remember. I saw the movie in my head. That seems to be gone. I'm not saying Geoff Johns isn't a talented guy, but the priorities obviously are very different. Maybe there are people who know who Mr. Terrific is and who know who the Carters are right away, but that group keeps getting smaller and smaller. We're just playing amongst ourselves here, now.

Eric: The medium is back to where it was when the first comic book fans started to take over. In terms of the artists and writers of the 1970s, there are a lot of parallels.
JS: Because a lot of those people were fans. Some of them were very talented, but nobody was trained. I think I'm one of the few guys who were trained. Roy got trained by Stan to some extent. I worked with Stan really closely for years on the strip and, then, when he was around the office . . . Then, after that, often—even when he was out in LA, I would go out there, or he would come out here. Whenever he did, we would spend time together and talk about stuff—did a lot of theory. I spent five years at boot camp with Mort Weisinger. I'm one of the few guys who really went through an apprenticeship.

Eric: You put Frank Miller on *Daredevil*, right? With Roger McKenzie?

JS: Sort of. Miller would show up with samples and stuff. I gave him a try-out job. He butchered it. I said, "Your stuff is a little rough. You have to bring me layouts." He showed me layouts, and they looked great. Then he made the mistake of coming over and showing Neal [Adams]. Neal said, "Why are you doing all this Kirby grid and stuff? What's up with this?" Frank said, "That's what Jim told me." Neal's my buddy, but he said to never pay attention to editors. He said, "Do it right. Then they'll look at it, and they'll say, 'Oh, that's great,' because they're all stupid." Frank went and he threw all the layouts away. He took a pane of glass hung over it and broke it—that was how he laid out the page. He brings it in, and I looked at it. I said, "We'll pay for this, but we really can't use you." He said, "What do you mean?" I said, "You didn't do what I said." It comes out that Neal told him not to. I said, "Who signs your check? Is it Neal? I'm going to slap that guy around. Come on, Neal, don't do this to me." Miller—he's always tense—he says, "Give me another chance." We give him something. He did what I told him, and he did it well. He still didn't quite grok the storytelling part. But every time he did something, he grew by leaps and bounds.

Then we needed an artist for *Daredevil*. I think I was the one who asked Denny [O'Neil], "Can you use this Miller guy?" He agreed. Frank was doing *Daredevil* with Roger McKenzie. Frank wasn't really happy with it because he didn't like the stories. Frank was slow—he wasn't that good, and he hadn't caught on yet. He really shouldn't have been making ultimatums. But he said to Denny, "You've got to get rid of this guy, or I'm going." Denny comes to me and says, "What do I do?" I said, "Whoever gives you the ultimatum goes." Goodbye Miller. He goes back, and Frank rethought that. He stuck around. But Roger was so insulted—because word got back to him—that he quit. Denny says, "I've got to get a writer for this series." Then he comes in and puts a plot on my desk: "Read that." "Yes, sir!" I read it. It's good. I said, "This is good. What's your problem?" He says, "He has no right to be that good on his first try." I said, "Who?" He said, "Miller." I said, "Oh! Good."

Both Denny and I had been talking about story and structure and that stuff. This was the first Elektra story, and it was great. He started writing it and drawing it. That's when I started winning more of the debates upstairs because I said, "You wait. You'll see." Chuck Rozanski was out in Denver, and he said, "I trust your judgment. What's the next big thing?" I said, "*Daredevil*." He said, "*Daredevil*?" I said, "Yeah, *Daredevil*." He said, "I'm going to bet on your judgment." He started buying up *Daredevil*, and he made a fortune. That's why

Frank took all those back issues—because they wound up being super valuable. He's still making money off them. He still sells those things.

Frank was a nut. He was real intense. One day, he comes in. He's all dirty. It's six in the morning. I was always in early, so I was there. He comes in all filthy. He says, "You know what I did last night? I prowled the rooftops in Hell's Kitchen." Then he would go up on the rooftops and draw.

Each story he did was exponentially better than the one before. Up until the day when he said he got that we're telling stories, he didn't know what to put in his pictures. He didn't draw all that well. The thinking wasn't there yet. It went on like a lightbulb. When he did the first one right, he was remembering: you got to establish the character, shot so that I can recognize them. Going through it all—all the drawing stuff—and then when it finally occurred to him. After that, man, everything got better and better, with more nuance, more thought.

Jason: He's one of the few guys who you lost when DC threw money at him to do *Ronin* and *Dark Knight*.

JS: I didn't really lose him. He was under contract. His contract was coming up. He, Starlin, and Simonson—we were already doing creator-owned in Epic. The three of them came to me, and they said, "We want to do creator-owned comic books." I said, "Okay, let's do it." We go into Mike Hobson's office, and I say, "These guys have ideas for creator-owned comic books that we publish and they own, just like the book publishers." Mike says, "I guess we'll need some contracts. I'll help you with those." They're all looking at each other like, "Wow, I guess we're going to do this."

We did. Walt, actually—at the same time, we were starting to do the graphic novels. Walt ended up doing *Star Slammers* instead as a graphic novel. He never got around to doing his other comic. Starlin did the first, *The Death of Captain Marvel*, but then he wanted to do *Dreadstar* as a comic book. Frank was going to do something, but at that time, he had really gotten hot. Jenette Kahn was always calling to take him to lunch and all this stuff. Finally, he says, "I don't want to sign any contract. I want to do a job at DC." I say, "Okay. Listen, Frank. I don't want you to feel like you're trapped here. Go there; find out that we're better." He says, "You're not mad?" I said, "No, just do it. Why do you want to do *Ronin* at DC? You could do it here. Forget the monthly contract. You could just do a graphic novel." He says, "I know you told me you were going to do this with these contracts, but over there I'm dealing with the president and publisher. Over here, you're the editor-in-chief, but what if you can't pull it off?" I say, "I can. But if they're giving you a better deal, go with it."

They gave him a worse deal. DC owns *Ronin*. Frank owns a decent amount of it, but basically it's a deluxe work-for-hire contract. Walt owns *Star Slammers*. Starlin owns *Dreadstar*. Our deal was much better than theirs. He came back. Also, *Ronin* was a disaster. They sold it real well because it was Frank, but it didn't sell through. Bud Plant[1] said he was rolling them up and selling them as firewood because he had tons of them. Of course when Frank later became more of a superstar, all those old things became more valuable, but at that time they weren't. Then he came back and said he wanted to do an *Elektra* graphic novel. I said, "Okay, but not like *Ronin*." He said, "What do you mean?" I said, "It's unreadable. If you're going to tell a story, fine. If you're going to do it like you used to do stuff and just be clear, fine. If you want to do *Ronin*, forget it." He got all huffy with me, and he stormed off. That night, he had a meet up with Will Eisner. He's telling Will what an asshole I am. Eisner asks, "Why?" "*Ronin*. He said it was unreadable." This is what Will said—and this is a quote: "Frank, it's unreadable horseshit." Unreadable horseshit. You don't get mad at Will. Frank got a little huffy, and he goes home. He took *Ronin* which he hadn't looked at for months, off the shelf. *He* had trouble reading it. The reason I know that is that he called me the next morning and asked if we could go to lunch. He told me the rest of the story. He said, "I want to do it, and I'll do it. I'll tell the story. I'll do it straight. I'm not going to get weird and experimental." I said, "Done deal." We signed the deal. It took him two years to do it, but he finally did it.

It was really funny because he started working with Sienkiewicz. At that point, after doing *New Mutants*, Sienkiewicz was always on constant experimental mode. So now it's like Frank has all these difficult-to-write pictures. He's trying to pull it all together. He said, "It's like God is punishing me." But he did pull it together. Bill gives you great images, even though he was going a little more *New Mutants* than I would have preferred. I would have rather had panels. But Frank pulled it together.

Eric: I interviewed Mark Badger recently and he pointed to your lecture as being one of the more influential things in his career.

JS: $1.98 storytelling. I convinced them all to tell a story. That's my bedrock. You've got to tell the story. You don't have to reinvent everything. You can learn from the people who came before. People always throw Will Eisner up and say, "Will always did this crazy experimental stuff." I say, "Yes, on *The Spirit*. Look at his Westerns. Look at anything else that he ever did." He's Will. He can get away with it.

Dominick: *The Spirit* was also a newspaper insert. It's a different format.
JS: Totally different. Then, I used to have kids—we used a lot of Kubies [Kubert school graduates]. They had been taught professionalism if not very much about comics. But I'd also have kids come over from the Eisner school. He had classes there. He taught these kids. I had these kids come to VALIANT. They'd show me stuff. Their stuff was pretty, but I'd say, "But here's what I want you to do. Use the Kirby grid, rectilinear panels, keep the stuff in the panels. Use no overlapping or little insets unless I tell you." They'd look at me; then they'd do whatever they want. I'd say, "You're not doing what I said." They said, "I'm doing it the way Will told me." I'd say, "Is Will signing your check?" I'd fire every one of them. Pay them for whatever page they did, and they'd go.

I kept telling Will, "You've got to stop telling these kids that they can manipulate time by the shape of the panel." I said, "*You* can manipulate time by the shape of the panel. They can't. When they get to be you, then they can do it. Teach them some fundamentals." He says, "Some of these guys have some real potential. Maybe if I can get that spark going, then—" I said, "But what you're doing is you're getting a lot of kids unemployed because they won't do what you ask them to do. When you ask them to do it, they say, 'I was taught by a genius.' You know, you can shut up, now." I'm like, "No, you're doing it my way, pal, or you're not doing it"—especially at VALIANT because I didn't have money. I didn't have anything except man-hours. I got a little wiser about creation, so I'd say, "There are rules. We're going to do this. When someone picks up a VALIANT book, I want them to know what it's going to be like inside. I want them to know that it's going to have rectilinear panels. It's going to have a lot of story in it. It's going to be a good story. It's going to be straightforward. It's about telling a story because none of you guys are Jim Lee." I enforced that. There we really did have a house style. We had to because we didn't have anything else.

Barry [Windsor-Smith] used to argue with me all the time because he was a superstar, and he wanted to do insets and have overlapping panels. I said, "No." He would say, "I'm Barry Windsor-Smith." "Go be Barry Windsor-Smith somewhere else. It would be a great loss, but either do it the VALIANT way, or don't work here." He'd show me a *Conan* page he did, and he'd say, "See, it expands the size of the image—the inset." I'd say, "No. You know what, Barry—it shrinks the size of the image. Because all this space around the inset, with leaves and stuff, it's meaningless. It even looks bad. You have basically cut off that corner of the page with this inset. What good is it to me? Why don't you just draw the picture? You know, it's what's in the painting—do what's in the painting. When you get to be Will Eisner, be Will Eisner."

Eisner and I would always get together at conventions. We'd get talking, and I remember one time, I said, "Three times in your career, this industry has almost died. Eight times in mine." We'd talk about it, and basically, we agree about story and storytelling. Usually what happened was a Stan Lee would come along, a Jack Kirby would come along. A change in distribution would come along at the same time. With me, it was the direct market. In the '60s, it was Stan and Jack, who got distributed by DC's distribution house. It was always some combination like that that kept us alive.

To me, it still seems that publishing is dying. I look at sales, and there were three books over a hundred thousand in the March *Previews*. The break-even in my day was sixty to seventy thousand. That was a low to break-even. It would just cover costs. We were making money. They were always saying you could make more money. Because you could.

Eric: The whole paradigm has changed.
Jason: They're IP-generation companies.
JS: Which is sad to me because, to me, the way to do that is to do it the way we did. The characters of the 1990s lasted because they were good characters well-realized and good stories . . . occasionally good art.

Eric: What's especially striking about now is that these superhero movies are incredible blockbusters, yet it's done virtually nothing for the medium.
JS: Because the books aren't really much like that.

I get really sick of the dark. You know—the hero loses, the building burns, the baby dies, the bad guy gets away with it and then laughs all the way to the bank. Come on guys. I'm not saying it has to be happy stuff, but could we have a good guy win maybe once? He would win in the movies. One of my themes is overcoming these odds rather than losing. There are too many of these guys who grew up thinking of the most shocking things they could do. Really, that's what it's about: What's the most shocking thing that we could do? I know, we broke his back; now, let's tear his eye out. The crap is out there.

Jason: Weisinger was an ass, but one thing he did do was to force you to increase your quality, to create something that people outside your niche of friends would like.
JS: He absolutely did. I think there aren't editors anymore. There are expediters. They just process the stuff through. I'm not seeing anybody teaching anybody. I'm not seeing anybody actually taking an editorial hand. When I walked out on our little hall of editors, we had fourteen, and I would walk

down the row. Larry Hama, Archie Goodwin, Ann Nocenti, Tom DeFalco, Bob Budiansky, Denny when he was on, who else? Boy, we had some really good editors. Even ones who weren't great editors, they always had a specialty. Like Milgrom—he was not a great editor, not a great story guy, but I could help him with that. He was really good with the artists, and he was really good at finding artists and developing them. I knew with him I had to be a little more involved with the stories. Whereas with Larry, I just had to stay out of his way. Archie knew more than I did.

It's funny. If you mention the name Archie Goodwin to fans, they'll say he was pretty good, but if you talk to professionals like Moebius you'll hear a different story. When you're in a room with Moebius and other greater artists, like Frazetta and all these other people, Archie is revered. Epic reprinted the Moebius stuff. Archie took this stuff, and he used it. Stan was afraid that there was too much nudity and violence. He said, "I don't know." I said, "But it's a magazine, so it doesn't have the same laws." But I was only associate editor. Archie was the editor at that point. Stan had cold feet. I don't care if he was the boss or not. He was Stan. If he told me to join the Boy Scouts, I would, and I would rub sticks together. He didn't want to do *Heavy Metal* at Marvel. That team went to Twentieth Century Communications, the *National Lampoon* people, which was right around the corner from us. They started publishing *Heavy Metal*. Then Stan was all hot for us to do something, something more story driven with less sex and violence. We cooked up the idea of coming up with this softer *Heavy Metal* [*Epic Illustrated*] with more emphasis on story.

Before Archie started on it, and I was temporarily trying to keep it moving, I called Frank Frazetta to see if I could get a cover for the first issue. Because that would be really cool. Ellie Frazetta was the gatekeeper. She answers the phone. I said, "Hi, I'm Jim Shooter from Marvel Comics." Not interested. Click. I told Archie, "Geez, before you got here, we were talking about trying to get Frazetta on the covers. I tried to call, and she hung up on me." He says, "Oh, I'll call her. . . . Hey Ellie, it's Archie." They chat for a while, and he agrees to two covers. Everybody loved Archie. He knew everybody. This was the right move. You know, if you get Archie, stay the hell out of his way.

Dominick: Since Epic was a creator-owned line, it required less editing, right? It was more hands-off.

JS: It was more hands-off. That was one thing Archie was terrific at. A creator would come in, and, without the guy feeling oppressed, Archie would help him get his points across. Archie was pretty good at picking good guys. He was perfect for that because he would work with these creators who were guns you couldn't aim, and he'd get them to nudge the gun a little bit this way.

Jason: You created a slew of characters that were either completely unfamiliar or new to readers, from New Universe to VALIANT to Broadway Comics and also the Gold Key revival at Dark Horse. It's throughout your career.

Eric: Then you had the Big Bang too, the idea that you would start over with a clean slate.

Jason: You've had the chance to put these ideas in motion. It sounds like that's maybe one of the key things you want a writer to know these days, that they need to get the reader engaged in creating a coherent world but also to give the reader entry points.

JS: DC, when they announced the New 52, it was all about how the start of the DC Universe again would give readers an entry point to the DC Universe. I wrote on my blog in big, red letters: "Every issue should be an entry point!" Every one. It was with Stan's stuff, and I tried with mine. One of the troubles I've had, since I'm not editor-in-chief anymore, is I don't really have much control over the art. You should see my scripts; they're like telephone books. They're all full of reference. A lot of photo reference. Then still the artist draws whatever he wants. Sometimes I'm counting on the picture to tell part of the story, and it isn't there.

I had this artist on *Turok* [Eduardo Francisco]. He's good. He's a talented guy. He's also Brazilian. He didn't speak a word of English. Chris Warren, the editor at Dark Horse, said, "It's okay; I've got a translator. It's going to be fine." I'm writing all this fight choreography and stuff. Then I found out from Chris that he found out that the translator would read all this stuff and tell Eduardo, "They fight." Is it his fault? No. Basically it was a failure to communicate. To the best of my ability, I try to do all that stuff. Sometimes it doesn't happen.

Eric: In most of your interviews, your own work tends to get glossed over. Is there any one work of yours that you find to be the most personal?

JS: This sounds like a cop-out, probably. Basically I find that whatever I'm writing at the time—because I devote myself to it and research it—that becomes the most interesting thing in the world to me. Nothing else. If I'm writing *Captain America*, then it's the greatest character I ever invented. I'm loving it, and I can't understand how any character could compare to it. Then the next week I'm writing *Spider-Man*; I feel the same way. I get this immersion in it, and that's the only way I can do it. Maybe other people can sit there and calmly

From *Harbinger* 1 (1992). Art by David Lapham and John Dixon. © 1992 VALIANT.

type this stuff. I'm one of those people who'll put "Flight of the Valkyries" on when I'm writing a fight scene to get the mood going.

I guess the first seven issues of *Harbinger* is kind of the mark. I liked that. I had good art. I had David Lapham. At that time, he couldn't draw like Neal. He couldn't draw that well but, boy, could he tell a story. Boy, could he deal with the subtleties. I'd ask him for an expression or an emotion, and he could do it.

When I do my storytelling lecture, I'll show somebody something, and I'll cover the balloon. I'll say, "What's this person saying?" If it's Kirby, you know exactly what they're saying. But if it's not Kirby, it's just a face.

Jason: One of the beauties of the first seven issues of *Harbinger*, really all the way up to and including *Unity*, was that these characters really grow and change. You can see an arc develop for them. That makes for intriguing characters.

JS: One of the things I decided to do at VALIANT is I was going to do a kind of *Gasoline Alley* thing. At Marvel, I inherited it, but some things there were not wise to change. Some of the characters existed timelessly. If Spider-Man really had that many battles, he would be 132 years old. We did evolve them slowly. I kept telling people, "Develop them inward. Don't keep killing Aunt May and having Jonah Jameson growing horns. Just do things that enrich the characters as opposed to—You have to move them forward all the time." That's Marvel.

But now I'm building my own company, and I'm going to do the *Gasoline Alley* thing. Everything has a day and a time. I said to myself there are a couple of characters here. It's really all about their own personal interior narrative. Like Solar, his point of view is what makes this interesting to me. I'm going to use captions for those, for his thoughts. Other than that, I'm not going to use captions. There were a couple cases where I had to but very few. I kept the captions down to "Where are we?" "What time is it?" "What day is it?" I can't even think of an exception—I hope there isn't an exception. I wanted to do that.

In VALIANT, it was proper for the characters to continue evolving at what I considered a normal pace. I like that. I thought that was good.

Eric: You introduced real time with New Universe.
JS: I tried to do it there. That was too hard. New Universe was a disaster. It was dead on the ground when it started because it was another one of those deals where I got called upstairs. With Nancy Allen, promotions, the licensing

people, other executive types. The discussion was "what are we going to do in terms of our twenty-fifth anniversary?" They're all like, "Well, Jim?" One of the first things I said is "I have talked about this Big Bang thing, and, if DC doesn't want to do it, we could do it." The circulation guy looks at me and says, "We've got something that's selling gangbusters for 70 percent of the market, and you want to stop it and start over?" I got shouted down. I said, "It's not as important for us as it is for DC. We're okay. Why don't we create a new universe? Celebrate the birth of this one with the birth of another one." They liked that.

I had about $120,000 to develop the characters. We were going to guarantee royalties because why would someone like Walt leave *Thor*, where he knows he's going to get royalties, and do something where he's not sure what's going to happen. They were going to put money into it because we were making so much money. Fine. We start on it. Then not too long after that, that's when they made the move to start selling the company. I get called upstairs. My budget's cut—badly. A week later, I'm called upstairs again. My budget is eliminated. I say, "You mean, you don't want to do this?" They said, "No, you have to do it. You have to do it with staff people." If you look at a lot of the New Universe stuff, it's assistant editors, Archie Goodwin. New artists you've never heard of, some of whom turned out to be Whilce Portacio and some of whom were Mark Texeira. It was a sinking ship, and everyone knew it.

Eric: It was all part of the company's plan to make Marvel look more profitable than it was, so they could sell it.

JS: When you're going to sell a company, every penny on the bottom line, you get a multiple. All of a sudden they're counting paperclips every night. It went from "let's spend money and build something else great that makes lots of money" to "let's not spend a dime because we want to protect that bottom line. We got a lot of money coming in. Let's not spend any." Basically, I still had to do it, but I had to do it on a shoestring.

I was doing this character called the Star Brand. Archie gave me that name. I did the rest. I'm writing the plots for this, and John Romita Jr., who was doing *Iron Man*, comes in and says "I want to draw your book." I said, "You don't want to do this. You're making good money. Stay where you are." He says, "No, I want to draw your book." I said, "You're out of your mind." He said, "Give me a plot." Later that day, I get a call from Al Williamson. He says, "I want to ink your book." I said, "You guys are nuts." He said, "Naw, I want to work with John and you." I had great art. I had John Romita and Williamson. It turned out to be a good combination. They came to my rescue a little. A lot of people thought that I pulled rank and used my authority to get these artists.

Jason: By common acclaim and my opinion, that was the best or one of the best of the New Universe titles. One of the reasons was that it felt like a really personal project for you. It was one of the few ideas that you had for the New Universe titles that was delivered in the form you wanted.

JS: Everything I do, I give it my best shot. I was doing my best, and I had good people to work with. Then that stuff started coming in, and I'm looking at it. It's amateur art, and the writing is by assistant editors. We were so dead. But the thing is, at that time not only were they starting to sell the company, and therefore got cheap on me, they also got cheap on everything. They cashed everybody out of the pension fund. They stopped the 401k program where they put in matching money. They changed the insurance. We had decent insurance before. We were self-insured, and they changed it to some crummy HMO. They were being as cheap as they could in every way they could. They were basically selling the people down the river.

At one point, Galton, Kaplan, and [Executive Vice President, Cadence Industries Joe] Calamari called me into this meeting, and they'd decided that they were going to stop paying royalties that month. That means that nine months of work by people that thought they were getting paid royalties did not get it. It got ugly. I threatened a class action lawsuit. I said, "I'm going to go to a lawyer, and we're all going to sue you." They caved on that. That was one of the few things that I won. That meant that they didn't like me very much.

All of a sudden, Carol Kalish was very important because they didn't know anything about the comics. They had to rely on me for that. She seemed to know comics pretty well. She became the fair-haired child.

They started to rely more on Carol Kalish's point of view and then they got [Tom] DeFalco. They figured, "He's been working with Jim for a long time, and he could probably do it." I can't get anywhere up there. They're, at that point, trying to ruin me. Galton said, "Just stay with me until we complete this sale. I swear to you. As soon as this sale is done and we're safe, we'll pay these guys. We'll take care of all this stuff. We'll make it right." I said, "All right." He had never actively lied to me before. I will quote what he said on the day that the sale was complete. I said, "It's time to start taking care of this stuff." He said, "Fuck you." That was that.[2]

Around the time they decided they were going to go ahead and try to sell Marvel, I met this guy named Mercer Mayer [best known as a children's author and illustrator]. He owned a company called Angelsoft [gaming company founded by Mayer and John R. Sansevere]. I was at the AV day, and he had a booth. I'm walking around, and there he is. He had one of those deals where they had a TV camera filming people as they walk by, and then they can see themselves on the TV. I'm walking by, and I'm looking at myself—looking at the camera, looking at myself. He said, "What's wrong with you?" I said, "It's taking a picture of me." He said, "No shit." I said, "It's color separating. You see; it takes the picture, and it makes it into little dots." He said, "Yeah, so?" I said, "Why can't we do that with comics? Why don't we take the art, have a camera like that—instead of it being on a TV screen, have it make film. You have to obviously go to RGB from the light to the pigments. That could be done. That's math." He's like, "You're crazy. That can't be done." I said, "All right. You're the software expert." Two weeks later, he called, and he says, "I can do that." I said, "Really?" He says, "You've got to come up here. I've got to show you this."

Mike Hobson and I went up to his place in Connecticut someplace. He's got all these blackboards and charts, pads and stuff. He says, "I can do this. I don't even have to invent anything." He said, "I have to do the software, but, basically, all the equipment exists. It's just a matter of sticking it all together." I said, "What would the cost per page be?," because at that time our camera separation costs were in the thousands of dollars. Our regular page cost was $175 or something like that. He said, "Cost of the film, cost of the electricity, and somebody to watch the machine." I said, "We could color separate our books for a $1,000 a year." He said, "Pretty much." I said, "Great."

We went back and talked to Galton. This is just before they decided to sell the company. We were ready to buy that equipment and be partners with him, doing color separation not only for ourselves, but to do it for other people and charge them enough to make money for it. It was going to take $300,000, which for Marvel, easy check. No problem. We decided to do that. Then, when they decided to sell the company, they thought, "Why are we investing in the future of a company that we are not going to be in?" I got called into another meeting. I was told what they were going to do was they were going to turn the project over to World Color Press. Let them do it. They turned it over to World Color Press.

I remember there was a meeting in Danny Crespi's office. The people from World Color Press came. It was Bob somebody from World Color Press. Ed Whitbread, who ran the hand separation operation up in Connecticut. While they were explaining all this to him, he was crying because he thought it was the end of his career. Because it's over, right? They took over. I think Mercer dropped out. They didn't do it the way that I wanted. They started doing polygon shapes and filling them in. They did it differently, but they did shift from hand separation to computer separation. There was a company in Ireland that did it, too. Then the advances in scanning equipment over the course of a few years made the Mercer Mayer idea obsolete. But we were going to do that, and that all blew up and was turned over to World Color.

Jason: Shortly before you left Marvel, you had a fateful meeting with Steve Massarsky that changed your next few years.

JS: What happened was Galton hated me. Calamari didn't like me. Kaplan liked me but realized that I was persona non grata. But the people who didn't stop thinking I was great were the licensing people because I kept making them all these deals. They would take me to all these meetings, and I would sell the thing because they didn't know that they didn't own Wonder Woman. They liked me.

Around the time I was leaving, when I was about to be fired, that's when I met Massarsky, who had been a road manager for the Allman brothers. He was a lawyer, too. He did legal work for them. He did legal work for Bob Marley and his kid. He did Aerosmith. He did Cyndi Lauper. Having been a road show manager, he thought, "Why don't I do a touring show?" He was looking for something he can get rights to. He had a partner at a company called TM Productions, a shell company. He had some money from a partner and went to Marvel. He wanted to get the live-action rights for an arena show that he would take around the country for Marvel characters and was stupefied when they offered all Marvel characters—all—for two years for $25,000. He said, "Oh, that's a lot, but sure."

While he was talking to them, he was talking to licensing people. He was saying, "I can't just find some writer. I've got to find somebody who knows the characters. Do you have anybody that I can use?" The licensing people told him—and I've heard this both from him and from them—"Get Jim to do it. If he does it, it's automatically approved. It'll be great. You can't go wrong. He's our editor. He's a genius. It's going to be great." I wasn't, but that's what they said. Sure enough, he comes in and he signs the deal. He says, "I'd like to meet this Jim Shooter guy." They say, "Oh, we fired him yesterday." "What?" "But still, go get him, and he'll do a good job for you. Guarantee, if he does it, it'll be right. There won't be any approval process problems." He called me up and asked me if I would write an arena show. I said, "Eh, I don't know. I've never actually seen an arena show." He paid for me to go see *Thundercats*, which also had in it Gumby and Pokey. They're all on roller skates. It was the stupidest thing I ever saw in my life. I call him, and I say, "I can't do this. I couldn't do this on the worst day of my life." He said, "Why not?" I say, "It's stupid." He says, "I know. A lot of these are like Bugs Bunny jumping up and down on a trampoline to the tune of 'Beat It.' I don't want to do that. I want to do *The*

Wizard of Oz with Marvel characters—something like that." I said, "Now you're talking."

He paid me $25,000 for it. I wrote a script called *Spider-Man and the League of Doom.* This took some months of course. He takes it to Marvel for approval, and they reject it because the licensing people took it downstairs and gave it to Tom DeFalco to review. DeFalco rejects it because my name was attached. At first, when I got fired and they gave DeFalco the job, for two weeks, he was calling me up in the middle of the day, asking me what to do or telling me he felt funny because he was sitting in my chair, and it was really my job. He wasn't up to it and this and that. I'm like, "It's okay, do what you do. You'll be fine. If you have a question, call me."

Then one day, I get a call from Stan. Stan is like—he was all tragic—"You're the best we ever had. I'm so sorry it happened." All to do with the sale of the company. I was all, "Nothing much could be done about it." Ten minutes later, DeFalco calls me. He says, "Oh my God! I just got this call from Stan. He thinks I'm doing such a great job. He's always thought I was terrific." I never got another call from Tom. When I did this thing, I don't know why he suddenly had this thing. Okay, fine, now you're the editor-in-chief. Why are you mad at me? He rejects it.

Massarsky asks if we can have a meeting. It's Massarsky, me, DeFalco, Gruenwald, who was the encyclopedic guy, and the licensing guy whose name I think was McKenzie. We're sitting there, and Massarsky says, "Walk us through this. Tell us what you don't like." The marketing guy starts talking about things that have to do with stagecraft. Massarsky says, "Whoa—whoa. That's not for you. You tell us about what your objections are to our use of Marvel characters. You're not going to tell me you know more than the director I'm going to hire about how this is staged." He's looking for things, and he says, "Oh, these characters aren't introduced." I say, "Like who?" He names a character. I say, "Page 16." "What about this one?" "Page 26." I'm like, "What the hell's wrong with you?" Finally, he comes to this thing. He says, "This character says he saw Spider-Man pick up a bus once. Spider-Man can't pick up a bus." I say, "First of all, it's a civilian talking. Maybe they're exaggerating. Second, have you ever looked at the Spider-Man Sunday strip, upon which Spider-Man has been picking up a bus for the last fifteen years in the lead panel?" He says, "I don't care. He still can't lift a bus." I say, "Okay, I'll change it to a car. Is that all right? A car? Is that good? Fine." McKenzie says, "You know what—this meeting's over." We walk out, we go to his office, and he signs the approval. He says, "I'm never going to show anything to that asshole again." It's like, okay, fine.

A couple guys like [Jim] Salicrup—they called me up and asked me to do some work. Then, eventually, I was told I wasn't welcome there. I did one story for Salicrup. It was a fill-in *Spider-Man*. I managed to burn my bridges there pretty good.

Dominick: Is there anything that you would have done differently in your last couple years at Marvel?

JS: No. I wish I was smarter. I wish I was faster. I wish I could get it done better than I did. I did the best I could. At each point along the way, I tried to do the right thing. Sometimes doing the right thing wasn't very popular with the people upstairs. They managed to make me unpopular with the people downstairs.

Toward the end, in the last couple months, I was so busy fighting with them and trying to do the things I had to do and going on these licensing trips and stuff that I got out of touch with what was going on on my own floor. I had seventy-five people working for me. Right toward the end, I remember looking around. I remember looking in offices, and there were people I don't know: "Who are you?" "I'm the new editor." They started hiring people without my knowledge. Bob Harras is suddenly promoted to something or other. All this stuff is going on. Basically they squeezed me. By the time I was fired, I didn't even know some of the people who worked there.

Jason: Was that part of why it was so important for you to have a cohesive group at VALIANT with the Nob Row that was in a big, open space?

JS: It was important to me to earn a living. I went about it the best way that I could. That open space just happened. We rented this loft space, 60' by 40'. I liked it. I liked the idea that we could shout out—I'd say, "I need the name for a girl." "Shaniqua!"—stuff like that. I didn't want to use Shaniqua, but the artist who gave it to me, it was his daughter's name. I couldn't say, "Nah, it's no good!"

Eric: In a 1994 *Wizard* magazine article Massarsky is quoted as saying, "In reality, we were never in the final bidding to purchase Marvel in 1989." Can you share your side of the story of that bid?

JS: It doesn't necessarily mean that he's lying. The thing is when I got thrown out of Marvel, I still kept track of it in the newspapers, the *Wall Street Journal*. I was probably the only creative guy in comics who ever read the *Wall Street Journal*. I started keeping track of it. I also knew a lot about what had been going on there. This was back in the junk bond era. New World Pictures, which had been New World Entertainment, had raised $361 million in high-interest junk bond money. Then they went out and started buying stuff, including Marvel. Most of what they bought turned to disasters. Marvel wasn't doing so well for a little while there—not that it was terrible. They fell off the top there a little bit.

I'm keeping track of this, and I realize that New World is losing a million dollars a day. That means that they've got not that much life left before they're broke—not Marvel—New World. I talked to a friend of mine who's knowledgeable about this kind of thing. He said, "You should talk to Jim Custer. He's a friend of mine who works at Chase." I say, "Okay." I talk to him after work–it was a little private meeting. He said, "Maybe it would be possible to put together a bid. It's possible that Chase might be interested in helping." I said, "All right." I thought about it and talked to my friend, Clark, who is knowledgeable. I decided—I got a high school education. I went to walk in there and tell them, "I'm going to tell them I'm going to buy this company." I thought I'd better have some support troops.

I knew Massarsky from the arena show thing. Up until that point, I thought he was an honorable guy. He told me his various adventures, and he seemed very genuine. I met some of his friends. We went backstage at an Aerosmith concert together. Everybody seemed to know him. I thought he was an okay guy. I asked him, "Are you interested in making a run at Marvel?" He said, "We have to get a financial guy." I said, "That's next on my list." My friend, Clark, introduced me to his uncle, who was a senior financial officer at Time Inc., named Winston Fowlkes. He had just taken an early retirement and had a nice package. We became the Marvel Acquisition Partners. We went and met with Chase. Sure enough, Chase agreed to be our financial advisor and our lending partner definitely. Then we needed an equity partner. We went through a number of tries with this one and that one that didn't work out. We'd meet. We'd think we'd have a deal. Then they'd say something that was unacceptable to us. We ended up with a company called Shenkman Capital.

It was an eleventh hour deal, but we'd finally found somebody who was willing to go in with us. All right. Chase had a problem because they were also doing business with [fellow competitor for Marvel purchase Ron] Perelman. They had to do what they call a Chinese wall, keeping those guys over there and us over here.

At first, we made an offer, and we were told, "Not for sale." The Chase guys were like, Chinese wall my ass. Wink-wink, nudge-nudge, it's for sale. We persisted. Then we were told that they were going to have an auction. Fine. We pursued it with Chase. I was told that it was a big enough deal that I would have to get the approval of Tom Reifenheiser, who's the head of media and entertainment for Chase.

I'm summoned to lunch at this big round table. There's Reifenheiser and the bankers we've been working with. Winston was there with me. Massarsky wasn't. I think there were eight of us. I go in, and I was, like, thinking that Winston would sit next to Reifenheiser. Winston's like, "No, sit over there." "Okay." I sit beside Reifenheiser. We're having lunch. He's talking about the Yankees and the Mets and "Where are you from?" We're just talking and stuff, "How'd you get into this?" He's asking me about Marvel and the studio and what were they thinking with that. I'm talking with him, then lunch is over, everybody gets up, and we're walking out. We get to the elevator lobby. He's going up. We're going down. He sticks out his hand. He says, "You can count on our support." That meant $75 million. He gets in the elevator. I say, "Winston, what just—" He says, "Shut up. Shut up. Don't say anything until we're out of here." I say, "Okay." It could be wired. I don't know. We get out, and we're far away from the building. He says, "Feel your calluses." You know the Disney story? Walt Disney went to Bank of America to borrow the money to launch his studio. The guy felt his calluses from where he held the pen, and that's why he gave him the loan. I said, "How?" He said, "Without you even realizing it, he had you explaining animation, accounting, production, editorial, licensing." He says, "You pretty much explained everything to him: marketing, promotions." I learned a lot of that from Mort. Winston said, "I heard you explaining animation to Reifenheiser." He says, "Reifenheiser knows more about animation than you ever will in your life. He wanted to see what you knew. He was pretending he didn't know anything." I didn't even realize he was doing it. Boy, he was smooth.

Then we had them. We eventually got Shenkman Capital—at the last minute. We put in a bid. Our bid was $81 million. There were nine bidders, except that eight of them dropped out. We were the only bidder. The reason I know they dropped out is because every one of them called me. Because they didn't have management, they all called me. When they couldn't get me, they dropped out. All of them. We were the only bid, so we won. Winston and I and the Shenkman guy went. We signed a letter with them that bound us, but it had an out for them. For a week, we thought we won.

Then one morning, Winston called and said, "Have you read the *Journal*?" I said, "No, I have not. You woke me up." He said, "Perelman bought Marvel. He was an insider at the selling company—20 percent of New World. In order for him to buy it, he needed an arm's length bid, which we provided." They just needed a stalking horse. We went through the whole auction—it wasn't like—

Jason: Which is why they beat you by a million and a half dollars or something.

JS: Oh, they paid $82-and-a-half million. However, as part of the deal, Perelman was holding $12 million worth of worthless paper from New World that was redeemed at face value. He actually paid $70 million. On top of that, he borrowed $75 million. He actually put $5 million in his pocket—and had horrible comics.

I know some of this stuff because, shortly after that, Bill Bevins, [Perelman's] CEO, interviewed me to be management and to come in as president. We were talking about it. I said, "A lot of people here don't like me. You might want to consider that." He said, "As far as I'm concerned, you were the editor-in-chief. If they didn't like it, that meant you were doing your job. You've got to tell these guys *no* sometimes. They don't like to hear that word. Not talking about the downstairs anymore. What would happen if you walked in there as the president?" I said, "Someone would leave. They would jump out the window. Some would run, and some I would fire." He said, "I'll tell you this." This is a quote, "If all the Marvel executive staff drowned in the East River today, it'd be a week before anyone noticed. It's the worst collection of losers I've ever seen in my life. However, we're going to go public. If we start with a bloodbath, that doesn't look good." The same thing that [New World Pictures President Bob] Rehme told me, more or less. He said, "But maybe down the road, we're getting rid of all these people. We're going to filter in our own people." That's what Rehme said, exactly the same thing. It must be an MO. They did. Eventually, they got rid of Galton and brought in Terry Stewart.

I used to run into Barry Kaplan on my way to VALIANT because he would come from the PATH Train from New Jersey. He was like, "Things are great. This is terrific. They gave me $3 million! They're doing all this great stuff!" Then one day I meet him, and he looks all, like, shell-shocked. I ask him, "What happened?" He says, "I went into work yesterday, and my passcodes didn't work. They were putting someone else in my office. I was moved to this little room." I knew exactly which room. It was right beside where the lawyer was. He said, "I can't even get into the computer system. I don't have a job. I have a contract for another year, but I don't have a job." I said, "Oh, well." I didn't want to say I wasn't surprised, but I wasn't.

To Barry's credit, he made himself a job. He realized that no one was taking care of the custom comics. He started doing that. He started hunting down custom-comics deals. He hustled his butt, got them some deals, and did business for them. When his contract expired, they got rid of him. They actually did filter their people in. They got rid of the deadwood. Mission accomplished, I guess.

I ran into Terry Stewart in Frankfurt. I guess I was at VALIANT at that time. In 1990, he had started *Spider-Man* over from number one. The next year, they published *X-Men* and *X-Force*. I ran into him there. He was busy flirting with Heike, who was a girl who worked at my friend Wolfgang's booth. He was annoyed when I interrupted. Then he saw my name tag. He says, "I feel like I won the lottery two times in a row. First with *Spider-Man* last year,[3] and this year with the X books. You're supposed to be the big comics guru. Now what do we do?" I said, "Punt, because you've got nothing left. You've now pulled all the easy triggers. You can get small bumps like that, but you've used all the big ones. The only thing you can do is you've got to create things. But frankly you don't have the horsepower because you lost all your good creators." He had systematically driven them away: Claremont—Byrne was gone—Stern; Michelinie, the Simonsons, Hama. Anybody who was any good, who was likely to create something, they weren't there anymore.

Jason: Then they lost the younger creators, too.

JS: He said, "I've got that covered. Stan is creating something." Stan was the greatest ever for a long time in the '60s. He can't do anything. He said, "Oh, yeah. He's doing this great new thing for us." I said, "Tell me about it." He says, "It's called Marvel 2099." I said, "It's like Marvel, but it's a hundred years from now." He said, "Yeah." I said, "You're going to have a Spider-Man? That's derivative. You're not creating anything. That's all you guys do. You keep playing with the same toys. You're going to have to create something." He said, "It's going to be a hit." Of course, like anything Marvel does . . . it crashed and burned. So predictable.

Jason: The stuff with VALIANT, DEFIANT, and Broadway was an attempt to get away from that.

JS: I just wanted to make a living. I just wanted to do it well.

Here's another thing, back when I was at Marvel, before they decided to sell the company, they went through several suitors, one of whom was Western Publishing, run by Richard Bernstein [chair of Western Publishing, 1984–1996]. He was serious. He actually carried out the whole due diligence process and was on the verge of buying Marvel. He had had several meetings with me as part of due diligence. At the last meeting, he said to me, "The more I learn about this place, the more I feel like I'm buying you and a bunch of used furniture." Now, by me, he meant the creative guys. You plural.

It went down to the wire. The thing is, Shelly Feinberg and Galton and the rest of the six guys who own Marvel, they took it private. Shelly is a major weasel. Bernstein told me, and I can just picture it, that every time they would have it all settled, Shelly would come up. He wants a nickel more, a nickel more. They were having what was supposed to be the final meeting for the third try. He starts this nickel-more things once again. Bernstein said, "That's it, I'm done." He walked out. He said, "It cost me $500,000 in lawyers and accountants, and I walked away from it."

That's why, when I was out of Marvel and I was a pariah and no one would hire me, I went to Bernstein. He liked me. I went to him. He was happy to see me. I sat in his office, and I said, "Are you aware that you own some comic book characters?" He said, "No, I do?" I said, "Yeah. They're very good ones. I would really like to get my hands on them and publish them." He says, "We'll license them to you. Do you have a publishing company?" I said, "Not yet." He said, "Oh, okay, I tell you what—we'll start a company." We went through this little dance for a while where he wanted to get Western to restart Gold Key Comics. His people didn't want to do it. His upper management people resisted it tooth and nail. He told me, "This isn't worth it. If we do this and these guys are all against it from the get go, it's not going to work." He says, "Tell you what: You go start a company, and when you're ready, you call me. I will hold those characters for you."

He held them for two years. This was when comics were going through another little boom. He got calls from Mike Richardson. He got calls from Marvel and DC, making him offers for this stuff. His licensing guy used to call me every week. "Are you sure you're going to do this? I've got all of these offers. I could be making a lot of money." I said, "Yes, I'm going to do this."

It took two years, and there was some dancing in between. We tried to buy Harvey. They couldn't prove they owned what they were selling. This guy out in California bought it anyway. Got together Stan Weston and some of his guys, and they couldn't make it happen. I finally found this company, Triumph Capital, and they ended up with a venture capital company that put up enough capital for us to start. That happened just before the ABA [American Booksellers' Association annual conference], which was late May, I guess. I was going to ABA. I went there. I somehow knew that Bernstein was going to be there. I walk there, and he says, "How are you, Jim?" I say to him, "I'm ready." He tells his licensing guy, "Sit down with him and make a deal. Do anything he wants. He'll tell you what the deal is, you just do it." We sat down. And I dictated a deal to him, but it was fair. You couldn't frontload any expenses. There were small advances and guarantees, bigger on the back end. But if I make it a hit, you'll make a lot of money. We licensed it, and that was going to be the basis. Then we started the company.

Jason: You started with the Nintendo and wrestling comics. That was a fiasco.

JS: I started with the comics I set out to do. Then Massarsky got himself a gig as the entertainment lawyer for Nintendo. Meanwhile, he was supposed to have given up his law practice. However, shortly after we started, he informed me that he was sleeping with the venture capitalist, whose name was Melanie Okun. Literally in bed with her, and they got married eventually. All of a sudden, he's not my partner. He's her partner. My other partner, Winston, objected that this was a conflict. They convened the board. They wanted to fire him, but they couldn't do it without me. I said, "I'm not going to go along with it." They said, "We're going to close the whole thing down." I said, "You can close the whole thing down." They said, "Then you'll owe us your $50,000 guarantee. You'll owe us this amount." "Sue me. What have I got? Nothing. Take it all." They said, "What do you want?" I said, "Winston tells me he's okay with it, that he's happy and satisfied on the financial side, I have to accept that. On the other hand, until he tells me he's happy, I'm not going to vote for it."

They went into a negotiation with him. He negotiated himself a wonderful deal. He ended up keeping half of his stock. Me, Massarsky, and him—we each had 20 percent, so he kept 10 percent, unrestricted. He had no vote, but it was unrestricted stock. He had a three year contract, and they paid out his contract. Then, just to piss them off, he filed for unemployment. Winston was a very wealthy man, but did it to stick it to them.

Jason: That means he made money when VALIANT was eventually sold to Acclaim.

JS: Oh, yeah. He made more than Massarsky because when it sold to Acclaim, it was sold for $65 million of Acclaim stock. But Acclaim's stock—because they bought VALIANT, it rose. He was able to sell at the peak of the market. Just before they sold it, they dividended themselves out of about $20 to $30 million worth of cash. He got a piece of that, too. He sold at the peak of the market. Meanwhile, Massarsky and the others, they vested over five years. By the time it got to the point that they were selling much of their stock, their price had plummeted. Acclaim actually went out of business.

Massarsky made millions of dollars, but Winston made more, which delighted him. He was so happy with that because Massarsky sleeping with Melanie was what got Winston out of there. When Winston told me he had negotiated a great deal and he was happy, I said, "Yeah, okay."

Jason: Once you'd cleared out the Nintendo/WWF comics, you were finally able to do the comics that you really want to do, following the pattern of the New Universe.

JS: Right, Massarsky became the entertainment lawyer for Nintendo and made a deal with himself. He was on both sides of the table. All of a sudden, this little, tiny, undercapitalized company of mine . . . we're giving $300,000 to Nintendo for licensing these characters I don't want. But he got paid well, so he didn't give a shit.

Then, same deal with the wrestling. We met the people at the LCI whom I knew. They represented wrestling, and he was able to get in touch with the wrestling people. Before you know it, he's representing them for media and entertainment. He does it again, and he makes a deal with himself! He gets paid a lot of money. All of a sudden, my capital is going to advances for shit I can't sell.

We did the best we could. I would have quit, but the fact is, number one, where am I going to go? Nobody wanted me. Number two, the only people who would come to work for me were friends. JayJay Jackson, Don Perlin. I told Don, "Don't leave Marvel. God, you're an old guy. If this doesn't work out, what are you going to do? There, you get paid well. It's secure." He said, "Ah, I'm sick of that place. I want to work with you."

JayJay Jackson, Debbie Fix, and a couple other people I knew came with me. Then Bob Layton. We were in the new office so that would have to be six, seven months into it. His contract expired with Marvel, and they didn't want him. Marvel had had their fill of him. He had previously burned bridges at DC, so he had no place to go. He shows up on my doorstep with a suitcase and not a dime in his pocket. I said, "You can ink for us, but you'll have to do it on staff and just flat rate. You show up every day. You get paid what you get paid." We paid him reasonably, but we didn't have a lot of money. He came in. When Perlin came in, I thought, "Great. He's an adult. He's a regular guy." My plan was that he was going to run the bullpen, and Bob was going to be a staff artist. Guess what? Perlin didn't turn out to be really good at the bullpen. It was too confusing for him. What he wanted to do was sit there and draw. But Bob actually had a knack for keeping the trains running on time. Totally organically, nobody decreed it, they shifted jobs. That worked out pretty well, and Bob was still doing some inking.

Then we had this little crew. But the thing was that, if I quit, they'd close the place, and all these people would be out of work. Because they'd dared to work with me, they would be unemployable. They were blacklisted. Ralph Macchio over at Marvel had his wall—Jim Shooter's Wall of Shame. You know, with all the enemies on it.

Jason: Like Nixon's enemies list?

JS: Yeah. My plan was . . . so, what am I going to do? I'm doing all this crap that we don't want to do. I've got all these people here. They're depending on me. There's Massarsky and his wife-to-be. They want money. They don't give a shit about comics. What if I make this successful? What if I make a lot of money? What if, therefore, I can go back to Reifenheiser and say, "I want to buy these turkeys out?" It seemed like a plan. All I had to work with was Nintendo and wrestling. I did the best I could with it. We did some okay stuff.

Nintendo reneged on everything they promised us. They were going to give us their mailing list. They were going to have us packaged with their games. They were going to have us on display with their games. No, nothing. The same with wrestling—sell at events, help us promote it, mailing list. They reneged on all of it. I think Massarsky promised it to himself, and then he couldn't deliver. We couldn't really make a go of that stuff. Finally, I got to do my stuff. That was a struggle for a while.

Jason: I recently spoke with Dinesh Shamdasani, who's the current CEO at VALIANT. He was making a strong case that this was really the only set of intellectual properties to come out of the 1990s that still survive today.

JS: Somebody voted *Harbinger* the comic of the decade.

Jason: The Gold Key books did well. *Harbinger, X-O,* and all the books that came around with those seemed to touch a chord.

JS: *Magnus* came out first. It was selling reasonable numbers, like seventy or eighty thousand. *Solar* came out second, and it started at fifty to sixty thousand and then trickled down to forty thousand. *Harbinger* was next. *Harbinger* never did sell well. It started out at thirty, forty thousand and then trickled down. It actually got as low as twenty-six thousand on the fourth issue.

We did *X-O*. It did, like, *Solar* numbers, but then it started to catch on. All of a sudden, things started to take off. We came out with *Shadowman,* and that started doing well. We started out in March of '91. By February '92, we were turning a profit. Then there were a couple months where we broke even. When *Archer and Armstrong* came out, that was a big hit. We made good money on that month. After that was *Unity,* and that's when it really starting rolling. I was making $2 million a month pre-tax!

Jason: The graph of the industry-wide sales is amazing because the industry starts the decade at about $190 million. Then about the time you're talking about, the spike goes way up to about $400 million, industry-wide sales. It continues to go up until the return of *Superman* and then essentially craters out. Of course, you lived all this, so I'm not telling you anything you don't know. By the end of the decade, sales were actually cumulatively lower than they were at the beginning.

JS: From the very peak to the bottom, at least the following year, it went from one hundred percent to eighteen percent.

But the thing with the VALIANT books, we were publishing eight titles a month by the time they got rid of me, and we were making way more pre-tax profit than Marvel was with 156 books. That says something. Part of that spike was VALIANT. Part of it was Image.

Jason: It was a hit with the younger generation. There was a sense of revolution where this is something that our parents don't get, and we like that. This is a new world, and it's throwing away everything that came before. Similarly, when Jim Lee and Rob Liefeld and the rest of the group created Image, it was a sense that "We're casting aside all this stuff. This is a new generation, and we're the new thing." What's interesting is that—a lot of their stuff now, you look at it now, and it's terrible. But you were producing this work that was fundamentally sound.

JS: The thing is, I remember when the Image guys left Marvel. They went off to start their own thing; who do they call? They call me asking, "How do you get lettering done?" They're asking me questions. I talked to a couple of them, but finally I put them on the phone with JayJay Jackson. She explains production to them. We did the same thing with Milestone when they started out. They didn't have a clue. JayJay and I would spend a day in there.

Eric: You should have become a consultant.

JS: Yeah, really. We did it for free. We were having fun.

At VALIANT, we spent all our money on Nintendo and wrestling, and it had gone into Massarsky's pockets. First of all, he did not give up his law practice. He did nothing with VALIANT, except come in every day and do his law stuff. He used our postage meter, which pissed me off.

The thing is, I've got no money. I've got no weapons to fight with except man-hours. I would be the first one there, Debbie would be second, and we would be there until late at night. She was commuting back and forth from Nyack. I, at least, lived in the city. At one point, I counted, and I worked five hundred thirty–something straight days, including Christmas, Thanksgiving, New Year's, everything. My hair got long because I had no time to get a haircut. I was writing most of it, and the only thing I had to fight with was story. I can't get hot artists. I was very lucky that Perlin came because he did a great job. Layton was there because there was no place else for him to go. Windsor-Smith wound up with us because he had also burned his bridges at Marvel and DC. He had no place to go. He knew me, of course, but he also knew Bob, so he turned up . . . other than that, David Lapham.

Eventually, we started getting some guys. But at first we had guys out of the Kubert School. David Lapham—he was delivering newspapers for a living when we got him. He wasn't really good, but like Miller he learned quickly. We had these Kubert guys. We had this new artist named [Joe] Quesada [who later became editor in chief at Marvel], who did *Captain N* for us.

Mostly, we got people no one else wanted. We got Ditko. Ditko came in; he looked miserable and asked, "Do you have any work for me?" I looked at him, "You're Steve Ditko. You're not leaving here without a job."

Eric: You put him on *ROM: Space Knight*, right?
JS: Right. Yeah. I actually got him to come back to Marvel, but one of the problems was that he didn't want to do any of the—

Eric: He didn't want to *Spider-Man*. Right.
JS: Not *Spider-Man*. What he wanted to do was a character with clear morals. If it was a hero, they had to be all noble. Mister A. There is white, and there is black. There is no gray. The only character we could come up with that was noble enough was *ROM*. But he liked that, and he had fun with it. He did great stuff with it, I thought. Then, after I left Marvel, they threw him out. He came, and I would not say hat in hand, but he was not happy. He was really depressed, and he wanted to know if we had any work. I said, "You're not leaving here without a job." He turned out to be really great at the wrestling comics—the good guys, the faces, and the heels: white, black. Then eventually he did Magnus and some other stuff for us. I had to talk him into Magnus being a noble character, but he bought it.

Jason: He did some *Plasm* work, too, right?
JS: He did *Dark Dominion*, but in the middle of that, he quit. I said, "Steve, finish the first book. You can't walk out in the middle." The reason he quit was—he said, "I can't do this." I said, "Why not?" He said, "It's Platonic. I'm Aristotlean." I said, "What? You're going to have to explain that one to me."

He said, "Aristotle believed that what you see is what you get. Plato believed in the real world and the unseen world." He says, "I'm not Platonic. I don't want that." I said, "I talked to you when I was coming up with this book. I asked you all the things you wanted to draw in a comic book. You told me. I pitched this to you. You liked it. Now you're telling me it's too Platonic!" He said, "All right, I'll finish the first one." He did. I guess he did other stuff for us. But at that point, he was getting some stuff from Dark Horse and other places.

We got Ditko. We got Stan Drake. Nobody wanted Stan Drake. Are you kidding me? We got John Dixon, who's Australian. He's a great artist, and nobody wanted him either. I had all these old guys that no one wanted. We had a party one time just for the old guys so the young kids could meet the old guys because the old guys didn't really come into the office. Stan Drake was paying alimony to like five women, and he was like, "I can't. I've got to work every day. I've got all this stuff I've got to do. I'm doing *Blondie*. I'm doing this. I'm doing that. I'm doing your stuff." I said, "Do you eat lunch?" He said, "Yeah." I said, "How about this—I've got a car waiting for you right outside your studio. When it's time to eat lunch, you go and get in the car, which will drive you here. You come up and have lunch with us." I say, "The car is waiting. It takes you back. You lose a half an hour. Come on." He said, "All right, I'll do it." We did that. I did this on my Visa card. This wasn't company-paid.

We have him and all the other guys. I'm leaving some out. Maybe Herb Trimpe was there. There were a few people there maybe that didn't even work for us. Ralph Reese was there. There was a bunch of old guys. The nice thing about the Kubert School kids is they don't know which end of the brush to hold, but, man, Joe made them professional. They respected their elders. If you asked them to do something, they'd say "Yes, sir." Then you'd turn the brush around for them. But the thing is—they didn't come out educated in the craft of it, but Joe taught them to be respectful. All these old guys, they were in pig heaven. They were loving it, getting to meet Stan Drake, for Christ's sake. Ditko wouldn't allow us to take his picture. We took pictures of everybody else. Steve said, "Don't you take my picture." I said, "Relax, it's me you're dealing with. It's okay."

Jason: You had a really great run at VALIANT. The early X-O is really an interesting character, a man lost out of time. The first run of *Rai* is about as dark and as despairing a comic as I have ever read. You really had something going there, and unfortunately, it—

JS: What happened was, Massarsky was married to the venture capitalist. Once we really turned the corner, which was in February, they wanted to sell the company. They were threatening me, saying, "You're $4 million in debt. We're going to shut you down." I said, "I don't believe you. Why would you shut us down when we're finally able to pay you?" We got into this little match. Melanie's brother worked at Allen & Company. Previous to that, he had worked at the IBM pension fund. Melanie and Michael started out working for a bank; I'm not sure which. They used to do two-person teams at this bank, and they did venture stuff and investment banking. They had a string of successes, and they thought, "Why are we doing this for the bank? Let's do this for ourselves."

They went out, and they tried to raise money. They had difficulty until Melanie's brother got IBM to invest $10 million. Once IBM invests $10 million, other people think, "IBM is here." But it was because of the brother. He left there, and he started working at Allen & Company. They said they wanted out, and they said they proposed to sell the company. I said, "Tell me what the terms are. Tell me the deal." They kept not telling me the deal.

But we kept getting taken to lunch by these people from Allen & Company, selling the sizzle that because Allen & Company is involved in entertainment, there will be movies; there will be this; there will be that. They said, "We're involved with Toys 'R' Us, so there will be toy deals." I'm like, "What's the deal? What are the terms?" They said, "It's going to be great; it's going to be great." It's like a soft cram-down is what it's called. They're doing this, and I'm like, "Tell me the terms. Okay, fine, you guys own the majority, and you want to sell. Fine. I want to know what's going to happen to all of us—to me."

Then, they're really starting to cram it down my throat. The deal was going to be that Allen & Company was going to buy a stake in VALIANT, and then they were going to sell it. It came down to this thing where they told me, "If you don't sign these documents by Monday, we're going to close this up." They handed me the documents on Friday evening when I was leaving to go to the Diamond Distributor conference for the weekend, hoping that I wouldn't be able to read the things and that I'd be forced to sign something I didn't read. I'm not signing something I don't read. I did read it. I'm one of those guys who stays up all night and reads it. It's a big, thick contract. It included a ten-year contract for me that specified no salary. It specified no title. It specified no duties. In it, was a section where, if I fail to report to the CEO—who was going to be Massarsky's brother—if I fail to obey the CEO, or if I fail to engender good morale, they could claw back 100 percent of my stock. Hmm. You'll keep me around until you sell the thing for the big flip. The next day I'll piss off somebody, and I'm gone. You get all the stock. On top of that, they had all these reps and warrantees they wanted me to sign that were false. Guess what, if anything ever blows up, it's my fault. I'm CEO and president, and I signed stuff, so it must be my fault. All this stuff.

I have a letter from them. When they first started doing this, they had to give us a letter. To have a clean balance sheet, they had to give us a letter that waived all the events of default. I have that letter. As soon as this started, I took that letter home, along with some other documents. Layton had a key to my place, so I had the locks changed because I didn't trust anyone. By that time, he'd moved into the same building. I took that letter home. I came home the next morning, and you could tell that somebody had been going through all my stuff. I'd done the James Bond thing—I'd left things in a certain way. They'd clearly been trying to find that letter. I had that letter waiving all events of default. If they could get that letter back, they could claim default that stock is worthless, and they could get rid of me. I'm supposed to sign these documents. All these reps and warrantees and the evil, horrible terms. Fuck that noise. My choice is I die today or I help them make a lot of money, and then they kill me. I said, "No." Then they convene the board. They had to add another member to have enough votes to fire me. They had enough votes to add a member, but they didn't have enough to fire me. They add Fred Pierce, and they fired me. I'll never forget: Fred said, "Jim, it's just business." That's his words exactly. I thought, "Oh, okay. I'm fired." When they were firing me, I was sitting there, like, "I don't have to stay up all night tonight" because I was still doing all the work.

They got away with it. They were willing to falsify documents, lie under oath. They sued me. I spent $70,000 defending myself against having to pay my $50,000 guarantee. They didn't care about the $50,000. They spent $140,000 suing me to get $50,000. The reason they did that was because, if they could get the judge to say that there was a default, then that accomplished what they were trying to do, which was to make sure my stock was worthless, so that they could then go ahead and not have to pay me anything. I won that one because I had the letter.

Jason: A lawsuit hampered DEFIANT right from the beginning.
JS: Marvel with the Plasmer thing.

Eric: They even brought a title into print for a few issues.
JS: They had to register their intent to use in England. When we searched it, we didn't come across it. They had the name and nothing else.

It had nothing to do with the American company. Then we did our *Plasm* card set. Our stuff was all created. As a matter of fact, I created them in 1987.

Because when I didn't have anything else to do, I worked on stuff I might sell some day.

We won in court, but the best thing was our lawyers met with their lawyers and worked out a settlement that we would change the name from *Plasm* to *Warriors of Plasm*. We had a document, we signed it, we sent it to them, and they never returned it. A month passes. We concluded that they were going to wait until our book was just about to ship and then get a temporary restraining order. If you do that to a little start-up, you're expecting a big check, and your book is held up, it puts you out of business, which was their goal. I called one of the distributors, and I said, "What can we do?" Marie Jose Danielle said she'd take care of it. She interlaced our books with all the Marvel books—every pallet of them, every pallet of Marvel Comics had *Warriors of Plasm* in it. They could stop our book, but they would have to stop all of theirs. Every single Marvel Comic would not ship.

They withdrew the temporary restraining order, and they went after a temporary injunction. We eventually go to court. The judge was Michael Mukasey.[4] In the morning, he's trying the first World Trade Tower bombers, and in the afternoon, it's comics. There are three tests for a temporary injunction—we won every point of every test. At the end of the trial, he calls their lawyers up. He covers the mic, but I can still hear him, and he says, "If you ever use my court as a business weapon again, you will regret it. You better not appeal." They didn't. They withdrew the suit. It cost me $300,000 to win.

Eric: Was he the one who compared Marvel to Goliath and you to David?
JS: In the opinion.

Jason: The shame is that you get out to the market finally, and it's so depressed that there's not as many buyers.
JS: The month we launched, Bill Schanes guaranteed that we would sell one million copies. We sold six hundred thousand copies, but that was the very moment that the industry fell off the table. Bill was shocked and apologized, saying, "I don't understand. All the orders are down." I said, "I can understand. Everyone's choking on the inventories. They're all stuck with fourteen million copies of *Superman*. You can roll them up and sell them as cord word."

We soldier on for a while. We had an offer from New Line for $9 million, but the guy who put up the money wanted more. It's stupid; we're going to go out of business. Then they go away. Then I get a call from Victor Kaufman [former Tri-Star and Columbia Pictures chair; at the time, president of Savoy Pictures]. The receptionist, Sheila, says "There's a Victor Kaufman on the line. Do you want to talk to him?" I say, "Yes, I will talk to Victor Kaufman!" I talk to him, and he says, "I want to talk to you about buying your company." I say, "Great, when can you meet with me?" He says, "Now. Come on up. Get in a cab."

I go up to his office, and I took Winston, who was my financial guy still, with me. He came back with me in DEFIANT. We go into this conference room. In walks [President and Chief Operating Officer of Savoy Pictures Lewis J.] Korman and Kaufman, and Victor Kaufman says, "Hey, Winston, buddy! How are you doing?" Old buddies. They made us an offer for $11 million. Once again, the venture guy wanted more. He had the sweetest deal in the world, and he kept doing that nickel more, nickel more thing. Victor Kaufman called me up and said, "Come back some day without this idiot." Of course, eventually, they went out of business, too. You can't take $300,000 out of a little start up like that.

Jason: Back in that line of comics, I feel like it was able to achieve some of the potential that you saw in the properties.

JS: *Plasm* came out okay, mostly because of David. I wrote good stuff, I think, but he really made it happen. The first designs he did, I kept telling him "all organic, everything's alive. The rug is alive. The chairs are alive." The first thing he brings back is these guys with these metal guns. I said, "No metal. Everything is alive." Finally, the light bulb comes on. He started doing all this great stuff. He actually started writing it for a while. He got his feet wet. He wasn't great right off the bat, but like Miller he started to develop really quickly.

Other than that, most of what we did was regrettable. *Dark Dominion* had a few moments because we got this guy, J. G. Jones, working on it. He's great. He came to Broadway. He did *Fatale* there. They were good ideas. We didn't have the manpower, the money. I couldn't do another five hundred straight days of staying up all night.

Eric: We all seemed to sense a satirical vein throughout your own work, starting with *Secret Wars II*. It seems to come to fruition with the Broadway material, a self-awareness that was commenting on the medium.

JS: We were making fun of the bad girl stuff. We did a bad girl who couldn't run if she didn't have her high heels on and put her arms over her chest if she was running.

At Broadway, we wrote as a team. I thought, "let's try this like TV writers." We had four people writing, and every once in a while, we'd have a guest person who we called the fifth chair. When you're in a group like that, joking around, we made a little fun of that. We make fun of the Image comics with "Till Death Do Us Part" [storyline in issues 1–5 of *Shadow State* (1996)]. We had a bit of fun.

Page from *Fatale* 1
(1996), art by J. G.
Jones and Frank
McLaughlin. © 1996
Broadway Comics.

Also, in *Secret Wars II*, we had gone through this whole thing with Steve Gerber. In the first issue of *Secret Wars II*, I made fun of Steve. He wrote me a lovely fan letter. It was great. He was actually really pleased with it.

Eric: Actually, it was ironically almost like a Steve Gerber homage because that was something Steve would do. A lot of people missed that. They saw it more as an acidic thing. I saw it as mostly playful.

JS: Steve loved it. Shortly after that Steve settled with Marvel. Part of that was, he was going to write [Howard] the Duck. His first issue of the Duck that he sent me was a scathing attack on anyone else who ever touched the Duck: Claremont, Mantlo, Wolfman. It was not subtle. It was horrible. It was mean-spirited in a big way. It starts out with Howard on that bus with the Kidney

Lady. It starts off with him on the bus, and this gang of thugs—[Bill] Mantlo, Wolfman, Claremont—are punching Howard. Howard somehow recovers, then evil things happen to these evil people. He really makes them evil, and they get their just desserts. I said, "Sorry, Steve. Can't do this. No."

Eric: You probably did him a favor, actually, because part of what's great about his writing was that his satire was nuanced.
JS: This wasn't. This was a sledgehammer. I told him *no*, and then we get into this fight. He decides that he's going to sue Marvel again. One of the things that he brings up is the fact that we lampooned him in *Secret Wars II*. I gave our lawyer the fan letter. End of suit. Shut him up. Oops.

Eric: *Secret Wars II* was a real interesting piece. It was a sequel to one of the most successful comics up to that time.
JS: It did well, too.

Eric: But it was almost the antithesis of the first one. There were no real major battles. It was more philosophical. There was a lot of social satire in it. Were you consciously working against form in that? Did you say, "I'm going to do something completely different"?
JS: Oh, absolutely. Also, when I came up with the branching thing, I wanted to set up stuff for them to solve in their issues. There was enough action, I thought, but that wasn't—it wasn't the Battleworld thing at all. That was on purpose. Some state-wide science fiction New Jersey fan club gave me an award for the best science fiction comics series of the year. Okay.

Actually, the first issue was drawn by Sal Buscema. That's why Sal hates me to this day. I chose him because we needed somebody fast, because they wanted it chop-chop, to make those revenues. I thought, "Who can do this fast enough? Sal. Sal can do this fast enough." I called him up and said, "Look, I've got this project. But this isn't just another comic book. You're going to have to really put your heart into this. I don't want any stock shots. I don't want any shortcuts. It's a lot of characters. The reward is that you'll get really good royalties." I was pretty sure I could guarantee really big royalties. If you spend twice as much time on this, and you get four times the royalties, you're ahead. He said, "Okay. Fine."

I send him the first plot. He does the first issue: absolutely standard, Sal Buscema hack-work. Sal hacked at a very high level because he was really talented. But he churned it out. He did that floor level thing so he didn't have to do perspective. He had all these little stock shot things that he would do. Sal did the whole first issue. I thought, "There's no way I'm letting him do the first issue and get the big royalty check for doing this crappy job. Then having to get somebody else." I scrapped it, and I had [Al] Milgrom do it over. Milgrom is not as good an artist, frankly, but, boy, he worked his ass off. It would have been great to have George Pérez or somebody doing it.

Eric: You were actually never able to get Pérez to work at Marvel.

JS: Pérez worked at Marvel when I started there. DC offered him to come over there and start doing *Justice League*. *Justice League* was his lifelong dream. He'd always dreamed of being on *Justice League*, from a little kid. He apologized, but he said he really wanted to do it. I said, "I get it. I understand. Go ahead with my blessing." He did. Pretty soon after that, he wound up on *Teen Titans* and that took off. Everything was great. But I did work with him for a little while. He did the first couple issues of "The Korvac Saga," which was basically his idea. This is another *Secret Wars* predecessor. He said, "I want to do a story with everyone in it."

Jason: One of the things that jumped out at me about "The Korvac Saga" was the way that you were able to keep the characters clear, put them in situations that made them interesting, and then have the storyline play itself out as part of larger, more complex saga.

JS: There was a lot of good stuff in there, I think. Somebody wrote a scholarly thing about it and sent it to me. He analyzed it like it was a Shakespeare play. A lot of what he noted was, "He got it!" Every once in a while, he'd say the subtlety of, like, this, and I'd say, "Yeah, I meant that."

Jason: Eric brought up *Secret Wars II*, but it leads into what I thought was interesting that spans "The Korvac Saga" and also Erica Pierce in *Unity* and also the latter version of *Solar, Man of the Atom*. Which is the banality of these people who have these amazing powers. *Unity* obviously had these incredibly powerful people, but they are placed in a very normal world. You have Erica Pierce, who seems very banal in her thoughts. Even Star Brand has amazing powers, but he can't get out of his own head. That's a theme that you come back to again and again.

JS: If I do have a theme that comes out a lot, it's probably common people rising to exceptional challenges. My plan for Star Brand was to start him as some clown who's fooling around on his girlfriend and then have him grow into the part, which is what I did with Leeja in *Magnus*. Because, I'm going to do Magnus, so I'm going to do it all my way. I'm going to do what Russ Manning did, and I'm going to take it where I want. When Russ Manning did it, Leeja was a bimbo.

She almost deliberately gets into trouble, so Magnus will come and rescue her. She's impetuous, she's childish. By the end of that story, she's grown up.

I liked to do that. Erica Pierce went through the first thirty-some years of her life being a regular person. She doesn't suddenly decide to build her galactic world ship. She does eventually, but it takes her until the year 4000.

I liked to write about not only common people having to rise to exceptional heroism, but common people given power and then becoming evil. My theory—and I've been saying this for a million years—and now, everybody says it: power doesn't corrupt; power magnifies. If you're a good person—if you're Mother Teresa, and you get power, you're a better Mother Teresa. If you're the average person, you're perhaps self-indulgent. If you're a person like Erica Pierce, who's got issues, then you're a terror. To me, it magnifies who you are because now you're operating on a grander scale—somebody who's powerless and, therefore, relatively benign but is seething inside. Give them power; see what happens. You've got the Molecule Man.

Jason: Not to get too analytical about this, but a lot of your stories about people who have a lot of money reflect that, too. They have this power, and they use it for their own selfish ends.

Tell us how you got involved with *Unity 2000*.

JS: I got a call from this guy Mike Martz, who was working at Acclaim. They were publishing comics. I guess they had bought VALIANT. It had crashed and burned, and they were trying to work with it again—trying to use Shadowman and build something. I don't know who came up with the idea of hiring me, but they realized that I had predicted that Shadowman would die in 1999 in the *Unity* story. What they wanted to do was to clean house in their universe and do another *Unity* and also do the death of Shadowman, as promised.

When I was at VALIANT and all these books started selling huge numbers, I actually had people say to me, "If they keep selling like this, you couldn't possibly cancel it." I said, "Oh, yes, I will. I bet you we will. We will make history, you know: 'Book canceled due to death of character!'—and stick with it. It'll shake everybody up. It'll blow the fans' minds: 'They cancelled a book selling half a million copies because he said so!'"

Jason: That's what happened with *Rai* after number eight.

JS: It wasn't quite the big hit that I was thinking *Shadowman* might be. Because I thought that, if we dare do that, who would dare look way? Number one. Number two—we could do it again. They can't, we can.

When I first started, I couldn't get artists. It was me, fighting with story, keeping people there at all hours of the day and night, fighting with man-hours because we had no money to pay anybody. I drew some stuff—I can't draw—but I drew it because there was no money. I couldn't pay anybody—couldn't get any artists. So, I'm drawing, like, the fifth issue of *Magnus*. Fortunately, between Bob and Don Perlin, they could touch it up a little bit. Bob would ink—he actually inked the faces. If you look at it, anything that's smaller than a big head looks like it was inked by an amateur. The point is that we would have done that. He called me up and said, "Let's do that." I said, "Okay." I wrote a six-issue story. Three actually came out. He said, "Who can we get to draw it?" I said, "I don't know. Seems to me that Starlin's always looking for work." He says, "Oh, Starlin! You could get Starlin?" I said, "I guess so; I'll call him." Sure enough, he was looking for work and was happy to do it. It was a little weird because, with him, I had to do it Marvel-style because he didn't want to be tied down too much. He's good, and he basically did what I wanted. It was kind of a good story, and it was going to accomplish everything that I wanted to accomplish and maybe help them do a relaunch. But they were running out of money, and they were dying. Only three issues came out.

Jason: That was the third revival of the Acclaim Comics line, so it was literally them going down for the third time.

JS: I wrote all the plots in detail. I wrote five of the scripts. Never did write the last script. Got paid for what I did. Then they were gone. But that was the idea. Later, Martz was one of the guys at DC when I worked on *Legion*. He was the editor. That didn't work out. It was terrible. It was ugly.

The thing is, I was writing full scripts for that stuff. Then the artist randomly decides to change things. I go, "Who made him editor? The editor actually read this script and approved it. Why are you changing it?" I've got to tell you—the craft has gone to hell.

Back when I worked in the ancient days of Woody [Wally Wood] and Curt Swan and even lesser lights in that pantheon . . . I'm fourteen, and Woody is listening to me. He's doing what I tell him. I already gave him a rough indication with the layout, but they left space for the copy. Most of them faked in lettering to make sure they left enough room—Curt, especially, because he was a great letterer. These guys now, I give them a description. They draw whatever they damn well please. They put the guy who speaks first on the lower right-hand corner of the panel. There's never time to redraw it, but there's always time for me to rewrite it. Then I've got to rearrange the dialogue so that this guy speaks last. I wrote every book twice. Because I write it, I get it; it's all finished, and there's no time to redraw it or do anything. I have to go through my script and try to cobble it together and make it work. Then if you so much as say anything to these guys, they get all huffy about it. I keep saying it, again and again: clear. Anyone in the world who looks at this image, even if they don't know the characters, they should know, "Oh, that guy hit this guy." But you get stuff that's meaningless. Then they get annoyed when you mention it.

Dominick: Is that a holdover still from the whole Image thing where basically what it looked like mattered more, but the story was irrelevant?

JS: Yeah, but those guys were making pages to sell in the aftermarket. It was all flash and dazzle and not much story. That's another reason, at VALIANT, we tried to go story-intensive because I didn't have the artists to compete with. I couldn't do flash and dazzle. The only thing I had to fight with was story.

I thought about Stan's stuff back when I was a kid, where you'd pick one of those up and it was a lot of story. You felt like it was a movie. It was satisfying. It was clear. I didn't ever feel like I had to stare at and puzzle over what it was. I thought, "If I can, no one else is doing that, so that'll make us stand out. If I can do it well enough, then we win." It took us a year, but we won. We won; I lost.

I was killing myself, and I tried to get other people to write. I tried this lady, Faye Perozich. I ended up having to rewrite a lot of that. It wasn't that good. Then I tried Steve Englehart. That was a disaster because Steve is one of those big guns that you can't aim. He's going to do whatever he wants. I say, "Steve, I'm trying to do continuity here." He said, "Here's how it works. I do whatever I want, and you adjust to me." I said, "No, I do whatever I want, and you go away." Big stink over that.

Finally, I got Roger Stern, which was a gift from God. Roger was not only great, he did a tremendous job. Roger—he'd catch my continuity mistakes. We had David Michelinie—talented guy. Professional. He got off on this political intrigue thing—probably not the best move. But talented guy.

Jason: At this point in your career, what do you see as your greatest accomplishment?

JS: The creator-rights stuff. I think that the fact that I came into Marvel and, in those days, it was strictly work-for-hire. You do a page; it's a page rate; you get your check. That's it. You're done. What I did was pretty much the same laundry list of stuff that Neal wanted. I managed over some time. I had the continuity bonus. I finally got the royalties, which we called sales incentives because royalty implies ownership. That was because of the Kirby thing.

I got improved reprint payments. I doubled the rates, and I doubled them again. I kept raising them. I had my budget, and I pushed it to the limit. I said, "If this is work-for-hire, then it must be work-for-hire. I can't change that. But if this is work-for-hire, it has to be fair work-for-hire, good work-for-hire."

We had life insurance for freelancers. You had to do about $7,500 a year in jobs—that's about three jobs. Okay. You're covered under our life insurance, a $10,000 life insurance plan. If you did $7,500 in work, you were covered under our major medical as freelancers. Of course, the contract people got all this stuff, too. I standardized that so that Joe Sinnott got at least the same vacation as Mike Esposito did. That, of course, got me better creators. I kept whipping and flogging them, trying to get them to tell stories.

It started to grow because we started to get the Who's Who of comics. You walk up and down the hall, and there's Michael Golden, there's Bill Sienkiewicz, there's Walt, there's Louise, there's Archie. There's Larry Hama. All these great talents.

I tried to get out of the way for the ones who knew what they were doing and tried to help the ones who were beginners or who needed help. Then occasionally argue with the Chris Claremonts who were great, but they sometimes wanted to do weird stuff.

A lot of good stuff happened, and we did a lot of really good work. I had a pretty good time doing it. We worked our tails off, even at Marvel—long hours. I can't tell you how many times I'd walk out of that building at 2:00 in the morning, ten blocks home. We did some all-nighters there, too. We worked really hard, and we goofed off a lot, too. Whenever we could, we'd have some fun.

Notes

1. Bud Plant is a long-time comics retailer who sold many comics through mail order catalogs.

2. The following additional information was provided by Shooter following an initial review of the draft manuscript of the present text:

   Because the creators I'd assembled and the direction I'd given accomplished great things, and we were successful, too successful, by middle-to-late 1985 the principals at Cadence saw opportunity. They'd hidden crown-jewel Marvel as a division of Cadence rather than a subsidiary, so no independent SEC filings, 10-Q's or 10-K's, were required. Outsiders had no way of knowing how well Marvel was doing. Profits were buried under "corporate overhead." The board of directors of Cadence formed CMI (Cadence Management Incorporated) and sought to take Cadence private. Corporate raider Mario Gabelli somehow saw through their scheme and tried to steal the deal. That's why I was compelled to do a lot of "junk publishing." Galton ordered me to bring in extra revenues fast to fight Gabelli's attempted hostile takeover. We published *The Marvel No-Prize Book*, the *Marvel Fumetti Book*, reprints, and such to raise quick-money millions for Cadence to defend against and, ultimately, buy off Gabelli. Then, the board, having deliberately depressed Cadence's stock price, took the company private for chump change. So, instead of being a publically traded company, Cadence was owned by seven men, CMI, who quickly stabbed one of their own in the back, and then there were six. The six, two of whom, Galton and Calamari, were Marvel execs, quickly sold off what remained of Cadence and pocketed millions. Curtis Circulation was sold for receivables (as such service companies are) and finally Marvel was put on the block. When unscrupulous owners are trying to sell a business, nothing matters but the bottom line, because non-service, and especially intellectual property/entertainment businesses, are sold for a multiple of earnings. If you are a vice president or "key man," as I was, in that situation, you have two choices: you can play along with the owners, help them sell your people down the river and be richly rewarded—Barry Kaplan told me they gave him $3 million for his cooperation—or you can become a labor leader. I chose to be a labor leader. I fought against the owners' depredations. They quickly came to hate me, but as Joe Calamari once told me, they couldn't fire me because none of them knew anything about the comics and, per Joe, "You're the only guy who can tell us who could replace you." The owners eliminated the pension program, eviscerated the healthcare, ended the 401K matching plan and cut every expense possible to put more money on the bottom line, even if it was temporary, so their multiple would be bigger. They tried to eliminate the royalty plan retroactively! That fight I won because their lawyers said fighting me, and a class-action suit I initiated, would go badly for them. Here's an example of their perfidy: Walt Simonson was sent a copy of *Star Slammers* published in France by a friend there. He asked me why he'd received no foreign royalties. I went upstairs and was told by Barry Kaplan that he had been ordered not to pay foreign royalties "unless they show up with their lawyer." That's a quote. So then what? Tell Walt Marvel is screwing him? So then he goes to DC and the way idiots like you report it is "Jim Shooter drives away another talent." So I told him there was some confusion and I'd try to sort it out. I fought like a wolverine. Futilely. Meanwhile, the owners didn't sit still. They worked at undercutting me, fostering the notions that the problems with Kirby and Gerber were my fault, blamed everything they could on me, cultivated DeFalco as a replacement and Carol Kalish as their "comics expert." Anyone I wanted to give a raise didn't get it. Anyone who spoke against me did. People were hired in my department without my knowledge or consent. They promoted

Bob Harras, who was and remains clueless. Step by step they obviated me. In December of 1986 I went to Galton and told him I couldn't stand it, I quit. He begged me to stay. He said the deal with New World Pictures was almost done but if I left, "key man" me, (that's what they'd told New World!), the deal would fall apart. He guaranteed me that as soon as the deal closed Walt would be paid, everybody would be paid, we'd all have NWP [New World Pictures] benefits and everything would be fine. Someone smart like Paul Levitz would have brought his lawyer in and gotten himself a golden parachute, but Galton, for all his faults, had never overtly lied to me before, so stupid me, I bought it. The day the deal closed, early January 1987, I went to Galton and said, "We owe Walt money. There are a lot of things that need to be set right." He said, and I quote, "Fuck you." He had his share of the 46.5 million Marvel brought in and cared about my issues not at all. I considered throwing him out his tenth floor window, but instead went back to my desk and started writing my resignation letter. I changed my mind and wrote to the NWP CEO Bob Rehme instead, blowing the whistle on the CMI thieves. Lots of perfidy to report. Long story, but Rehme investigated, found out I was right, that Galton and company were unscrupulous and incompetent scumbags but his choice was this: fire all of them, which would look bad to the shareholders of New World Entertainment (they changed their name after the acquisition of Marvel), or fire just me. No choice. Fire me. Rehme also said he thought I was a "genius"—that and a buck eighty-five will get me a Starbucks. He said they'd do what is common in the film biz, set me up as an independent producer, provide me with a budget, offices and a staff so I could create and publish comics distributed by Marvel, which Marvel and I would share ownership of. Meanwhile, he'd slowly filter in his own management people and get rid of the incompetent scum like Galton and Calamari without a bloodbath that might make him look bad, and we'd all live happily ever after. Galton and company, however, angry because I'd ratted them out, dug their heels in and prevented Rehme's plan. It wasn't that important to Rehme in the scheme of things, I guess, so he didn't force it. He had a lot on his mind because New World Entertainment was saddled with junk bond debt and losing, . . . ready? A million dollars a day.

3. *Spider-Man* #1 sold over 2.5 million copies in 1990.

4. Michael Mukasey is a federal judge who went on to serve as attorney general during the George W. Bush administration.

SELECTED RESOURCES

Books

Barbanell, Jeff. "Shooter's Marvelesque," in Timothy Callahan, ed. *Teenagers from the Future: Essays on the Legion of Super-Heroes*. Edwardsville, IL: Sequart Research and Literary Organization, 2008, rev. ed. 2011, 63–84.

Cadigan, Glen. *Legion Companion*. Raleigh; NC: TwoMorrows Publishing, 2003.

———. *The Best of the Legion Outpost*. Raleigh; NC: TwoMorrows Publishing, 2004.

Dallas, Keith, ed. *American Comic Book Chronicles: The 1980s*. Raleigh, NC: TwoMorrows Publishing, 2013.

———. *American Comic Book Chronicles: The 1970s*. Raleigh, NC: TwoMorrows Publishing, 2014.

Darowski, Joseph, ed. *Ages of the Avengers: Essays on Earth's Mightiest Heroes in Changing Times*. Jefferson, NC: McFarland Publications, 2014.

Eury, Michael. *The Krypton Companion*. Raleigh; NC: TwoMorrows Publishing, 2003.

Irving, Christopher, and Seth Kushner. *Leaping Tall Buildings*. New York, NY: Powerhouse Books, 2012.

Print Sources (Journals, Fanzines, Magazines)

Anon. "The Beginning of the Valiant Era," *Wizard Presents the Beginning of the Valiant Era*. Congers, NY: Wizard Press, 1994.

———. "Jim Shooter: Editor in Chief," *Comics Feature* #35 (December 1986):

———. "Jim Shooter: He Keeps the Epics Coming," *Comics Feature* #44 (May 1986): 32–33, 42, 43.

———. "Newswatch: Jim Shooter Fired," *The Comics Journal* #116 (July 1987): 13–14.

Archer, Miles. "Jim Shooter on Broadway," *Hero Illustrated* #3 (August 1995): 50–52.

Baker, Bill. "Storyteller: Jim Shooter," *Comic Book Marketplace* #97 (December 2002): 67–69.

Berman, Phyllis. "How Not to Start a Company," *Forbes*, June 21, 1993.

Butler, Dan. "Jim Shooter's Dark Dominion: An Interview," *Comic Buyer's Guide* #1038, October 8, 1993: 96, 100, 104.

Childress, Jan. "The One," *Overstreet Comic Book Monthly* #4 (1993): 14–18.

Cudlipp, Edyth. "Talent Unlimited: James Scooter (sic): He writes and draws comic books," *Cincinnati Enquirer*, September 17, 1967, n.p.

David, Peter. "*Marvel Age* Interview with Stan Lee and Jim Shooter," *Marvel Age* #8, November 1983.

Dean, Darren. "Dissertations, Disclaimers, Defiance: An Interview with *Jim Shooter,*" *Amazing Heroes Interviews* #3: 6–35.

Doran, Michael. "Jim Shooter Gets Daring," *Comic Buyer's Guide* #1291, August 14, 1994: 6.

Grant, Paul J. "From the Hip: The Jim Shooter Interview," *Wizard* #45 (1995): 70–76.

Greenberger, Robert. "Marvel Turns 20," *Comics Scene* #1, January 1982: 11–18, 64.

Groth, Gary. "Pushing Marvel into the '80's: An Interview with Jim Shooter," *The Comics Journal* #60 (1980): 55–85.

Hart, Ken. "It's Not Over Yet!," *Amazing Heroes* #67 (1985): 21–26.

Kaye, Ethan. "Unlocking the Gold Key," *Wizard* #227 (2010): n.p.

Lustig, John. "New Universe," *Comic Buyer's Guide* #651, May 9, 1986: 1, 3.

Martin, R. S. "All Quacked Up: Steve Gerber, Marvel Comics, and Howard the Duck," http://rsmwriter.blogspot.com/2016/04/all-quacked-up-steve-gerber-marvel.html, accessed April 27, 2016.

McTigue, Maureen. "Defiant Steps," *Comics Scene* #36 (1993): 37–40, 62.

O'Neill, Patrick Daniel. "Atom Smashing," *Comics Scene* #20 (1991): 17–20.

———. "Magnus Robot Fighter 4001 A.D.," *Comics Scene* #18 (1991): 14–17, 66

———. "Straight-End Shooter," *Wizard* 24 (1993): 42–46.

Park, W. H. "Jim Shooter Defiant," *Cryptych* 7, July 1994: 76–79.

Salicrup, Jim. "Marvel Super Heroes Secret Wars," *Comics Interview* #14 (1984): 6–21.

Schuster, Hal. "Doug Moench, Jim Shooter, and Death in the Marvel Universe." *Comics Feature* #21 1982): 5–7.

Shooter, Jim. "How I Spent My Summer Vacation," *The Legion Outpost* #10 (1981): 12.

Smith, Andrew. "Dark Horse Holds the (Gold) Key," *Comic Buyer's Guide* #1669, (2010): 6–14.

Thompson, Kim. "An Interview with Marvel's Head Honcho," *The Comics Journal* #40 (1978): 38–45.

Thompson, Maggie. "From Editing to Freelancing," *Comic Buyer's Guide* #1469: 29.

———. "The Unityverse," *Comic Buyer's Guide* #963, May 1, 1992: 26–28.

Online Sources

Coville, James. "An Interview with Jim Shooter," *Coville's Clubhouse*, September 1998, http://www.collectortimes.com/1998_09/Clubhouse.html.

Dilworth, Joseph. "Jim Shooter Talks Gold Key at Dark Horse," *Pop Culture Zoo*, http://popculturezoo.com/2010/05/interview-jim-shooter-talks-gold-key-at-dark-horse.

Eberson, Sharon. "Pittsburgh-born Marvel Writer Hasn't Lost Thrill for Comics," *Pittsburgh Post-Gazette*, November 11, 2010, http://www.post-gazette.com/ae/art-architecture/2010/11/11/Pittsburgh-born-Marvel-writer-hasn-t-lost-thrill-for-comics/stories/201011110424.

Irving, Christopher. "Jim Shooter's Secret Origin: In His Own Words," *Graphic NYC* (July 20, 2010), http://www.nycgraphicnovelists.com/2010/07/jim-shooters-secret-origin-in-his -own.html?m=1.

Martin, R. S. "Jim Shooter: A Second Opinion," http://rsmwriter.blogspot.ca/2016/06/jim -shooter-second-opinion.html.

Mithra, Kuljit. "Interview with Jim Shooter," *Manwithoutfear.com*, July 1998, http://www .manwithoutfear.com/daredevil-interviews/Shooter.

Neprud, Sean. "Shooter and NYCC," *Only the Valiant*, http://onlythevaliant.com/epi sodes/22.

Renaud, Jeffrey. "Back to the Future: Shooter Talks 'Legion of Super-Heroes,'" *Comic Book Resources*, September 20, 2007, http://www.comicbookresources.com/?page=article&id =11512.

———. "Shooter Dishes on Legion's Demise," *Comic Book Resources*, October 29, 2008, http://www.comicbookresources.com/?page=article&id=18623

Robinson, Iann. "Exclusive Interview with Jim Shooter," *Crave*, May 11, 2010, http://www .craveonline.com/art/138906-exclusive-interview-with-jim-shooter.

Shooter, Jim. "A Look Back with Jim Shooter" https://www.youtube.com/watch?v =boMX4q5mUoo.

———. "Bullpen Bulletin Special," all Marvel Comics titles, August 1982.

———. "The Giants of Comic Book Publishing Panel with Jim Shooter and Bill Jemas," https://www.youtube.com/watch?v=EiFfl4Sf5v8, accessed March 10, 2016

———. "Jim Shooter on the X-Men," https://www.youtube.com/watch?v=BxJSL6uqiCM&list=P LIqgi6UcSQ9YB_VrsjgD17fG6jVd-oV9D.

———. *Shooter's Blog*, www.jimshooter.com.

Stroud, Bryan. "Jim Shooter Goes Back to the Beginning," http://www.wtv-zone.com/ silverager/interviews/shooter_1.shtml/.

Thomas, Michael David. "Jim Shooter Interview," http://www.comicbookresources.com/ ?page=article&id=146.

Trammel, Jimmie. "Q&A with Former Marvel Editor in Chief," October 23, 2015, http://m .tulsaworld.com/blogs/scene/popculture/jim-shooter-q-and-a-with-former-marvel-comics -editor/article_34c67552–1dcb-5273–981d-b673a85bf097.html?mode=jqm.

———. "What if Former Marvel Boss Jim Shooter Was in Charge of DC?" *Tulsa World*, Octo- ber 23, 2015, http://www.tulsaworld.com/blogs/scene/popculture/pop-culture-what-if -former-marvel-boss-jim-shooter-was/article_3ee053f0-ed58–5eab-9034–7f7b5a0a1d55 .html.

White, Aron. "Jim Shooter Discusses Solar, Magnus, and More!" *Comic Attack.net*, June 7, 2010, http://comicattack.net/2010/06/jimshooter/.

INDEX

CPSIA information can be obtained
at www.ICGtesting.com
Printed in the USA
BVOW09*1243140517
483691BV00004B/4/P